The Healing Art of Feminist Psychology

ABOUT THE AUTHOR

Dr. Faith Onyango, (Ph.D) specializes in research on Language and Cultures and the ways in which second language teching and learning is Influenced by Groplitics. A key areas of interest in particular is how sociolinguistic factors impact the acquisition of language and creole studies. He is bilingual in both English and French and currently resides in France where he is an adjunct professor at the Essex Business School and the University of Cergy-Pontoise.

ABOUT THE BOOK

Feminist psychologists have a wealth of knowledge on varied topics related to the psychology of women. These topics include but are not limited to feminist therapy, trauma recovery in the lives of women, mental health needs and services for diverse women, reproductive rights and violations and industrial /organizational psychology and women's career development. The Feminist Psychology Institute provides a premiere online resource for mental health professionals who would like to earn quality, affordable continuing education credits on feminist psychology. The institute's continuing education site now is available. Proceeds will support the work of the Society for the Psychology of Women. Feminist theory has explored the social construction of masculinity and its implications for the goal of gender equality. Masculinity is seen as a problematic gender role that associates males with aggression and competition, and which reinforces patriarchy and unequal gender relations. The concept of masculinity is also seen as harmful to men by narrowing their life choices, limiting their sexuality, and blocking full emotional connections with women and other men. Some feminists are engaged with men's issues activism, such as correcting legal and social imbalances in regard to father's rights, bringing attention to male rape and spousal battery, and addressing negative social expectations for men. This book offers a sampling of the many ways that gender affects experience. Whether the context is domestic or international, court-room or a business or a clinic, gender matters. It influences ideas and expectations, and they shape behavior and laws.

The Healing Art of Feminist Psychology

Dr. Faith Onyango

AMIGA PRESS. INC
Delhi -110051

AMIGA PRESS. INC
H.O :- 28-A, Indra Park, Chander Nagar
Delhi :- 110051 (India)
Tel :- 011-22504028, +91-98736-57000
Email :- info@amigapress.co.in
amigapub@gmail.com
Website :- www.amigapress@co.in

This edition is published by Amiga Press.Inc

ISBN : 978-93-87295-14-8

First Published 2019

Printed and bound by Amiga Press Inc. New Delhi-India

Preface

Feminism is a collection of movements aimed at defining, establishing and defending equal political, economic, and social rights and equal opportunities for women. Its concepts overlap with those of women's rights. Feminism is mainly focused on women's issues, but because feminism seeks gender equality, some feminists argue that men's liberation is therefore a necessary part of feminism, and that men are also harmed by sexism and gender roles. Feminists—that is, persons practicing feminism—can be persons of either sex. Feminist theory emerged from these feminist movements and includes general theories and theories about the origins of inequality, and, in some cases, about the social construction of sex and gender, in a variety of disciplines. Feminist activists have campaigned for women's rights—such as in contract, property, and voting—while also promoting women's rights to bodily integrity and autonomy and reproductive rights. They have opposed domestic violence, sexual harassment, and sexual assault. In economics, they have advocated for workplace rights, including equal pay and opportunities for careers and to start businesses.

Feminists—that is, persons practicing feminism—can be persons of either sex. Feminist theory emerged from these feminist movements and includes general theories and theories about the origins of inequality, and, in some cases, about the social construction of sex and gender, in a variety of disciplines. Feminist activists have campaigned for women's rights—such as in contract, property, and voting—while also promoting women's rights to bodily integrity and autonomy and reproductive rights. They have opposed domestic violence, sexual harassment, and sexual assault. In economics, they have advocated for workplace rights, including equal pay and opportunities for careers and to start businesses.

Feminist legal scholars contend that raising the social costs to rape perpetrators is essential to the prevention of future rapes. Rapists must know that rape is not condoned by our society, that rape is not sex, and that all legal sanctions will be brought to bear to punish perpetrators. Committing rape must be seen as a costly endeavor for the rapist. Identifying and reporting rape is essential to raising the costs of rape to rapists.

However, narrow legal definitions of rape conflict with survivor declarations of rape. Because most researchers, activists, and even women themselves define "real rape" as a forceful attack by a stranger on an unwilling victim, many victims are reluctant to report rape. This results in one of the lowest reporting rates for any violent crime, according to the Rape in America study. Only one in three rapes is reported, the lowest reporting rate since 1989. The closer the relationship of the victim to the offender, the less likely she is to report the rape to authorities. Although date and acquaintance rapes are no longer the hidden rapes that they have been throughout history, they are still functionally condoned by social myth. This is evidenced by the relatively low conviction rate even though the perpetrator is typically easily identified. Once reported, very few reported rapes ever reach the level of a trial, and the few rapists who are tried rarely serve prison time. Systems-level interventions are slow and difficult to achieve, but they can have a powerful impact on the successful outcomes of rape complaints for victims. The problem is multifaceted and will require resistance at multiple points.

Feminist criminology today is primarily concerned with the victimization of women. Other issues, such as female delinquency, prostitution and gender inequality in the law and criminal justice system are also receiving attention. Feminism seeks the elimination of all forms of gender inequality. The goal is not to push men out but to pull women in. Feminism is a set of theories about women's oppression and a set of strategies to change it. Remember that gender is not a natural fact (sex is) but a complex social, historical and cultural product. It is related to, but not simply derived from, biological sex difference and reproductive capacities.

However, narrow legal definitions of rape conflict with survivor declarations of rape. Because most researchers, activists, and even women themselves define "real rape" as a forceful attack by a stranger on an unwilling victim, many victims are reluctant to report rape. This results in one of the lowest reporting rates for any violent crime, according to the Rape in America study. Only one in three rapes is reported, the lowest reporting rate since 1989. The closer the relationship of the victim to the offender, the less likely she is to report the rape to authorities. Although date and acquaintance rapes are no longer the hidden rapes that they have been throughout history, they are still functionally condoned by social myth. This is evidenced by the relatively low conviction rate even though the perpetrator is typically easily identified.

This is a reference book. All the matter is just compiled and edited in nature, taken from the various sources which are in public domain.

This book provides deep insight to various dimensions of issues in this subject.

—Editor

Contents

1

Introduction

Feminism is a collection of movements aimed at defining, establishing and defending equal political, economic, and social rights and equal opportunities for women. Its concepts overlap with those of women's rights. Feminism is mainly focused on women's issues, but because feminism seeks gender equality, some feminists argue that men's liberation is therefore a necessary part of feminism, and that men are also harmed by sexism and gender roles. Feminists—that is, persons practicing feminism—can be persons of either sex. Feminist theory emerged from these feminist movements and includes general theories and theories about the origins of inequality, and, in some cases, about the social construction of sex and gender, in a variety of disciplines. Feminist activists have campaigned for women's rights—such as in contract, property, and voting—while also promoting women's rights to bodily integrity and autonomy and reproductive rights. They have opposed domestic violence, sexual harassment, and sexual assault. In economics, they have advocated for workplace rights, including equal pay and opportunities for careers and to start businesses.

In the West, the movements and theoretical developments were historically led predominantly by middle-class white women from Western Europe and North America, but, since then, more women have proposed additional feminisms.

The experiences of women are also shaped by absence and invisibility: what does not get noticed, discussed, valued, or included. This includes invisibility in the workplace. As Fletcher (1999) demonstrates, the relational work that women are expected to do does not quite make it into the job evaluation. It includes the "second shift" of the average working mother, which occurs after she comes home from her paid employment, when she has the primary responsibility for the care of the emotional and physical needs of family members (children, husband, elderly parents, or parents-in-law). She has this responsibility because she is female. She may ask for "help" in these duties, but that they are her responsibility is not likely to be questioned. It includes the routine exclusion of women as subjects in health care and drug research, because their inclusion makes the subject pool less "homogeneous" and more complicated statistically, even when women will be the consumers of the drugs.

In every context, we see the power of language to define experience. When it is men defining the experience of women, the results can be surprising. In the law pregnancy is not seen as a gender-related issue because health benefits divide employees into "pregnant people" and "nonpregnant people". Using this logic, a company can choose not to pay for the health care costs of pregnancy, even if it does cover illnesses related to the prostate. Under similar logic, erectile dysfunction is viewed as a health disorder for which insurance should cover the cost of treatments such as Viagra, while pregnancy is not a health problem and insurers should not be required to cover the cost of birth control pills. Those psychological and legal scholars who use a power and dominance model to explain gender relations will readily note the irony: that we are enabling men to have more sex and simultaneously making it more difficult for women to protect themselves from the consequences of that sex.

Jean Baker Miller (2003), a psychiatrist who has written about the psychological effects of gender, notes the following: Power is very real and is operating in front of us all the time. Quite amazingly, those who have the most power in our society almost never talk about it, and even more amazingly, they induce many of the rest of us not to recognize it, either. [Through distorted representations of groups in film] we absorbed... untruths routinely every week.... This is one example of how the "cultural materials" of a dominant group mystify its operation of power.

For various historical reasons, a dominant segment in any society tends to divide people with less power into groups by race, class, gender, sexual preference, and the like. The dominant group often gains tremendous power over the less powerful groups in economic, social, political, and cultural realms. But dominant groups do not usually say, "I have great power over your life; I want to keep it and, if possible, increase it because I'm afraid of losing any of it to you."

It is important to recognize that there are different kinds of power. We use the term "power-to" to mean the ability to make a change in any situation, large or small, without restricting or forcing others. The term "power-over" we apply to situations or structures in which one group or person has more resources and privileges and more capacity to force or control others. Structural power reinforced by power-over practices obstructs growth and constructive change.

Dominant groups usually manufacture false belief systems that act to perpetuate their power-over position and sustain their separation from subordinate groups. Patricia Hill Collins (1990), an African-American sociologist, discusses the impact of controlling images. She notes that dominant groups tend to create sets of images about themselves and about each of the "subordinate" groups. These controlling images are always false, yet they exert a powerful influence, holding each group in its place and maintaining the status quo. We absorb these images about others and ourselves, usually without fully realizing it.... This is part of the way dominant groups mystify their power-over practices and entice many of us into cooperation.

HISTORY

Feminists and scholars have divided the movement's history into three "waves". The first wave refers mainly to women's suffrage movements of the nineteenth and early twentieth centuries (mainly concerned with women's right to vote). The second wave refers to the ideas and actions associated with the women's liberation movement beginning in the 1960s (which campaigned for legal and social equality for women). The third wave refers to a continuation of, and a reaction to, the perceived failures of, second-wave feminism, beginning in the 1990s.

Waves of Feminism

The period described as first-wave feminism refers to feminist activity during the nineteenth century and early twentieth century in the United Kingdom and the United States. Originally it focused on the promotion of equal contract and property rights for women and the opposition to chattel marriage and ownership of married women (and their children) by their husbands. However, by the end of the nineteenth century, activism focused primarily on gaining political power, particularly the right of women's suffrage. Yet, feminists such as Voltairine de Cleyre and Margaret Sanger were still active in campaigning for women's sexual, reproductive, and economic rights at this time.

In Britain the Suffragettes, and possibly more effectively, the Suffragists campaigned for the women's vote. In 1918 the Representation of the People Act 1918 was passed granting the vote to women over the age of 30 who owned houses. In 1928 this was extended to all women over twenty-one. In the United States leaders of this movement included Lucretia Mott, Elizabeth Cady Stanton, and Susan B. Anthony, who each campaigned for the abolition of slavery prior to championing women's right to vote and strongly influenced by Quaker thought. Other important leaders include Lucy Stone, Olympia Brown, and

Helen Pitts. American first-wave feminism involved a wide range of women, some belonging to conservative Christian groups (such as Frances Willard and the Woman's Christian Temperance Union), others resembling the diversity and radicalism of much of second-wave feminism (such as Matilda Joslyn Gage and the National Woman Suffrage Association). In the United States first-wave feminism is considered to have ended with the passage of the Nineteenth Amendment to the United States Constitution (1919), granting women the right to vote in all states.The term *first wave,* was coined retrospectively after the term *second-wave feminism* began to be used to describe a newer feminist movement that focused as much on fighting social and cultural inequalities as political inequalities.

Second-wave feminism refers to a period of feminist activity beginning in the early 1960s and lasting through the late 1980s. The scholar Imelda Whelehan suggests that the second wave was a continuation of the earlier phase of feminism involving the suffragettes in the UK and USA. Second-wave feminism has continued to exist since that time and coexists with what is termed *third-wave feminism*. The scholar Estelle Freedman compares first and second-wave feminism saying that the first wave focused on rights such as suffrage, whereas the second wave was largely concerned with other issues of equality, such as ending discrimination.

The feminist activist and author Carol Hanisch coined the slogan "The Personal is Political" which became synonymous with the second wave. Second-wave feminists saw women's cultural and political inequalities as inextricably linked and encouraged women to understand aspects of their personal lives as deeply politicized and as reflecting sexist power structures.

Third-wave feminism is siad to have begun in the early 1990s, arising as a response to perceived failures of the second wave and also as a response to the backlash against initiatives and movements created by the second wave. Third-wave feminism seeks to challenge or avoid what it deems the second wave's essentialist definitions of femininity, which (according to them) over-emphasize the experiences of upper middle-class white women.

A post-structuralist interpretation of gender and sexuality is central to much of the third wave's ideology. Third-wave feminists often focus on "micro-politics" and challenge the second wave's paradigm as to what is, or is not, good for females. The third wave has its origins in the mid-1980s. Feminist leaders rooted in the second wave like Gloria Anzaldua, bell hooks, Chela Sandoval, Cherrie Moraga, Audre Lorde, Maxine Hong Kingston, and many other black feminists, sought to negotiate a space within feminist thought for consideration of race-related subjectivities.

Third-wave feminism also contains internal debates between difference feminists such as the psychologist Carol Gilligan (who believes that there are important differences between the sexes) and those who believe that there are no inherent differences between the sexes and contend that gender roles are due to social conditioning.

Post-Feminism

Post-feminism describes a range of viewpoints reacting to feminism. While not being "anti-feminist", post-feminists believe that women have achieved second wave goals while being critical of third wave feminist goals. The term was first used in the 1980s to describe a backlash against second-wave feminism. It is now a label for a wide range of theories that take critical approaches to previous feminist discourses and includes challenges to the second wave's ideas. Other post-feminists say that feminism is no longer relevant to today's society. Amelia Jones has written that the post-feminist texts which emerged in the 1980s and 1990s portrayed second-wave feminism as a monolithic entity and criticized it using generalizations.

Movements and Ideologies

Several overlapping movements of feminist ideologies have developed over the years. Liberal feminism seeks individualistic equality of men and women through political and legal reform without altering the structure of society.

Socialist feminism connects oppression of women to exploitation, oppression, and labor. Marxist feminists feel that overcoming class oppression overcomes gender oppression; some socialist feminists disagree. Radical feminism considers the male-controlled capitalist hierarchy as the defining feature of women's oppression and the total uprooting and reconstruction of society as necessary and has branched into such as anti-pornography feminism, opposed by sex-positive feminism. Anarcha-feminists believe that class struggle and anarchy against the state require struggling against patriarchy, which comes from involuntary hierarchy. Cultural feminism attempts to revalidate undervalued "female nature" or "female essence"; its critics assert that it has led feminists to retreat from politics to lifestyle. Separatist feminism does not support heterosexual relationships. Lesbian feminism is thus closely related. Other feminists criticize separatist feminism as sexist. Womanism emerged after early feminist movements were largely white and middle-class. Black feminism argues that sexism, class oppression, and racism are inextricably bound together. Chicana feminism focuses on Mexican American, Chicana, and Hispanic women in the United States. Multiracial or "women of colour" feminism is related. Standpoint feminists argue that feminism should examine how women's experience of inequality relates to that of racism, homophobia, classism, and colonization. Postcolonial feminists argue that colonial oppression and Western feminism marginalized postcolonial women but did not turn them passive or voiceless. Third-world feminism is closely related. These discourses are related to African feminism, motherism, Stiwanism, negofeminism, femalism, transnational feminism, and Africana womanism.

Conservative feminism is conservative relative to the society in which it resides. Libertarian feminism conceives of people as self-owners and therefore as entitled to freedom from coercive interference. Individualist feminism or ifeminism, opposing so-called gender feminism, draws on anarcho-capitalism.

Postmodern feminists argue that sex and gender are socially constructed, that it is impossible to generalize women's experiences across cultures and histories, and that dualisms and traditional gender, feminism, and politics are too limiting. Post-structural feminism uses various intellectual currents for feminist concerns. Many post-structural feminists maintain that difference is one of the most powerful tools that women possess. Contemporary psychoanalytic French feminism is more philosophical and literary than is Anglophone feminism.

Ecofeminists see men's control of land as responsible for the oppression of women and destruction of the natural environment, but a criticism is that ecofeminism focuses too much on a mystical connection between women and nature.

Theoretical Schools

Feminist theory is an extension of feminism into theoretical or philosophical fields. It encompasses work in a variety of disciplines, including anthropology, sociology, economics, women's studies, literary criticism, art history, psychoanalysis and philosophy. Feminist theory aims to understand gender inequality and focuses on gender politics, power relations, and sexuality. While providing a critique of these social and political relations, much of feminist theory also focuses on the promotion of women's rights and interests. Themes explored in feminist theory include discrimination, stereotyping, objectification (especially sexual objectification), oppression, and patriarchy.

The American literary critic and feminist Elaine Showalter describes the phased development of feminist theory. The first she calls "feminist critique", in which the feminist reader examines the ideologies behind literary phenomena. The second Showalter calls "gynocriticism", in which the "woman is producer of textual meaning" including "the psychodynamics of female creativity; linguistics and the problem of a female language; the trajectory of the individual or collective female literary career and literary history". The last phase she calls "gender theory", in which the "ideological inscription and the literary effects of the sex/gender system" are explored". This model has been criticized by the scholar Toril Moi who sees it as an essentialist and deterministic model for female subjectivity and for failing to account for the situation of women outside the West.

Societal Impact

The feminist movement has effected change in Western society, including women's suffrage; in education; in gender neutrality in English; job pay more nearly equal to men's; the right to initiate divorce proceedings; the reproductive rights of women to make individual decisions on pregnancy (including access to contraceptives and abortion); and the right to enter into contracts and own property. Feminists have struggled to protect women and girls from domestic violence, sexual harassment, and sexual assault, emphasizing the grounds as women's rights, rather than as men's traditional interests in families' safety for reproductive purposes. On economic matters, feminists have advocated for workplace rights, including maternity leave, and against other forms of gender-specific discrimination against women. They have achieved some protections and societal changes through sharing experiences, developing theory, and campaigning for rights.

Civil Rights

From the 1960s on, the campaign for women's rights was met with mixed results in the U.S. and the U.K. Other countries of the EEC agreed to ensure that discriminatory laws would be phased out across the European Community. In the U.S., the National Organization for Women (NOW) began in 1966 to seek women's equality, including through the Equal Rights Amendment (ERA), which did not pass, although some states enacted their own. Reproductive rights in the U.S. centered on the court decision in *Roe* v. *Wade* enunciating a woman's right to choose whether to carry a pregnancy to term. Western women gained more reliable birth control, allowing family planning and careers. The movement started in the 1910s in the U.S. under Margaret Sanger and elsewhere under Marie Stopes and grew in the late 20th century.

The division of labor within households was affected by the increased entry of women into workplaces in the 20th century. Sociologist Arlie Russell Hochschild found that, in two-career couples, men and women, on average, spend about equal amounts of time working, but women still spend more time on housework, although Cathy Young responded by arguing that women may prevent equal participation by men in housework and parenting. In international law, the *Convention on the Elimination of All Forms of Discrimination Against Women* (CEDAW) is an international convention adopted by the United Nations General Assembly and described as an international bill of rights for women. It came into force in those nations ratifying it.

In the final three decades of the 20th century, Western women knew a new freedom through birth control, which enabled women to plan their adult lives, often making way for both career and family. The movement had been started in the 1910s by US pioneering social reformer Margaret Sanger and in the UK and internationally by Marie Stopes.

Feminist Theology and Religion

Feminist theology is a movement that reconsiders the traditions, practices, scriptures, and theologies of religions from a feminist perspective. Some of the goals of feminist theology include increasing the role of women among the clergy and religious authorities, reinterpreting male-dominated imagery and language about God, determining women's place in relation to career and motherhood, and studying images of women in the religion's sacred texts.

Christian feminism is a branch of feminist theology which seeks to interpret and understand Christianity in light of the equality of women and men. Because this equality has been historically ignored, Christian feminists believe their contributions are necessary for a complete understanding of Christianity. While there is no standard set of beliefs among Christian feminists, most agree that God does not discriminate on the basis of biologically-determined characteristics such as sex. Their major issues are the ordination of women, male dominance in Christian marriage, and claims of moral deficiency and inferiority of abilities of women compared to men. They also are concerned with the balance of parenting between mothers and fathers and the overall treatment of women in the church.

Islamic feminism is concerned with the role of women in Islam and aims for the full equality of all Muslims, regardless of gender, in public and private life. Islamic feminists advocate women's rights, gender equality, and social justice grounded in an Islamic framework. Although rooted in Islam, the movement's pioneers have also utilized secular and Western feminist discourses and recognize the role of Islamic feminism as part of an integrated global feminist movement. Advocates of the movement seek to highlight the deeply rooted teachings of equality in the Quran and encourage a questioning of the patriarchal interpretation of Islamic teaching through the Quran, *hadith* (sayings of Muhammad), and *sharia* (law) towards the creation of a more equal and just society.

Jewish feminism is a movement that seeks to improve the religious, legal, and social status of women within Judaism and to open up new opportunities for religious experience and leadership for Jewish women. Feminist movements, with varying approaches and successes, have opened up within all major branches of Judaism. In its modern form, the movement can be traced to the early 1970s in the United States. According to Judith Plaskow, who has focused on feminism in Reform Judaism, the main issues for early Jewish feminists in these movements were the exclusion from the all-male prayer group or *minyan*, the exemption from positive time-bound *mitzvot*, and women's inability to function as witnesses and to initiate divorce.

The Dianic Wicca or Wiccan feminism is a female focused, Goddess-centered Wiccan sect; also known as a feminist religion that teaches witchcraft as every woman's right. It is also one sect of the many practiced in Wicca.

Gender-neutral Language

Gender-neutral language is a description of language usages which are aimed at minimizing assumptions regarding the biological sex of human referents. The advocacy of gender-neutral language reflects, at least, two different agendas: one aims to clarify the *inclusion* of both sexes or genders (gender-inclusive language); the other proposes that gender, as a category, is rarely worth marking in language (gender-neutral language). Gender-neutral language is sometimes described as *non-sexist language* by advocates and *politically-correct language* by opponents.

SEX DIFFERENCES OF SUFFICIENT MAGNITUDE

Not surprising, central to the controversy about the existence of sex differences is the disagreement among researchers about the consistency across studies and the magnitude of the differences that have been reported. Eagly (1995a) contends that many feminist researchers want to ignore or minimize sex differences for fear that they perpetuate social inequities. She summarizes the arguments put forth by the critics of the sex differences research: that differences are small and often inconsistent, results frequently are artifacts due to improper methods, and findings often conflict with stereotypes about sex differences, creating a second source of inconsistency. Eagly (1995a) counters each of these arguments; she asserts that the meta-analyses of traits, abilities, and behaviours have demonstrated a range of consistent findings with effect sizes comparable to those in most accepted areas of psychology. She estimates that most effects in psychology for well-known research are in the moderate range of around "one half of a standard deviation or less; considerably larger effect sizes are relatively unusual". Compared to this standard, she points out that several aggregated findings of particular sex differences show large effect sizes (examples include a test of visuospatial abilities, nurturance, and facial expressiveness), with most differences falling in the small-to-moderate range of effect sizes. Eagly points out that even small effect sizes can have significant cumulative real-world consequences and impact. To provide a context for the relevance of these effect sizes, Eagly (1995a) cites Cohen's explanation (1977) of the benchmarks pertaining to each effect size category: small effect sizes represent group distributions that are 85 percent overlapping and are more common in studies lacking good experimental or measurement control, such as new areas of research; moderate effects are 33 percent nonoverlapping and 67 percent overlapping and represent group differences that are noticeable in daily life; and large differences are highly visible (47 percent nonoverlapping and 53 percent overlapping). Thus, Eagly's assertion is that most of the sex difference literature has findings that at least are noticeable in ordinary life. With regard to the other critiques of sex difference research, Eagly (1995a) asserts that researchers have increasingly taken into account and controlled for experimental artifacts.

Hyde and Plant (1995) take issue with Eagly's assertions, first, that feminist researchers have one perspective about the value of identifying or minimizing the existence of sex differences, and second, that the effect sizes of aggregated research in sex difference research are equivalent to those in other major areas of psychology. Hyde and Plant (1995) maintain that feminist empiricists have existed along a continuum; in addition to those who argue that sex differences do not exist or that this research promotes inequity for women, there have been many feminist empiricists who have taken the position that clear differences between men and women exist, and still others who have taken a more mixed position—that some sex differences are in fact large, while others are quite insignificant.

The authors use Gilligan's work on moral reasoning (1982) as one example of a feminist researcher concluding that men and women fundamentally differ in moral reasoning, with men assuming a justice (agentic) perspective and women a care (communal) perspective.

Hyde and Plant (1995) also cite the research in sex differences in nonverbal behaviour as another widely accepted area of research by feminist scholars in spite of large sex differences. Examples include sex differences in touching behaviour, smiling, verbal interruptions, and other differences in conversational style and meaning. In addition, feminist psychologists disagree about whether differences in some abilities, such as cognitive abilities, represent substantial or insignificant differences.

Hyde and Plant (1995) reviewed the aggregated sex differences studies that had been conducted previously. They concluded that the effect sizes for the many sex differences reviewed in these meta-analyses were smaller than the figures given by Eagly (1995a) and smaller than the findings of meta-analyses of other psychological phenomena. They found that the magnitude of gender differences varied substantially from one variable to another, with one-fourth of the sex differences studies revealing effect sizes close to zero, 35 percent showing small effects, 27 percent moderate effects, and 13 percent large and very large effects.

They compared these results with the aggregated analyses of other established areas of psychology, where only 6 percent of the research fell into the close-to-zero category, 29 percent in the small effects category, 38 percent in the moderate category, and 27 percent in the large and very large group. They argue that these comparisons support their contentions that sex differences are generally not of the same magnitude as other psychological findings and the impact of these differences needs to be questioned.

However, these researchers still advocate for the understanding of the differences that fall into large effect sizes. "An important direction for research will be to sort out the larger from the smaller gender differences to give special attention to understanding the processes that create the larger differences".

It is important to note that even in areas of sex difference research showing robust effect sizes, men and women overlap in abilities, traits, attitudes, and behaviours more than they fall into two separate groups. It is this overlap that is the source of controversy. In some ways, the controversy about effect size boils down to the question of whether the glass is half empty or half full. On the one hand are researchers making the case that research on sex differences is an area worthy of study, with findings that will lead to our understanding of important phenomena. For example, is it not important to know that men are responsible for most of the violent crime in the United States if one is developing interventions or policies? Doesn't knowing that most sex offenders are male lead not only to better-targeted intervention and research efforts but to more informed legal and social policies as well? Wouldn't recognizing that women suffer more from depression aid in prevention and treatment efforts? Wouldn't awareness of sex differences in quantitative problem solving and visuospatial abilities lead to more effective teaching techniques for women? Aren't sex differences in cognitive abilities as important to understand as social class differences? Researchers who see the glass as half full line up on the side of these arguments, asserting that the differences found in research cumulatively "make a difference" in society.

Other researchers question why psychologists would attend to sex differences rather than individual differences given that men and women overlap so substantially on every trait studied. They remind us that for 60 percent of the psychological variables that show significant sex differences, the group distributions for men and women overlap between 85 percent and almost completely. For the large effect sizes found only for 13 percent of the attributes studied, a 50 percent overlap between men and women still exists. Thus, these researchers argue that knowing that a person is male or female provides very little predictive value on where he or she would fall on any particular trait.

The "half-empty group" argues that the continued focus on sex differences in the light of their insignificance contributes to the unequal status of women because the justification of sex discrimination and even unequal treatment under the law has been based primarily on sex differences. Hyde and Plant (1995) make this point: "Any possible bias that may have been introduced by minimalist psychologists [that is, those who minimize differences] is more than balanced by the effects of the popular media, which glamorize and magnify findings of gender differences and are bored to tears with findings of no difference".

CONTEMPORARY RESEARCH FINDINGS

Research on sex differences has only increased since Maccoby and Jacklin's book. Marecek (2002) estimated that by 1985, over sixteen thousand studies of sex differences were reported in the literature. A major change that has occurred since the publication of *The Psychology of Sex Differences* in 1974 is the shift in the method of reviewing results across studies from cataloguing those with significant results (*p* value) in order to locate trends or themes to using quantitative methods of meta-analysis. In the latter process, effect sizes (*d* value), derived from the standard deviation of the sex comparison for each study, are averaged.

This method is considered an improvement over earlier, more informal techniques of analysis because it evaluates effect size rather than statistical significance, which is tied to sample size, and because it involves establishing and complying with criteria-based rules for inclusion and aggregation that are uniformly applied throughout an analysis. This technique of aggregating and evaluating the effect sizes of studies in a particular research literature along a continuum has been applied to many areas of psychology, including sex differences, where meta-analyses of comparisons of men's and women's emotions, attitudes, traits, and behaviours across research studies have been conducted over the past two decades.

These meta-analytic techniques have not quelled the controversy about the existence or importance of sex differences. There is still little agreement on or clear direction about what traits, abilities, and attributes differ between men and women and about the size of these differences, their relevance to functioning in contemporary society, or their etiology.

Critics of this approach counter that it does not solve the "file drawer phenomenon," meaning that only studies with some positive findings are published and available for another researcher's meta-analysis, while the studies with no results are filed in researchers' drawers. Meta-analysis attends only to those that have seen the light of day. A second critique is that studies may employ very different measures to evaluate the same disposition, and these measures may be lumped together in meta-analysis without truly knowing whether they are measuring similar or different qualities.

Cognitive Abilities

Meta-analytic techniques have been used to evaluate hundreds of studies measuring cognitive and intellectual sex differences and have resulted in a range of interpretations of the results. Hyde (1981,1994) has argued that sex differences in verbal, quantitative, and spatial cognitive abilities are small and diminish in late adolescence and adulthood. Halpern (1992) has interpreted the data as demonstrating that stable and significant sex differences exist for particular cognitive abilities even when the overall levels of quantitative and verbal sex differences appear to diminish over time (for example, in adolescence and adulthood). She and others cite research that has been focused on the specific dimensions of verbal, spatial, and quantitative abilities that seem to account for stable sex differences, such as visuospatial ability involving the mental rotation of three-dimensional objects, where males score higher than females, verbal fluency, and quantitative problem solving.

Traits and Behaviours

Social and personality researchers have analysed sex differences using quantitative techniques on synthesized databases from a vast array of databases in social, personality, clinical, organizational, and sports psychology. Eagly (1995a) has made the case for their analyses confirming sex differences: "The psychologists who have conducted most of these syntheses of sex-related differences in social behaviour and personality are in general agreement that their meta-analytic findings yield evidence of differences. A major theme of much of the interpretive writing based on these new syntheses is that empirical research has provided evidence for numerous nontrivial differences in many aspects of behaviour". Eagly asserts that these researchers have provided evidence of sex differences in many more areas than claimed by Maccoby and Jacklin in 1974.

Costa, Terracciano, and McCrae (2001) analysed synthesized databases of the Revised NEO Personality Inventory from twenty-six cultures made up of 23,031 adults and college-age participants. The authors concluded that modest-sized but cross-culturally consistent gender differences were found that were similar to stereotypes held about gender differences. Women tended to score higher on agreeableness, warmth, openness to feelings, and neuroti-cism, whereas men scored higher on openness to ideas and assertiveness. This review supports earlier work by Fiengold (1994) and Nolen-Hoeksema (1987). Fiengold (1994) had previously used meta-analysis to review sex differences on nine of the thirty personality traits of the Revised NEO Personality Inventory. He found that men scored higher in assertiveness, whereas women scored higher on gregariousness, trust, and tender-mindedness. Nolen-Hoeksema (1987) found that women score higher in symptoms of depression cross-culturally Nevertheless, Costa et al. (2001) interpreted their findings as showing that individual variation within sexes is greater than the differences between the sexes on these personality traits.

Eagly (1995a) summarizes the vast array of sex difference research in the areas of social and personality psychology: "Thematic analysis of demonstrated sex differences in social behaviour suggests that they conform to stereotypic expectations that women are communal and men are agentic. In general, women tend to manifest behaviours that can be described as socially sensitive, friendly, and concerned with others' welfare, whereas men tend to manifest behaviours that can be described as dominant, controlling, and independent". For example, quantitative syntheses of nonverbal and vocal behaviours by Hall and her colleagues have concluded that women are better at decoding nonverbal expressions and smile more, whereas men touch women more than women touch men, use more dominant eye gaze patterns, and interrupt and hold the floor in conversation more than women.

In a vein similar to Eagly's statement already quoted, Cross and Madson (1997) consider the majority of social and personality sex differences to reflect differences in traits of independence and interdependence. They use the definitions proposed by Markus and Kitayama (1991) based on whether one views oneself as separated from (independence) or connected to others (interdependence). A person who values independence focuses on self-fulfilment, whereas one with an interdependent perspective emphasizes the fulfilment of one's place in the broader social context. Cross and Madson (1997) provide examples from the existing literature in social sex differences as support for their position. They note research findings showing that women cite interpersonal problems as sources of distress more than men do ; that women are more likely to talk about interpersonal subjects, whereas men talk about sports and politics; that women pay more attention to information related to relationships than men do; and that men attend to information pertaining to themes of social dominance.

Gabriel and Gardner (1999) suggest that both men and women are interdependent, but that their type of interdependence differs. They define *interdependence* as relational or collective and hypothesize that men demonstrate more collective (group-oriented and agentic) interdependence and women more relational (dyadic and intimate) interdependence. Their results across five studies investigating cognitive, emotional, and behavioural differences did not find sex differences in participants' tendencies toward independence versus interdependence. However, they did demonstrate sex differences in whether the type of interdependence manifested was relational or collective. Women described themselves in more relational terms, scored higher on a measure of relational "self-construal," reported more emotional experiences linked to relationships, appeared more attuned to information pertaining to the relationships of others, and were motivated to behave in ways that maintained close relationships. The male participants described themselves in more collective terms, scored higher on a measure of collective self-construal, reported more emotional experiences linked to groups, appeared attuned to information pertaining to group memberships of others, and were motivated to behave in ways that supported their groups.

MYSTIFICATION AND BIOLOGY

The concept of mystification helps us understand how gender stereotypes can be perpetrated, maintained, and internalized, until we are almost convinced they are true. We live in a culture that provides contradictory messages about almost everything, and gender is no exception. Any challenge to the status quo is met with opposition. Frequently, that opposition takes the form of biological mandates, or "natural law," which suggest that women are limited by the immutable characteristic of sex and it is the result of biology, nature, genetics, or, more recently, evolutionary forces that require women to be in a culturally inferior position.

When women began to assert their rights to education, property, and the vote, the science of the times warned of the health dangers of a higher education. The data were clear: women with college educations tended to have fewer children. In the late 1800s, the explanation was biological: education was literally impairing women's fertility, primarily by exhausting them with all that thinking.

If the health dangers were not enough to keep women from seeking an education, then the genetic explanation was available. The variability hypothesis argued that only males could be expected to achieve great things. This "scientific" hypothesis pointed to the data: the historical records demonstrated that only men had made great intellectual and societal achievements. It also demonstrated that there were more men than women institutionalized for "mental defects."

The conclusion was clear: men were genetically endowed with more potential to reach extremes in both directions, while women were resigned to mediocrity. The subtext was, Why bother educating women, who could achieve only modest goals ?

As late at the 1960s, women at Harvard Law School were formally required to justify their presence. Alumnae have described an annual ritual, a dinner hosted by the school's dean, Erwin Griswold, where the guest list included all of the women in each class (and none of the men), along with selected faculty and their wives. After dinner the students were called upon, one by one, to answer Griswold's horrifying question, "Why are you at Harvard Law School, taking the place of a man?". While the history of legal education in the United States was primarily that of exclusion of women, professional psychology was not dramatically more liberal. Women began earning Ph.D.s in psychology in the late 1800s, but they did it at the cost of a personal life. One could choose to be a professional or have a family, but not both. Institutions of higher education, even those most accepting of women as professors, required that they leave teaching once they married.

MYSTIFICATION AND THE PSYCHE

By the early 1900s, psychology was beginning to explain gender inequalities as the result of intrapsychic conflicts. It was not that there was inherently a problem with women's legal, cultural, or economic status. The problem was that women did not willingly accept their inferiority. Freud himself had warned his colleagues, "We must not allow ourselves to be deflected... by... the feminists, who are anxious to force us to regard the two sexes as completely equal in position and worth". Modern psychoanalysis continues to struggle with Freud's concept of penis envy. One strategy is to dismiss it as children's fantasy or magical thinking based on a child's naive understanding of anatomy. This leaves open the opportunity to outgrow the "natural inferiority" that little girls experience at the discovery that they are without a penis or to compensate by acquiring a man—and therefore vicarious ownership of a penis.

One strategy is to "equalize" the child's dilemma: girls wish they had a penis, and boys wish they could have babies, because children (and perhaps adults) do not want to acknowledge any limitations. All difference is loss at the preoperational level of cognitive development. In classical psychoanalytic theory, the core issue is power: who has the advantage between the sexes and who is lacking and therefore inferior. Girls make the heartbreaking discovery that they are not "as good as boys," and they spend their lives trying to make up for it. The question of sexual identity is thus complicated by the value judgment that says girls are lesser. Chodorow (1978) redefined the early childhood struggle as one of connection and separation. In this scenario, it is the boys who have the more difficult challenge of separating from the nurturing mother in order to identify with the same-sex parent. Boys have to give up the regressive pull toward mother in order to be "masculine."

Those who do not will face the ultimate criticism from peers: that they are weak, sissies—in other words, like girls. This model offers an explanation for the intensity of feeling around masculinity, and the ever-present fear of being emasculated, as if masculinity were a fragile and precarious state of being, subject at any time to being lost or stolen. Women do not worry about "losing" their femininity any more than they worry about misplacing an arm or a leg.

What these theories have in common is the locus of control. Feelings about gender identity come from within and are an inherent part of the developmental process of all humans. They are ultimately biologically based, the result of millions of years of evolution, and they are unlikely to be changed.

MYSTIFICATION OF POWER AND DOMINANCE

Jean Baker Miller (2003) reminds us that gender definitions have served as a means of domination and control, with this control often achieved through violence. To change the definitions of gender "appropriateness" is revolutionary and dangerous. Women have been killed for their difference (the witchcraft trials in Salem, Massachusetts, in the late seventeenth century). Women have been killed for their conformity (funeral pyres for the wives of deceased men). Women are killed for the behaviour of others (honour killings of rape victims). Women are still routinely mutilated in Africa, and they are routinely beaten in America (domestic violence).

Gender equality is not an academic or philosophical issue. It has life-and-death implications for women, whether it involves access to safe abortions in Western culture, access to medications needed to treat HIV in Africa, or protection from murder (as an adult female in rural India or as a newborn female infant in China).

In recent news stories, we have seen rape trials treated as "he said-she said" relational disputes. We have discovered numerous police departments that have hundreds of "rape kits" in storage that were never sent off for DNA analysis. The explanations were consistent: it was too expensive to analyse this evidence of a crime. The results were also consistent: alleged rapists went free or never went to trial in the first place. This is violence by omission.

MYSTIFICATION THROUGH INVISIBILITY

Law professor Leslie Espinoza (1997) describes the way in which even informed and well-intentioned professionals can disregard the perspectives and feelings of women: After a while, try as we might, domestic attorneys, whether we are clinical law professors or representing for-pay clients, become inured to the most shocking of social taboos. Abuse becomes normalized for us.

Rape of a child is awful, but it happens. Family law attorneys have routine ways of redressing the situation. This is the standard response: temporary protective orders in district court, divorce action filed in the probate court, and temporary orders during the pendency of the divorce providing for support, custody, and protection.

The temporary probate court orders become permanent upon the final adjudication of the case. The standard response is comforting to the attorney—you get to feel like the knight in white armour. It allows you not to think of the reality of what this family is going through.... A contextual understanding of what happened does not really matter. Only enough of the background to support the outcome is relevant.

... We do not wrestle with the impact of gender-related trauma. Likewise we do not recognize that race matters.... Our legal distance validates the dysfunctional normalization of abuse that usually occurs in abusive families.

...The stories of women who are traumatized by abuse are suppressed by the normalization of violence toward women and children. Subordination of women—treating them like objects of property—is our cultural legacy. Historically, this violence has been acknowledged as the private right of men ruling families. Violence and rape of women are now tacitly allowed by the suppression of knowledge about abuse and the failure of the society to redress abuse. When women and children do speak, their stories are distorted to make them willing victims, liars, provocateurs, and crazies. ... Who is listening and how they listen affect the ability of the speaker to talk. There is an interaction between speaker and listener. In a symbiotic way they can work together for deeper levels of understanding.

DISTINCTION BETWEEN SEX AND GENDER

The distinction between *sex* and *gender* is generally that *sex* is biological (e.g., chromosomal or morphological) while *gender* is social or cultural (e.g., how societies structure relationships).

Men and Masculinity

Feminist theory has explored the social construction of masculinity and its implications for the goal of gender equality. Masculinity is seen as a problematic gender role that associates males with aggression and competition, and which reinforces patriarchy and unequal gender relations. The concept of masculinity is also seen as harmful to men by narrowing their life choices, limiting their sexuality, and blocking full emotional connections with women and other men. Some feminists are engaged with men's issues activism, such as correcting legal and social imbalances in regard to father's rights, bringing attention to male rape and spousal battery, and addressing negative social expectations for men.

Male participation in feminism is encouraged by feminists and is seen as an important strategy for achieving full societal commitment to gender equality. Many male feminists and pro-feminists are active in both women's rights activism, feminist theory, and masculinity studies. However, some argue that while male engagement with feminism is necessary, it is problematic due to the ingrained social influences of patriarchy in gender relations. However, the consensus today in feminist and masculinity theories is that both genders can and should cooperate to achieve the larger goals of feminism.

Debates have emerged within feminism over whether patriarchy is the primary cause of women's oppression, as radical feminist theory asserts, or whether legal systems and class conflict play a large role as well, as is proposed in other feminist movements such as liberal feminism and socialist feminism. Some radical feminists have proposed that because patriarchy is too deeply rooted in society, separatism is the only viable solution. Other feminists have criticized these radical feminist views as being anti-men. Societal tension caused by second-wave feminism gave rise to backlash in the form of anti-feminist men's movements, such as Masculism, though today some see masculism as a complementary movement that does not oppose feminism. Some feminists have argued that associating feminism with misandry is an anti-feminist strategy to discredit the movement, even though misandry is not a part of feminism and feminists are not more likely to hate men than non-feminists, and that this characterization has contributed to both men and women's reluctance to identify as feminist despite agreeing with the movement's goals.

Architecture

Gender-based inquiries into and conceptualization of architecture have also come about, leading to feminism in modern architecture. Piyush Mathur coined the term "archigenderic". Claiming that "architectural planning has an inextricable link with the defining and regulation of gender roles, responsibilities, rights, and limitations", Mathur came up with that term "to explore...the meaning of 'architecture' in terms of gender" and "to explore the meaning of 'gender' in terms of architecture".

Women's Writing

Women's writing came to exist as a separate category of scholarly interest relatively recently. In the West, second-wave feminism prompted a general reevaluation of women's historical contributions, and various academic sub-disciplines, such as Women's history (or herstory) and women's writing, developed in response to the belief that women's lives and contributions have been underrepresented as areas of scholarly interest. Virginia Balisn et al. characterize the growth in interest since 1970 in women's writing as "powerful". Much of this early period of feminist literary scholarship was given over to the rediscovery and reclamation of texts written by women. Studies such as Dale Spender's *Mothers of the Novel* (1986) and Jane Spencer's *The Rise of the Woman Novelist* (1986) were ground-breaking in their insistence that women have always been writing. Commensurate with this growth in scholarly interest, various presses began the task of reissuing long-out-of-print texts. Virago Press began to publish its large list of nineteenth and early-twentieth-century novels in 1975 and became one of the first commercial presses to join in the project of reclamation. In the 1980s Pandora Press, responsible for publishing Spender's study, issued a companion line of eighteenth-century novels written by women.

FEMINIST SCIENCE FICTION

In the 1960s the genre of science fiction combined its sensationalism with political and technological critiques of society. With the advent of feminism, questioning women's roles became fair game to this "subversive, mind expanding genre". Two early texts are Ursula K. Le Guin's *The Left Hand of Darkness* (1969) and Joanna Russ' *The Female Man* (1970). They serve to highlight the socially constructed nature of gender roles by creating utopias that do away with gender. Both authors were also pioneers in feminist criticism of science fiction in the 1960s and 70s, in essays collected in *The Language of the Night* and *How To Suppress Women's Writing*. Another major work of feminist science fiction has been *Kindred* by Octavia Butler.

Sexuality

Lesbianism and bisexuality were accepted as part of feminism by a significant proportion of feminists, while others considered sexuality irrelevant to the attainment of other goals. Sexuality, sexual representation, sadomasochism, the role of transwomen in the lesbian community, and other sexual issues arose within acrimonious feminist debates known as the feminist sex wars. Opinions on the sex industry are diverse. They are generally either critical of it (seeing it as exploitative, a result of patriarchal social structures and reinforcing sexual and cultural attitudes that are complicit in rape and sexual harassment) or supportive of at least parts of it (arguing that some forms of it can be a medium of feminist expression and a means of women taking control of their sexuality).

Riot Grrrl Movement

Riot grrrl (or riot grrl) is an underground feminist punk movement that started in the 1990s and is often associated with third-wave feminism (it is sometimes seen as its starting point). It was grounded in the DIY philosophy of punk values. Riot grrls took an anti-corporate stance of self-sufficiency and self-reliance. Riot grrrl's emphasis on universal female identity and separatism often appears more closely allied with second-wave feminism than with the third wave. The movement encouraged and made "adolescent girls' standpoints central," allowing them to express themselves fully.

PORNOGRAPHY

The "Feminist Sex Wars" is a term for the acrimonious debates within the feminist movement in the late 1970s through the 1980s around the issues of feminism, sexuality, sexual representation, pornography, sadomasochism, the role of transwomen in the lesbian community, and other sexual issues. The debate pitted anti-pornography feminism against sex-positive feminism, and parts of the feminist movement were deeply divided by these debates.

THE ORIGINS OF SEX DIFFERENCES

Psychological theories pertaining to the causes of sex differences primarily fall into the biological and social psychological (constructionist) domains. Wood and Eagly (2002) broadly summarize these positions: "Essentialist perspectives emphasize the basic, stable sex differences that arise from causes that are inherent in the human species such as biologically-based evolved psychological dispositions.... Social constructionist perspectives emphasize the variation in sex differences across social contexts that emerges from the means of male and female within particular contexts". Although essentialist theories have been proposed from other perspectives, pertaining to parenting, moral development, and "ways of knowing", biological and evolutionary theories are the predominant ones.

Evolutionary theories postulate that basic sex differences are the result of the adaptations of ancient men and women to distinct survival problems. In brief, sex differences in psychological attributes stem from different reproductive pressures and levels of parental investment, and mate selection. Nur-turance and relational qualities were adaptive for women as they experienced pregnancy, childbirth, and child rearing. Women needed to be more selective about mates because they invested more in the offspring and preferred males who could provide and protect successfully.

Long-term mates were in their best interest and that of their offspring; thus, women historically have competed for more socially dominant, competitive, and aggressive men. As men competed for sexual access to women, aggressiveness, competitiveness, and risk taking evolved because these traits increased their chances of being selected. Men's control over women's sexual behaviour and their sexual jealousy came about to ensure their paternity. Evolutionary psychologists recognize that environmental conditions can influence the pattern of evolved traits but continue to attend more to demonstrating the universality of sex differences. Wood and Eagly (2000) dispute that cross-cultural data support the evolutionary perspective, showing instead greater flexibility in mate selection and social organizations than that argued by the evolutionary perspective. They contend that the conclusions of evolutionary psychologists far outstrip their findings. Others maintain that the evolutionary perspective becomes a way to rationalize male domination and aggression toward women.

Social structural and constructivist theories emphasize contextual and social psychological principles over biological determinism. Social role theorists posit that sex differences emerge from men and women assuming different family and occupational roles. The sex differences found in these family and occupational roles may occur for a number of reasons: from the greater status and power associated with men's roles, from sex-specific divisions of labour based on differing physical abilities, and from different economic and ecological contexts. Because these factors will vary across cultures and periods, the organization of the social structure and, thus, sex roles will differ as well. Structural theories argue that sex differences and roles are not universal but related to these contextual conditions.

Wood and Eagly (2000) have developed a biosocial model that integrates the essentialist perspective with a social psychological perspective. Their theory focuses on the "interactive elements between the physical attributes of men and women and the social contexts in which they live". This interactionist perspective is one in "which psychological and physical sex-linked attributes are repeatedly constructed or emergent in response to the evolved attributes of the species, the developmental experiences of each sex, and the situated activity of men and women in society".

The theory has the following elements:

1. Men and women are distributed differentially into societal roles, resulting in differences in social behaviour.
2. These differences in social behaviour occur through many processes, such as the formation of gender roles, where each sex is expected to have psychological dispositions congruent with the tasks usually performed by that sex.
3. These gender roles become stereotypical of women and men and guide social behaviour, shaped by various processes of socialization, expectancy confirmation, and self-regulation.
4. Biological processes such as hormonal regulation and changes work in unison with psychological processes to direct the sexes toward specific social roles and to improve their functioning in these roles.
5. These causes of psychological sex differences arise from other determinants that have defined the positions of men and women in the social structure: sex differences in physical attributes and the behaviours associated with these differences (such as women's child rearing and men's greater size and upper-body strength) and the contextual factors within a society. These determinants have influenced social roles because of the ability of one sex or the other to perform particular tasks more efficiently in a society that is based on complementary relationships.

Although the biosocial model includes biological components, it differs significantly from the evolutionary theories. Wood and Eagly (2000) dispute that the types of sexual selection pressures that contributed to physical sex differences are related to sex differences in dispositions. In their review of a considerable literature, they show that psychological sex differences in humans have not consistently covaried with physical ones or shared antecedents.

EPISTEMOLOGICAL, SOCIAL CONSTRUCTIVIST AND POSTMODERN PERSPECTIVES

This chapter so far has focused on the quantitative research pertaining to psychological sex differences. Many contemporary theorists question whether quantitative research is the only way, or even a valid way, to approach these issues. They argue that women can be understood only in a context that includes the intersection of structural variables such as social, economic, cultural, and ecological contexts. Any human can be understood only as a function of the interaction of race, ethnicity, gender, class, sexual orientation, disability, and age.

Many psychologists also dispute the objectivity theoretically inherent in quantitative research methodologies, arguing that one's social identity, values, and own social "location" shape all aspects of one's research and conclusions. For example, Minton (2000) has made the compelling argument that as North American psychology was emerging and searching for an identity, it adopted the androcentric biases emerging in early twentieth-century American culture. Leading psychologists of the time such as G. Stanley Hall and James McKeen Cattell were proponents of a cultural shift in the view of masculinity from the turn-of-the-century ideal of gentle introspection to a rawer, instinctually based ideal characterized by independence, aggressiveness, and competitiveness (epitomized by Teddy Roosevelt and the Rough Riders). One manifestation of this shift in psychology was its move away from its roots in philosophy to an empirical science where control and "objectivity" replaced introspection and qualitative methods. However, the shift itself occurred in the context of particular social identities and values and the power and status of individual men to define the field of psychology.

Marecek (2002) compares the efficacy of qualitative with quantitative research methods in truly understanding women. She describes qualitative inquiry as embedding "psychology in rich contexts of history, society, and culture. It not only re-situates people in their life worlds, but also regards them as reflexive, meaning-making, and intentional actors".

She contends that qualitative research frequently provides more accurate and meaningful information about people's lives because it captures psychological reality through the use of more natural language, allows more depth and input by participants, resulting in a more active collaboration, and dispels false notions of objectivity that often pervade one's methods, findings, and interpretations. Kaschak (1992) has concentrated on feminist epistemology and the deconstruction of patriarchal social structures. She uses an epistemological approach, or making known the rules or meaning of "meaning," to illuminate the rules behind the relationships between the sexes. She questions whether sex differences can even be discovered, because in a patriarchal society, "the masculine always defines the feminine by naming it, containing it, engulfing, invading, and evaluating it. The feminine is never permitted to stand alone or to subsume the masculine" (p. 5).

By taking the noun *gender* and transforming it into a verb form, Kaschak reveals the epistemology of gender. In a gendered, or "engendered," world, gender is not static. Gendering is an active, interactive, and continuous process that is embedded in all aspects of our existence, our relationships, and our meanings. To truly understand the embeddedness of gender throughout our social structures means to recognize that changes in these relationships and structures cannot occur within the context of the same rules. Regarding sex differences, Kaschak (1992) points out that women are penalized for being too feminine as well as too masculine. They are presented with the paradox that to follow the rules is to be confronted with negative consequences for being female, and not to follow the rules is to be confronted with negative consequences for not being female enough. As women walk this tightrope between expressing too little or too much femininity, there are few payoffs for doing what is expected.

Kaschak (1992) offers the Antigone myth as the embodiment of women's roles and sex differences within patriarchal family and cultural structures. It is emblematic of the realization that men exist always with the expectation that they are entitled to the love and caretaking of women, just as Oedipus expected his daughter Antigone to sacrifice her life to care for him.

In a patriarchal, gendered society, women's development is tantamount to preparation to serve men. Attachment to one's mother or other women or even conscious attempts to raise children in nonsexist ways cannot change these relationships or alter the course of gender in the broader context. In fact, in an Oedipal/Antigone world, women are separated from each other, as the role of mothers is to prepare their daughters for the same servitude.

Kaschak (1992) provides examples of the pervasiveness of the embeddedness of gender. Self-concept is "embodied" for women, meaning that it exists only within the context of the female body. For women, esteem is the result of the internalization of a social, rather than an individual, construct that revolves around the attributions given to women by men about women's bodies. *Relational,* according to Kaschak, is defined as being responsible for the success of relationships with others or for being sensitive to the needs of others, even when these needs go unexpressed or even unrecognized by men who assert their independence and separateness while expecting nurtu-rance and support.

Other feminist psychologists have considered language, or discourse, as the primary source of shaping gender relations (and sex differences) and subsequently of understanding them. From this theoretical perspective, language creates reality. Through language, men and women negotiate their relationships and are either enabled or restricted in what they perceive about themselves and their social relationships. In a patriarchal society, men define the roles of both men and women through discourse, determining when women will manifest feminine behaviour and when they are "permitted" to venture from strictly sex-typed roles.

Brown and Ballou have provided a feminist critique of sex differences in both personality theories and psychopathological constructs. In *Personality and Psychopathology: Feminist Reappraisals* (1992) and *Rethinking Mental Health and Disorder* (2002), they have exposed the inadequacy of traditional quantitative approaches for understanding women's distress, their psychological development, or the static construct called "personality" as it pertains to women. They have pointed out that no psychological theories or constructs that fail to account for oppression in the lives of women can ever effectively be used to understand or treat women.

Worell and Remer (1992) elaborated on the ways in which assumed sex differences in psychopathology have resulted in bias in the psychological assessment and diagnosis of women. They have described the process as similar to a self-fulfilling prophecy where the outcomes are determined by initial assumptions. Assumptions of sex differences have had an impact on our understanding of psychopathology because of researchers' "(a) disregarding or minimizing the effect of the environmental context on individual's behaviours; (b) giving different diagnoses to women and men displaying similar symptoms; (c) mis-judgments in selection of diagnostic labels due to sex-role stereotyped beliefs; and (d) using a sex-biased theoretical orientation".

Although the themes of these contemporary feminist theorists are wide ranging, there are common themes in the topics they have pursued. Attention to context, the diversity of women's lives, and the impact of multiple oppressions, such as race, ethnicity, class, or sexual orientation, on women are central to the work of these theorists. These authors have struggled to move beyond sex or gender as a dichotomous category to describe women's development, growth, and dilemmas in all of their complexity and depth.

2

Feminist Criminology

Feminist criminology today is primarily concerned with the victimization of women. Other issues, such as female delinquency, prostitution and gender inequality in the law and criminal justice system are also receiving attention. Feminism seeks the elimination of all forms of gender inequality. The goal is not to push men out but to pull women in. Feminism is a set of theories about women's oppression and a set of strategies to change it. Remember that gender is not a natural fact (sex is) but a complex social, historical and cultural product. It is related to, but not simply derived from, biological sex difference and reproductive capacities.

Liberal Feminism Freda Adler and Rita Simon

This is the most widely recognized feminist theory in North America. It emerged in the 1960's. Liberal feminists contend that women are discriminated against on the basis of their sex, so that they are denied access to the same political, financial, career and personal opportunities as men. This can be eliminated by removing all obstacles to women's access to education, paid employment and political activity, by enabling women to participate equally with men in the public sphere and by enacting legal change.

The problem for gender inequality can be solved by clearing the way for women's rapid integration into what has been the world of men. Adler and Simon challenged sexist assertions made by Lombrosian crimonologists. They argue that sociological factors, not physiology, best explain women's criminality. There is a strong relationship between women's emancipation and the increase in female crime rates. As women become more liberated and become more involved in full time jobs, they are more likely to engage in the types of crime that men commit.

But this lacks empirical support. Most of the crimes committed by women were not related to improved labour market opportunities. Even now women primarily commit petty property crimes, such as shoplifting, bad checks, and welfare fraud, which are offences caused by an increasing feminization of poverty. Women's crimes tend to follow their traditional roles as shoppers, consumers, and health care providers within the family.

They commit primarily feminine offences, they write bad checks and take items useful for them as homemakers and for feminine appearances. Female violent crime rates are significantly lower than male rates. But societal reactions to their behaviours have become more punitive, e.g., the public is more likely to report violent females, the police are more likely to arrest them. Women who challenge the traditional patriarchal gender role structure are viewed as unruly women worthy of punishment.

MARXIST FEMINISM JULIA AND HERMAN SCHWENDINGER

Marxist theory argues that the economic formation of a society is the primary determinant of other social relations, such as gender relations. Marxist feminism emerged in the late 1960's in response to the masculine bias in the Marxist social theory. Rather as simply ignoring women as did traditional Marxist theory, Marxist feminism agreed with liberal feminism that women are dominated by men and are prevented from full participation in all aspects of society. As Marxists, they believe that ultimately the key explanatory factor is the nature of the economy. The gender division of labour is viewed as the product of the class division of labour. Because women are seen as being primarily dominated by capital and secondarily by men, the main strategy for change is the transformation from a capitalist to a democratic socialist society. Rape is not common in all societies. Capitalist societies have the highest rape rates because they produce unequal gender relations that foster violence. The exploitative modes of production that have culminated in the formation of class societies have either produced or intensified sexual inequality and violence.

Radical Feminism

Radical Feminism has dominated feminist perspectives on woman abuse and it was the first radical perspective to criticize the assertions of liberal feminism as simplistic. Radical feminists see male power and privilege as the root cause of all social relations, inequality and crime. The most important relations in any society are found in patriarchy (masculine control of the labour power and sexuality of women). All other relations such as class are secondary and derive from male female relations. The main causes of gender inequality are (i) the needs of men to control women's sexuality and reproductive potential, and (ii) patriarchy. Their work has focused on female victims/survivors of male violence. Radical feminist theory contends that men physically, sexually and psychologically victimize women mainly because they need to desire to control them.

Socialist Feminism Piers Beirne And James Messerschmidt

It is informed by both Marxist and radical feminism. Class and gender relations are viewed as equally important. To understand class we must recognize how it is structured by gender, conversely to understand gender requires an examination of how it is structured by class. In sum, socialist feminists argue that we are influenced by both gender and class relations. Crime is mainly seen as the product of patriarchal capitalism.

A FEMINIST PERSPECTIVE ON WOMEN AND CRIME

Criminology refers to any kind of study concerned with crime and criminal justice. It is a term used to include a multitude of topics and approaches. Feminist perspectives, over the past thirty years have not only put some new topics under the criminological cover, they have challenged the theories, concepts, methods and assumptions of most of the people already involved in the study of crime. Criminology, has for most feminist writers and researchers been a constraining rather than a constructive and creative influence. Theories of criminality have been developed from male subjects and validated on male subjects. Whilst there is nothing wrong with this, the problem is that these theories have been extended generally to include all criminals, defendants and prisoners. It was assumed that the theories would apply to women; most do not appear to do so.

Usually feminism is included in chapters about 'Gender and Crime' and woman as offenders are more likely to be discussed within the boundaries of sexual and petty offences such as prostitution and shop lifting. Voigt et al, in their recent book called *Criminology and Justice,* make particular mention of the inadequacies of criminology texts suggesting that 'criminology is nothing more than specialised theories of male delinquency and crime'. In other words, the facts about crime tend to be based on the sex of the offender and not the crime itself. This 'sexism' in criminology is more in keeping with Gelsthorpe's critique of 'accumulated wisdom' about female offenders. She proposes that women are discriminated against in areas such as crime because of their sex and this sexism influences the sentencing, punishment and incarceration of women. She accuses many police, welfare institutions and judges among others as assuming 'sweeping generalisations' about crime as something*men* are expected to do, because they are men'. Women are not expected to be criminals and if they are, they may be described as '*mad* not *bad* '.

The perception that women may be *mad* because they 'dared to go against their natural biological givens such as 'passivity' and a 'weakness of compliance' ' appears to originate from the view that women who conform as pure, obedient daughters, wives and mothers benefit society and men. Women became 'doubly damned' that is, they are seen as weak and in need of protection while being judged as having 'uncontrollable sexuality' (prostitutes and delinquent girls). Results from studies conducted by Gelsthorpe showed how sexual promiscuity amongst girls resulted in them being institutionalised and treated for 'abnormal' behaviour. On the other hand male's sexual permissiveness was encouraged and thought to be 'natural' to the male persona (1989: 34). According to Cain, these equity studies were 'androcentric' as 'women and girls appeared to exist as Other'. Men were used as the 'yardsticks' against which actions and treatment were measured.

Such androcentric studies urged many feminist writers to develop theories that engaged in negative and/or reactive projects and/or criticised social, theoretical, and political relations, thereby challenging theories that currently existed. Critique and construct were important creative alternatives for the production of feminist, not simply anti-sexist theory, and without them according to Grosz, problems of the past, especially patriarchal assumptions, could have been repeated (1990: 59).

According to Spelman, feminist theory has not changed all that much and has neglected to include the 'problem of difference'. She suggests that 'feminists have extrapolated the condition of the most privileged type of woman-the white, middle-class, heterosexual-to all women' and the 'conflation of women in feminist theory has not produced a melting pot of different ages, colours and classes'. She also suggests that white feminist criminologists, although objecting to the 'stereotypical representations of female offenders', have had little to say about indigenous women or those from developing countries. To fail to see differences in racial groups is to 'reinstate the white woman's assumption that the problem is always first one of gender, never one of difference'. This apparent absence of race and other factors such as employment are mentioned in the following discussion.

Could women's emancipation account for the apparent increases in crime? If not, what has? The word 'feminism' today remains entrenched in some people's minds as the 'cause of most of societies problems'. Chesney-Lind suggests that 'the invention of the liberated woman' has forced women to bear the brunt of the hostility towards the women's movement (1980: 15). Prominent feminist theorists such as Freda Adler (1975) and her 'Sisters in Crime' seems to have done little to alleviate these negative assumptions. Real problems within the criminal justice system appear to have been obscured and such deflection may have provided those opposed to the women's movement with scientific evidence of the 'dark side of liberation' as is discussed below.

Freda Adler believed that the arrival of the Second Wave of Feminism during the 1970s consequently coincided with a 'dramatic' upsurge in women's criminal activity. She claimed while 'women have demanded equal opportunity in the fields of legitimate endeavours, a similar number of determined women have forced their way into the world of major crime such as white collar crime, murder and robbery'. That women criminals today represent a 'new breed' can be demonstrated, according to Adler, by evidence of the changing nature of female involvement in a wide variety of crimes. The emergence of this 'new female criminal' engaged in predatory crimes of violence and corporate fraud has broken into a man's world. For example, female white-collar crime has increased since the 'liberation' of women. Adler suggests that as women are 'climbing up the corporate business ladder', they are making use of their 'vocational liberation' to pursue careers in white-collar crime.

Adler's theory has invited much criticism from other feminist writers such as Brown. She describes it as an 'embarrassment to feminism' and argues instead that feminism has made female crime more visible through increased reporting, policing and sentencing of female offenders. She mentions that the degree of sentencing (more severe penalties) would be a more acceptable index of increases in offences among women rather than statistical measures as adopted by Adler. Carol Smart argues that Adler's theory is based on 'statistical illusions caused by a smallness of the base' (1979: 53). Carlen argues that Adler's 'new female criminal' is cast as the 'biological female' who is essentially masculine. The 'new female' criminal turns out to be the 'old maladjusted masculinist female' of traditional criminology, rejecting her proper feminine role such as institutionalising rather than incarcerating women who commit 'male' offences such as robbery. In other words, Adler's 'sisters in crime' appears to work within the frameworks of traditional criminology rather than a feminist one. Her perspective also seems to exclude factors such as race, ethnicity, age and class. Many feminist writers see these factors as very important. For example, Jane Chapman's (1980) studies of the connection between labour force participation and female crime revealed an increase in criminal activity during times of economic hardship. The smallest increases in arrests coincided with periods of the greatest increase in economic activity with the most common offence being that of shop lifting. These findings would seem to support a theory of a relationship between employment and crime (economic perspective) rather than that offered by the 'women's liberation thesis'. When times are good, the offending woman appears to stabilise rather than escalate. An absence rather than availability of employment opportunities (liberation thesis) would seem a more plausible explanation for increases in female crime. Naffine believes the criminal woman's motive appears more rational and straight forward than manifesting her gender-role concerns or seeking to compete with the criminal male (1987: 99).

Giordano and Cerkovich conducted studies in 1979 involving women between the ages of 17 and 29. Their findings suggested that the 'more liberated' the response to questions, the less delinquent participants were. For example, they found that women who believed women should enter the workforce and a woman's role was not necessarily that of housewife and mother, were the least delinquent. James and Thornton revealed from studies involving women prisoners that those incarcerated were primarily from impoverished and uneducated backgrounds. When asked why they offended, responses did not appear to be 'liberation' motivated (1980: 240). In other words, contrary to Adler's theory of emancipation, feminism appeared to be a positive force for conformity when there was opportunity to offend.

RAPE, THE WORST CRIME

It Isn't so much the possibility of a stranger lurking in the gullies you by-pass to reach home. There is a far greater chance it may be your neighbour or teacher, or even worse, your own brother or uncle. The year 2008, reported more than 20,000 rapes (and estimates say only about one in 69 cases is reported in India). In a staggering 92 per cent of the cases, the perpetrators were known to the victim.

One of the worst places for a woman to live in, in terms of personal safety and security, India records 57 rape cases per day, up by 800 per cent if one considers the seven per day recorded in 1971. This is excluding the several others that are muffled or pushed under the carpet for reasons of 'honour' and 'family name'. Rape is present as at least one of every four crimes recorded in India. Every hour, there are at least 20 crimes committed against women across the country. And out of all rape cases, only about 20 per cent actually see conviction for the offenders.

Are we ashamed? We ought to be. According to 2008 statistics, out of 35 cities checked for women's security, national as well as rape capital Delhi stood first, with an incredible one-third of total rapes happening here. If the capital of the country and one of its biggest cities does not guarantee safety, what will? And to think that these are estimates that don't even reveal the whole truth. If one were to have the 'real' figures in hand, one would realise that there is indeed truth in the claim that rape is India's biggest crime at the moment.

What compounds most of our problems is that we Indians tend to have stereotypes for everything. So, what would your typical rapist be like? The immediate thought that comes to mind is of a red-eyed, sinister-looking and lecherous guy who stares you at the bus stop or in the office or at the departmental store. We know little about him, except that we have comfortably assumed it is a rank stranger. Well, we couldn't be more mistaken. Research of several years has revealed that in India, you needn't be a stranger to perpetrate sexual crimes. Which is why women need to be afraid. You need to be alert to the male figures already around you, instead of assuming he will come from another planet.

A stupendous 92 per cent of all rape victims already knew and decently well, the ones than violated them. These figures are clearly indicative of the Indian social fabric indeed being so designed that it leaves little scope for a woman to express her resentment of anything, even intrusion in her own space. The knowledge that she will keep quiet for fear of being ill-treated and taunted is exactly what drives most rapists to their crime. And not only that, the rate of conviction of rapists is also insignificant. Put together, these two factors create a lethal combination that encourages rape, for the fear of being caught and punished is insignificant while the chances of getting away with the crime are very high.

Psychologists say it is a result of a dangerously lopsided equation between the sexes. Sexual harassment and rape are two sides of the same coin. Both showcase the power of man to dominate that of women. Both have one victim-'women'. Both are barbaric in nature; but many people extenuate sexual harassment to rape, just because the victims are not physically harmed. Whereas in rape-the victim is ravished like an animal for the fulfilment of desire and lust of another man. Both have the same object-to undermine the integrity of the victim, physically as well as mentally.

As observed by Justice Arjit Pasayat: " While a murderer destroys the physical frame of the victim, a rapist degrades and defiles the soul of a helpless female." Sexual harassment is nothing less than the showcasing of male dominance. Given an opportunity, such men (those committing sexual harassement) would try fulfilling their desire. However, it also not true that all cases of sexual harassement are such-where the accused is guilty of conceiving the intention of a sexual intercourse. But it also depends on each individual case and circumstances, because it may well be the case that the woman may also be at fault.

The question is not whether women have the right to bodily integrity, as this right is already adumbrated under Article.21 of the Constitution of India.

Article.21, which guarantees the right to life and liberty to men and women both alike-but whether it is really imperative to take a decisive step towards extirpating this evil and make the contemporary and future society a safe haven for women. According to the official statistics of 1991, one woman is molested every 26 minutes. These statistics refer to the reported cases. Whereas, if the unreported cases were to be included, it would be a matter of seconds-rather than minutes. investigation of Most cases are not reported by victims because of various reasons such as family pressures, the manner of the police, the unreasonably long and unjust process and application of law; and the resulting consequences thereof.

In instances where women have reported such illegal and unwelcome behaviour, there have been significant victories in the past decade or so. Also considering the fact the sometimes these victories are achieved after a wait of a decade or so.

In Rupan Deol Bajaj Vs. K P.S.Gill, a senior IAS officer, Rupan Bajaj was slapped on the posterior by the then Chief of Police, Punjab-Mr. K P S.Gill at a dinner party in July 1988. Rupan Bajaj filed a suit against him, despite the public opinion that she was blowing it out of proportion, along with the attempts by all the senior officials of the state to suppress the matter. The Supreme Court in January, 1998 fined Mr.K P S.Gill Rs.2.5 lacs in lieu of three months Rigorous Imprisonment under Sections. 294 and 509 of the Indian Penal Code. In N Radhabai Vs. D. Ramchandran, when Radhabai, Secretary to D Ramchandran, the then social minister for state protested against his abuse of girls in the welfare institutions, he attempted to molest her, which was followed by her dismissal. The Supreme Court in 1995 passed the judgment in her favour, with back pay and perks from the date of dismissal.

Vishaka's Case,

It was in 1997 in Vishaka Vs. State of Rajasthan and others, that for the first time sexual harassment had been explicitly-legally defined as an unwelcome sexual gesture or behaviour whether directly or indirectly as

1. Sexually coloured remarks
2. Physical contact and advances
3. Showing pornography
4. A demand or request for sexual favours
5. Any other unwelcome physical, verbal/non-verbal conduct being sexual in nature.

It was in this landmark case that the sexual harassement was identified as a separate illegal behaviour. The critical factor in sexual harassement is the un-welcomeness of the behaviour. Thereby making the impact of such actions on the recipient more relevant rather than intent of the perpetrator-which is to be considered.

In the abovementioned case, the judgment was delivered by J.S.Verma. CJ, on behalf of Sujata Manohar and B.N.Kirpal, JJ., on a writ petition filed by 'Vihska'-a non Governmental organization working for gender equality by way of PIL seeking enforcement of fundamental rights of working women under Article.21 of the Constitution.

The immediate cause for filing the petition was the alleged brutal gang rape of a social worker of Rajasthan. The Supreme Court in absence of any enacted law (which still remains absent-save the Supreme Court guidelines as stated hereunder) to provide for effective enforcement of basic human rights of gender equality and guarantee against sexual harassement, laid down the following guidelines:

1. All the employers in charge of work place whether in the public or the private sector, should take appropriate steps to prevent sexual harassement without prejudice to the generality of his obligation, he should take the following steps:
    a) Express prohibition of sexual harassment which includes physical contact and advances, a demand or request for sexual favours, sexually coloured remarks, showing pornographic or any other unwelcome physical, verbal/non-verbal conduct of sexual nature should be noticed, published and circulated in appropriate ways.
    b) The rules and regulations of government and public sector bodies relating to conduct and discipline should include rules prohibiting sexual harassment and provide for appropriate penalties in such rules against the offender.
    c) As regards private employers, steps should be taken to include the aforesaid prohibitions in the Standing Orders under the Industrial Employment Act, 1946.
    d) Appropriate work conditions should be provided in respect of work leisure, health, hygiene-to further ensure that there is no hostile environment towards women and no woman should have reasonable grounds to believe that she is disadvantaged in connection with her employment.
2. Where such conduct amounts to specific offences under the Indian Penal Code or any other law the employer shall initiate appropriate action in accordance with the law, by making a complaint with the appropriate authority.
3. Victims of sexual harassment should have the option to seek transfer of the perpetrator or their own transfer.

As stated by the Supreme Court, these guidelines are applicable to:

a) The employer or other responsible persons or other institutions to prevent sexual harassment and to provide procedures for the resolution of complaints;

b) Women who either draw a regular salary, receive an honorarium, or work in a voluntary capacity-in the government, private or organized sector come under the purview of these guidelines.

Preventive Steps:

1. Express prohibition of sexual harassment should be notified and circulated.
2. Inclusion of prohibition of sexual harassment in the rules and regulations of government and public sector.
3. Inclusion of prohibition of sexual harassment in the standing orders under the Industrial Employment Act, 1946 by the private employers.
4. Provision should be made for appropriate work conditions for women.

Procedure pertaining to filing of complaints:

1. Employers must provide a Complaints Committee which is to be headed by a woman; of which half members should be women.
2. Complaints Committee should also include an NGO or other organization-which is familiar with sexual harassment.
3. Complaints procedure should be time bound.
4. Confidentiality of the complaints procedure has to be maintained.
5. Complainant or witnesses should not be victimized Or discriminated against-while dealing with complaints.
6. The Committee should make an annual report to the concerned Government department and also inform of the action (if any) taken so far by them.

Miscellaneous Provisions:

1. Guidelines should be prominently notified to create awareness as regards the rights of the female employees.
2. The employers should assist the persons affected, in cases of sexual harassment by outsiders or third parties.
3. Sexual harassment should be discussed at worker's meetings, employer-employee meetings and at other appropriate forums.
4. Both Central and State governments are required to adopt measures including legislations to insure that private employers also observe these guidelines.

A K.Chopra's Case,

A K.Chopra's case, is the first case in which the Supreme Court applied the law laid down in Vishaka's case and upheld the dismissal of a superior officer of the Delhi based Apparel Export Promotion Council who was found guilty of sexual harassment of a subordinate female employee at the place of work on the ground that it violated her fundamental right guaranteed by Article.21 of the Constitution. In both cases the Supreme Court observed, that " In cases involving Human Rights, the Courts must be alive to the International Conventions and Instruments as far as possible to give effect to the principles contained therein-such as the Convention on the Eradication of All forms of Discrimination Against Women, 1979 [CE DAW] and the Beijing Declaration directing all state parties to take appropriate measures to prevent such discrimination."

The guidelines and judgments have identified sexual harassment as a question of power exerted by the perpetrator on the victim. Therefore sexual harassment in addition to being a violation of the right to safe working conditions, is also a violation of the right to bodily integrity of the woman.

Provisions of the Indian Pena Code

In cases where the accused sexually harasses or insults the modesty of a woman by way of either-obscene acts or songs or-by means of words, gesture, or acts intended to insult the modesty of a woman, he shall be punished under Sections.294 and 509 respectively. Under Sec.294 the obscene act or song must cause annoyance. Though annoyance is an important ingredient of this offence, it being associated with the mental condition, has often to be inferred from proved facts. However, another important ingredient of this offence is that the obscene acts or songs must be committed or sung in or near any public place. Section.509 of IPC, comes into effect when there is an intention to insult the modesty of any woman by the offender by uttering any word, making any sound or gesture or by exhibiting any object, with the intention that such word or such sound be heard, or that such gesture or object be seen by such a woman, or by intruding upon the privacy of such a woman.

Thus, this Section requires:

1. Intention to insult the modesty of a woman.
2. The insult be caused by
   i) Uttering any word or gesture, or
   ii) Exhibiting any object with the intention that such word, gesture, or object be hear or seen by such a woman, or
   iii) By intruding upon the privacy of such woman.

RAPE AS TORTURE

In the case *of Prosecutor v. Delalic et al.*, commonly referred to as the *Celebici* case, Zejnik Delalic, Zdravko Mucic, Esad Landzo, and Hazim Delic were charged with grave breaches and violations of the laws or customs of war, including torture. Some of the offenses charged were multiple rapes, public rape, gang rape, vaginal and anal intercourse, rape during interrogation, and multiple instances of rape. The judgment was rendered, in a nearly five-hundred-page document, on November 16,1998. In considering the charge of rape as torture, the ICTY adopted the broad definition of rape provided by the ICTR in the *Akayesu* case.

In addition to accepting the ICTR's broad definition of rape, the ICTY also agreed with the ICTR's new understanding of the crime of rape. The trial chamber stated in its decision that it "considers the rape of any person to be a despicable act which strikes at the very core of human dignity and physical integrity.... Rape causes severe pain and suffering, both physical and psychological". This signified a further shift away from understanding rape as a crime against women's honour and instead recognized it as a violation of integrity and a crime of violence.

In this way, building on the ICTR's *Akayesu* case, the ICTY recognized rape as torture. The tribunal stated that "there can be no question that acts of rape may constitute torture under customary law". It then went on to find Hazim Delic guilty of rape as torture as both a grave breach of the Fourth Geneva Convention and a violation of the laws and customs of war. In its judgment, the principle of command responsibility also evolved; the tribunal found Zdravko Mucic, the camp commander, responsible for crimes committed at the camp, including gender-based crimes.

Rape as Evidence of a Campaign of Terror

Although the first trial held by either tribunal was expected to be the first international war crimes trial to prosecute rape separately as a war crime, the prosecutor was forced to drop rape charges from two counts because the witness was afraid to testify. The ICTY's decision in *Prosecutor v. Tadic (1997)* nevertheless offered some "absolute gems" in terms of prosecuting rape during wartime. One of these is the fact that the tribunal accepted testimony about the sexual violence that occurred and "the enormous pain and suffering endured by the women and girls and the community at large" from medical workers who did not witness the sexual violence. The tribunal allowed this testimony under a hearsay exception and went on, in its decision, to quote that testimony at length. In addition, the tribunal interpreted testimony of rape as evidence of discriminatory intent and found that, based largely on the testimony of a rape survivor, "a policy to terrorize the non-Serb population... on discriminatory grounds is evident and that its implementation was widespread and systematic". Although the prosecutor did not prove that Tadic himself had committed rape, Tadic was still held liable for participating in a general campaign of terror, manifested by rape and other forms of violence. This decision signifies that anyone— including nonstate actors and low-level participants such as Tadic, who was a civilian traffic officer—can be convicted of aiding and abetting crimes of sexual violence through knowing participation in or tacit encouragement of such crimes.

Rape as Genocide and a Crime Against Humanity

The ICTR decision in *Prosecutorv. Akayesu* (1998) has been hailed as historic in its treatment of rape within an internal conflict. It marked the first time an international court punished sexual violence in a civil war and the first time rape was found to be an instrument of genocide. Unfortunately, the rape allegations almost were ignored entirely. When Jean-Paul Akayesu was charged in 1996, the indictment contained twelve counts, none of which included rape (Coalition on Women's Human Rights in Conflict Situations, 1998). It was largely due to a concerted effort and heavy international pressure from women's rights groups that sexual violence charges were added to the indictment. The ICTR acknowledged this in the final judgment: "The Chamber takes note of the interest shown in this issue by non-governmental organizations, which it considers as indicative of public concern over the historical exclusion of rape and other forms of sexual violence from the investigation and prosecution of war crimes. The investigation and presentation of evidence relating to sexual violence is in the interest of justice" *Prosecutorv. Akayesu*, 1998, para. 731)

It is important to note that at the time of the trial, there was no internationally accepted definition of rape. When considering this fact, the ICTR clearly departed from restrictive definitions of rape that exist in national law. Instead, the chamber defined rape "as a physical invasion of a sexual nature, committed on a person under circumstances which are coercive." This is a broad definition of rape, unrestricted to one gender or to particular body parts. In fact, the chamber stated that "the central elements of the crime of rape cannot be captured in a mechanical description of objects and body parts". The chamber also found that force need not apply. Rather, coercive elements could include threats and intimidation. In addition to providing a broad definition of rape, the ICTR indicated its understanding of the true nature of the crime. It moved away from the view formerly held in international humanitarian law that rape is a crime against honour. Instead, the ICTR looked to international definitions of torture. The ICTR declared that, like torture, "rape is used for such purposes as intimidation, degradation, humiliation, discrimination, punishment, control or destruction of a person. Like torture, rape is a violation of personal dignity". By reconceptualizing rape, the ICTR placed rape on equal footing with other serious violations that occur during armed conflict. These groundbreaking steps—broadening the definition of rape and assigning it equal status—allowed the tribunal to recognize sexual violence as a form of genocide and a crime against humanity and to prosecute the crime accordingly.

In its decision, the ICTR recognized sexual violence as an essential component of the genocide and found Akayesu guilty of genocide for crimes that included sexual violence. Although gender is not one of the enumerated groups protected from genocide, the ICTR found that when rape was used as a method to destroy a protected group by causing serious bodily or mental harm to the members thereof, it constituted an act of genocide. The ICTR found that in the Rwandan genocide, sexual violence was intimately linked to genocide and meant to destroy the spirit and will to live of its victim and the collective group. As the trial chamber declared in its judgment, "Sexual violence was an integral part of the process of destruction, specifically targeting Tutsi women and specifically contributing to their destruction and to the destruction of the Tutsi group as a whole". The chamber also recognized rape and other forms of sexual violence as independent crimes constituting crimes against humanity. It found that the rapes had been systematic and carried out on a massive scale and that Akayesu had witnessed, and even encouraged, rapes of Tutsi women while serving as communal leader.

Akayesu was sentenced to three life terms plus eighty years. For genocide, he received a life term for each of the three counts. For rape as a crime against humanity, he received a fifteen-year sentence. This sentence was equal to sentences received for counts of murder, signaling the ICTR's recognition of rape as a crime of equal status to murder.

Through its broad definition of rape, its reconceptualization of the crime, its jurisprudence regarding genocide and crimes against humanity, and its sentencing, the ICTR began creating a paradigm shift concerning the crime of rape in war and armed conflict. Fortunately, the ICTY recognized the importance of this shift and carried it further in later decisions.

Rape as a War Crime

The trial of An to Furundzija, a local military commander, gave the ICTY a chance to play an important role in the movement toward establishing rape as a serious violation of international humanitarian law. Furundzija was charged with a rape committed by his subordinate against a Bosnian Muslim woman during a single day of the conflict, which Furundzija witnessed and failed to disrupt or curtail.

The trial chamber, which delivered its decision on December 10, 1998, admitted that it was not possible to discern the elements of the crime of rape from international treaty or customary law, from general principles of international criminal law, or general principles of international law. It therefore concluded that it was necessary to look to major legal systems of the world in order to find common principles of criminal law. After surveying municipal rape laws, the trial chamber found what it deemed a trend of broadening the definition of rape to include other forms of sexual assault. Although it did broaden the definition of rape to include forced oral penetration, the trial chamber nevertheless delineated a surprisingly narrow and specific list of what it found to be the requisite elements of the offence of rape under international criminal law. Some have seen the trial chamber's elaboration of the elements of rape as a regression from the broad definition established by the ICTR in*Akayesu*

Nevertheless, the trial chamber in *Furundzija* agreed with the ICTR that rape and other forms of sexual violence must be recognized for the serious violations they are. In its decision, the chamber stated, "The essence of the whole corpus of international humanitarian law as well as human rights law lies in the protection of the human dignity of every person, whatever his or her gender". The trial chamber also affirmed, "It is indisputable that rape and other serious sexual assaults in armed conflict entail the criminal liability of the perpetrators" (para. 169). The ICTY therefore acknowledged the true nature of the crime of rape and the necessity of punishing perpetrators accordingly. The trial chamber went on to find Furundzija guilty, under Article 3 of the ICTY statute, of violating the laws or customs of war for torture and for outrages upon personal dignity, including rape. He was sentenced to ten and eight years' imprisonment, respectively, which he was to serve concurrently. Although this was not a perfect decision, *Furundzija* nevertheless served to move the treatment of wartime rape along its progressive trajectory by recognizing the violent nature of rape, recognizing a single incident of rape as a war crime, and furthering the liability of those who aid and abet wartime rape.

Rape as the Sole Charge

The decision of the ICTY was hailed as a groundbreaking case. When the indictment was issued, an article on the front page of the *New York Times* asserted, "This is a landmark indictment because it focuses exclusively on sexual assaults, without including any other charges.... There is no precedent for this. It is of major legal significance because it illustrates the court's strategy to focus on gender-related crimes and give them their proper place in the prosecution of war crimes". Indeed, this case represents the first time that an international tribunal brought charges solely for crimes of sexual violence against women. The indictment charged all of the accused with various counts of violations of the laws and customs of war and crimes against humanity, and charged Dragoljub Kunarac and Zoran Vukovic with grave breaches, all stemming from crimes of sexual violence.

In its decision, rendered on February 22, 2001, the ICTY took the opportunity to clarify the definition of rape in international law. It decided that part of the definition stated in the *Furundzija* decision was "more narrowly stated than is required by international law," in that it did not refer to factors other than coercion, force, or threat of force, "which would render an action of sexual penetration *non-consensual or non-voluntary* on the part of the victim." In order to develop a more appropriate definition of the crime in international law, the trial chamber determined that it must look to certain basic principles among the national legal systems. The trial chamber went on to say that the "true common denominator which unifies the various [national legal] systems may be a wider or more basic principle of penalising violations of sexual *autonomy*".

The trial chamber then surveyed national legislation regarding three factors—force or threat of force; specific circumstances, which go to the vulnerability or deception of the victim; and absence of consent or voluntary participation—to make clear its point about autonomy. The trial chamber determined that these factors indicate that in international law, "serious violations of sexual *autonomy* are to be penalised".

The judgment then offered a slightly broader definition of rape than in *Furundzija.* This broader definition allowed for the rejection of Kunarac's claim that because one of the victims, D.B., took an active part in taking off his trousers and kissing him before having vaginal intercourse with him, she consented to sexual intercourse with him. Instead, the trial chamber found that D.B. did not in fact freely consent to any sexual intercourse with Kunarac, given the context of the surrounding circumstances, and that Kunarac had full knowledge that she did not freely consent. In so deciding, the court made clear that sexual autonomy is intrinsically connected to human dignity and bodily integrity, furthering the paradigm shift in international humanitarian law.

In addition, this was the first time the ICTY found rape and sexual enslavement to be crimes against humanity. The trial chamber was satisfied that rape met the elements of a crime against humanity: it was a widespread and systematic attack directed against any civilian population during an armed conflict. Notably, the trial chamber stated that no nexus between the acts of the accused and the armed conflict was required: the "armed conflict requirement is satisfied by proof that there was an armed conflict at the relevant time and place".

There was found to be an armed conflict and the underlying crimes were related to the armed conflict. In considering the charge of rape under the provisions governing violations of the laws or customs of war, the trial chamber was satisfied that rape met the requirements for the application of Common Article 3 of the Geneva Conventions, including that it is a serious offence.

In its decision, the trial chamber convicted Kunarac, Radomir Kovac, and Vukovic of various counts of crimes against humanity and violations of the laws or customs of war for rape, torture, or enslavement and sentenced them to twenty-eight, twenty, and twelve years' imprisonment, respectively. According to prosecutor Peggy Kuo, the prosecution was "pleased with the court's decision because the sentences show that the court took the crimes very seriously". The founder of a support group for women who have suffered trauma in war also praised the convictions: "I'm so glad, we've been waiting so long for such clear language and convictions".

RAPE AS A CRIME UNDER THE LAWS OF WAR PRIOR TO THE 1990S

The laws of war, both formal and customary, have prohibited rape for centuries. In 546 A.D. the Ostrogoth who captured Rome forbade his troops to rape Roman women. Richard II's Ordinances of War, issued in 1385, prohibited the rape of women and stipulated that offenders were to be punished by death. The 1419 Nantes Ordinances of Henry V drew on these rules and also proscribed the rape of women. English ordinances issued in 1639,1640, and 1643 stated similar prohibitions on rape 7 Several scholars, including the Italian Alberto Gentili (1552-1608) and Dutchman Hugo Grotius advocated the prohibition of rape in wartime and peacetime.

More recently, the Lieber Code of 1863 explicitly prohibited "all rape" and punished its commission with death. In the trials of World War II war criminals, the Nuremberg Tribunal received reports of sexual assault. In addition, under Article 2 of Control Council No. 10, signed in 1945 by the four occupying powers of Germany, rape was explicitly listed as a crime against humanity. Most notably, at the Tokyo Tribunal, rape was prosecuted successfully as a war crime under prohibitions against "inhumane treatment," "ill-treatment," and "failure to respect family honour and rights". An unequivocal prohibition of rape was established in 1949 in the Fourth Geneva Convention, which characterizes rape as an attack on women's honour. Additional Protocols

I and II to the Geneva Conventions also protect women from rape, declaring that women deserve special respect and listing rape alongside other forms of attacks on dignity. Despite these prohibitions, soldiers and combatants have committed wartime rape with impunity for centuries. Indeed, the history of wartime rape reflects a tolerance for such actions. The founding of Rome began by the rape of the Sabine women.

In ancient Greece, rape was "socially acceptable behavior well within the rules of warfare [and] an act without stigma for warriors." Christian rape and pillage of Muslims marked the Crusades. Similarly, it was accepted, from the Age of Chivalry (1100 to 1500) through the Age of Napoleon (1792 to 1815), that if a town was taken by siege, women could be raped. And although Henry V sought to protect women and impose discipline among his soldiers by issuing ordinances banning rape, there is evidence that he knew his rules were being breached and that his desired protection for inhabitants "remained largely unaccomplished".

Rape continues to be accepted as an inevitable by-product of war and armed conflict. Examples of mass rape abound in modern wars and armed conflicts: in the actions of the Germans in World War I; by the German, Japanese, and Russians during World War II; in Bangladesh during the 1971 armed conflict; by Americans during the war in Vietnam; and by the Indonesians in East Timor. These crimes have gone largely unpunished, despite the written prohibitions and customs that penalize rape during war and armed conflict.

CONTINUED EXISTENCE OF WARTIME RAPE

Although written and customary prohibitions of rape exist, they have not captured the true nature of this crime. Rather than identifying rape as a crime of violence, the prohibitions of rape classified it as an offence against women's honour. Defining rape in this way is problematic because it inextricably links a woman's dignity to her sexuality. This contrasts with other serious crimes like murder and torture, which are understood as violations of an individual's fundamental right to bodily integrity and security. Defining rape as a crime against honour means that "nowhere are the discriminatory and violent nature of the offence recognized". These definitions in international humanitarian law mischaracterize and obscure the crime of rape. Rape is more than merely a crime against a woman's honour, and it deserves the same condemnation and punishment as those war crimes that more commonly happen to men. Unfortunately, because of the definition given rape in international humanitarian law, rape was placed on an unequal footing with other serious violations that occurred during war and armed conflict.

This insufficient definition of rape developed largely because of the absence of women's rights and perspectives within the framework of international human rights and humanitarian law. Feminists have decried international law as male dominated and reflective of a male point of view. One explanation for women's absence is that women's issues are seen as "private," whereas the "public" sphere "is regarded as the province of international law". Indeed, in international law, rape is often considered a private act by individual men, in contrast to the state violations of human rights, which are recognized and addressed at the international level.

Because sexual violations against women were not afforded equal status, they similarly received unequal punishment. For example, the 1907 Hague Convention Respecting the Laws and Customs of War on Land does not list rape as a violation but rather provides general protection for family honour and rights. This provision has rarely been interpreted to cover rape. In addition, although evidence of rape and sexual assaults was presented to the Nuremberg Tribunal after World War II, defendants were never charged with rape as a war crime. In fact, neither the Nuremberg Charter nor the Tokyo Tribunal Charter enumerated rape as a crime against humanity.

Likewise, the Fourth Geneva Convention, despite establishing an unequivocal prohibition of rape, does not explicitly include acts of sexual assault within its provision on grave breaches, which are subject to universal jurisdiction. This failure to prioritize the punishment of wartime rapists created implied rules of war that permit, encourage, and condone sexual violence against women. The willingness by states to tolerate sexual violence against women despite explicit prohibitions in international humanitarian law provides soldiers with a "license to rape because of their military association". They are shielded from prosecution and provided with impunity because rape has proven to be a valuable war strategy. Rape is used in war as a means of vengeance, a tool of propaganda, a way to signify power to the opposing side, a reward for weary troops and a way to build morale, and, increasingly, a strategic tool of ethnic cleansing or genocide. Rape is an effective way to subjugate and terrorize a population and is a means of communication from conquering men to the conquered. In this way, women as individuals are absent from the equation; their bodies are merely used to pass on a message or are seen as spoils of war.

The international community has finally begun to recognize the true nature of the crime of rape, signaling its intention to end the practice of using rape as a weapon of war by punishing the crime equally with other war crimes. This change came about largely as a result of the alarming prevalence of sexual violence inflicted on women in the former Yugoslavia and in Rwanda.

SPOUSAL ABUSE

Spousal abuse refers to a wide spectrum of abuse. This includes physical abuse, sexual abuse, emotional abuse, economic abuse and financial abuse. The abuser can be the husband or wife as can the victim.

Common Misunderstandings

Most of the information today confuses spousal abuse with domestic violence, which is only part of the whole spectrum of abuse. 'Domestic violence' is a specific form of violence in which physical or sexual abuse is perpetuated by one spouse upon another, or by both partners upon each other. The term was coined in the late 1970s once such crimes were given wider attention in society. There are separate legalities and punishments applied to such a crime as opposed to random assault or assaults of another nature.

Spousal abuse is committed by both males and females in intimate relationships.

Gender of Assailant

In the most serious cases of violence men dominate. Women are much more likely to be murdered by an intimate partner, regardless of who started the fight. Among the persons killed by an intimate partner, about three quarters are female, and about a quarter are male: in 1999, in the US, 1,218 women and 424 men were killed by an intimate partner, regardless of which partner started the violence and of the gender of the partner. In the US, in 2005, 1181 females and 329 males were killed by their intimate partners.

Dr. Martin Fiebert, from the Department of Psychology of California State University, has compiled an annotated bibliography of research relating to spousal abuse by women on men.

This bibliography examines 155 scholarly investigations: 126 empirical studies and 29 reviews and/or analyses, which demonstrate that women are as physically aggressive, or more aggressive, than men in their relationships with their spouses or male partners. The aggregate sample size in the reviewed studies exceeds 116,000. Very few studies have shown men to aggress more frequently than women. However, until recently the bulk of domestic violence research did not even ask about woman-on-man violence. It has also been found that many kinds of behaviour, such as pushing and slapping, are experienced by both genders, but are mainly called "violence" by female victims. Early studies that merely asked "have you been a victim of domestic violence" did find far lower levels of male victims; but when they asked about specific behaviours ("have you been slapped, punched,...), the numbers evened out.

Justice Department studies show that men are 32% less likely than women to report any form of violent victimization.

Straus and Gelles found in couples reporting spousal violence, 27% of the time the man struck the first blow; the woman in 24%. The rest of the time, the violence was mutual, with both partners brawling. The results were the same even when the most severe episodes of violence were analysed. In order to counteract claims that the reporting data was skewed, female-only surveys were conducted, asking females to self-report, and the data was the same.

The simple tally of violent acts is typically found to be similar in those studies that examine both directions, but some studies show that men's violence may be more serious. Men's violence may do more damage than women's; women are much more likely to be injured and/or hospitalized, wives are much more likely to be killed by their husbands than the reverse (59%-41% Dept of Justice study), and women in general are more likely to be killed by their spouse than by all other types of assailants combined. Coramae Richey Mann, a researcher at the Department of Criminal Justice, Indiana University/ Bloomington, found that only 59% of women jailed for spousal murder claimed self-defence and that 30% had previously been arrested for violent crimes.

Women charged with killing their husbands were acquitted in 12.9% of the cases, while husbands charged with killing their wives were acquitted only 1.4% of the time. In addition, women convicted of killing their husbands receive an average sentence of only six years, while male spousal killers got 17 years, according to an LA Times article citing Department of Justice data.

These findings, however, may have other problems. Women are far more likely to use weapons in their domestic violence, whether throwing a plate or firing a gun. Women are also much more likely than men to enlist help if they wish to kill their spouse; but such multiple-offender homicides are not counted toward domestic-violence statistics. In addition Farrell points out that there are several "female-only" defences to murder charges, such as the posthumous allegation of abuse; in short, our data on rates of domestic homicide are incomplete.

In their study of severely violent couples, Neil Jacobson and John Gottman conclude that the *frequency* of violent acts is not as crucial as the impact of the violence and its function, when trying to understand spousal abuse; specifically, they state that the purpose of battering of whatever direction is to control and intimidate, rather than just to injure.

There is a whole source of new evidence to suggest that some of the research into family abuse has been politicized. Sam and Bunny Sewell, Family Resources & Research state that "However, misleading statistics are a deliberate fund raising tactic for women's shelters. The shelter movement almost never mentions scientific studies".

Classification

All forms of domestic abuse have one purpose: to gain and maintain *total control* over the victim. Abusers use many tactics to exert power over their spouse or partner: dominance, humiliation, isolation, threats, intimidation, denial and blame. The form and characteristics of domestic violence and abuse may vary in other ways. Michael P. Johnson argues for three major types of intimate partner violence. The typology is supported by subsequent research and evaluation by Johnson and his colleagues, as well as independent researchers.

Distinctions need to be made regarding types of violence, motives of perpetrators, and the social and cultural context. Violence by a man or woman against his intimate partner is often done as a way for controlling "their partner", even if this kind of violence is not the most frequent. Other types of intimate partner violence also occur, including violence between gay and lesbian couples, and by women against their male partners.

Distinctions are not based on single incidents, but rather on patterns across numerous incidents and motives of the perpetrator. Types of violence identified by Johnson:

- Common couple violence (CCV) is not connected to general control behaviour, but arises in a single argument where one or both partners physically lash out at the other. Intimate terrorism is one element in a general pattern of control by one partner over the other. Intimate terrorism is more common than common couple violence, more likely to escalate over time, not as likely to be mutual, and more likely to involve serious injury.
- Intimate terrorism (IT) may also involve emotional and psychological abuse.
- Violent resistance (VR), sometimes thought of as "self-defence", is violence perpetrated usually by women against their abusive partners.
- Mutual violent control (MVC) is rare type of intimate partner violence occurs when both partners act in a violent manner, battling for control.

Another type is situational couple violence, which arises out of conflicts that escalate to arguments and then to violence. It is not connected to a general pattern of control. Although it occurs less frequently in relationships and is less serious than intimate terrorism, in some cases it can be frequent and/or quite serious, even life-threatening. This is probably the most common type of intimate partner violence and dominates general surveys, student samples, and even marriage counselling samples.Types of male batterers identified by Holtzworth-Munroe and Stuart (1994) include "family-only", which primarily fall into the CCV type, who are generally less violent and less likely to perpetrate psychological and sexual abuse. IT batterers include two types: "Generally-violent-antisocial" and "dysphoric-borderline". The first type includes men with general psychopathic and violent tendencies. The second type are men who are emotionally dependent on the relationship. Support for this typology has been found in subsequent evaluations. Others, such as the US Centres for Disease Control, divide domestic violence into two types: reciprocal violence, in which both partners are violent, and non-reciprocal violence, in which one partner is violent.

Physical

Physical abuse is abuse involving contact intended to cause feelings of intimidation, pain, injury, or other physical suffering or bodily harm.

Sexual

Sexual abuse is common in abusive relationships: The National Coalition Against Domestic Violence reports that between one-third and one-half of all battered women are raped by their partners at least once during their relationship.

Any situation in which force is used to obtain participation in unwanted, unsafe, or degrading sexual activity constitutes sexual abuse.

Forced sex, even by a spouse or intimate partner with whom consensual sex has occurred, is an act of aggression and violence. Furthermore, women whose partners abuse them physically and sexually are at a higher risk of being seriously injured or killed. Categories of sexual abuse include:

1. Use of physical force to compel a person to engage in a sexual act against his or her will, whether or not the act is completed;
2. Attempted or completed sex act involving a person who is unable to understand the nature or condition of the act, unable to decline participation, or unable to communicate unwillingness to engage in the sexual act, e.g., because of underage immaturity, illness, disability, or the influence of alcohol or other drugs, or because of intimidation or pressure; and
3. Abusive sexual contact.

Emotional

Emotional abuse (also called *psychological abuse* or *mental abuse*) can include humiliating the victim privately or publicly, controlling what the victim can and cannot do, withholding information from the victim, deliberately doing something to make the victim feel diminished or embarrassed, isolating the victim from friends and family, implicitly blackmailing the victim by harming others when the victim expresses independence or happiness, or denying the victim access to money or other basic resources and necessities. People who are being emotionally abused often feel as if they do not own themselves; rather, they may feel that their significant other has nearly total control over them. Women or men undergoing emotional abuse often suffer from depression, which puts them at increased risk for suicide, eating disorders, and drug and alcohol abuse.

Verbal

Verbal abuse (also called reviling) is a form of abusive behaviour involving the use of language. It is a form of profanity that can occur with or without the use of expletives. Whilst oral communication is the most common form of verbal abuse, it includes abusive words in written form.

Economic

Economic abuse is when the abuser has control over the victim's money and other economic resources. In its extreme (and usual) form, this involves putting the victim on a strict "allowance", withholding money at will and forcing the victim to beg for the money until the abuser gives them some money. It is common for the victim to receive less money as the abuse continues. This also includes (but is not limited to) preventing the victim from finishing education or obtaining employment, or intentionally squandering or misusing communal resources.

Stalking

Stalking is often considered a type of psychological intimidation that causes a victim to feel a high level of fear.

FEMALE CRIMINALITY

In the wake of industrialization, westernization and urbanization, Indian society has been passing through drastic and fundamental changes both in the structures, socio-economic and cultural spheres which not only produced a changed physical environment and a new form of economic organization but also affected the social order, solidarity, human conduct and thought. Traditionally women, whose role was mainly confined to the domestic area has now switched over to productively job sector. She is found to be actively participating in area sphere of professional life along with the male counterparts. The urbanization, industrialization, liberalization, globalization, and market friendly policies have resulted in increased opportunities for employment to women. Moreover, women centred policies; programmes and projects accelerated the process of women empowerment. Women are participation in economic activities, political insulations and a social sphere has increased to the greater extent.

However, because of family disorganization, marital discord, high aspiration level and frustration due to non fulfillment, stress and failure in coping process and alteration women are found to getting involved in criminal activities more in number in the present day society. Statistics on female criminality reveals that female criminals contribute a numerically smaller proportion than that of male offenders. But at present, there is upward trend in the number of crimes committed by women. According to crime in India Report, the female percentage for arrested persons at all India level was at 4.7. An increasing trend in the female criminality has been found considering their involvement in total cognizable crimes from 3.1 per cent in 1990 to 4.1 per cent in 1995 and finally to 4.7 per cent in 1996.

At the same time 10 states and 3 Union Territories recorded more than 5 per cent female arrests in total arrested persons during 1996. Again, report reveals that Manipur and Himanchal Pradesh recorded higher female arrested percentage.

During 1995, 2.29 taken females were arrested while in 1996 the figure slightly dropped to 2.05 lakh. Most of the females were arrested against prohibition Act. However, women were also arrested against serious crimes. Women are arrested mainly under the different kinds of crimes i.e. riots, murder, cruelty by husband, dowry death, hurt/serious hurt etc. A significant number of women arrested are below 16 years and 16-18 years.

Majority of the arrested women are belonging to age groups of 18-30 years and 30-50 years. While women belonging to age group of 50 years and above constituted just 10.15 per cent in 1996. The states of Kerala and Tamil Nadu registered higher female convicts inmates in their prison in 1995. In percentage term Manipur, Mizoram and Karnataka, recorded higher percentage of female convicts to the convicts held in prison. So far as the women under trial in jails are concerned, their number was highest in the state of Tamil Nadu followed by Kerala and Karnataka.

In percentage terms, the share of women undertrial prisoners was high in Mizoram, Tamil Nadu, Kerala and Meghalaya. During June, 1997, 7268 females were reported in jails and out of total women prisoners, 5658 were under trials. In the state of Uttar Pradesh, 902 women prisoners were reported and most of them were undertrial. Again, 885 children were reported in jails and most of the children were living in jails of Uttar Pradesh, Madhya Pradesh, Andhra Pradesh, Maharastra, Bihar, Delhi, West Bengal and Rajasthan. In nine states no child was reported living in jail. The number of women prisoners is fluctuating since most of the women prisoners are under trials. However, number of children living with their mothers in jails is still high in some of the jails of Uttar Pradesh.

State of Jail Administration

The Indian correctional system is one of the oldest and one of the largest in comparison with many other countries of the world. It comprises of vast paraphernalia of infrastructure, through out the country, in terms of many institutions such as central jails district jail, sub jail etc; land and buildings etc. About 8.6 million people are held in penal institutions through out the world and about 3.81 lakh prisoners are incarcerated in India.

The prison population rate i.e. defined as the number of prisoners per lakh of the total to population of that country. This rates is far behind to USA, UK, Australia, Russian Federation, China, Singapore, Srilanka, and Pakistan. Of the 3.81 lakhs of the prisoners incarcerated in Indian prisons, majority of them are undertrials, and convict prisoners only forms a small minority.

In an average Indian prison, a typical prisoner is likely to be a male, a first offenders, and will be mostly an under trial. The rate of increase of prison population in India is up by a factor of 2.83. If this trend continues, there will be about 12 lakh prisoners by the end of this decade. Though, the prison infrastructure available in India is huge but the main problem of the prisons is overcrowding due to under trial prisoners. The occupancy rate has been reported to be 128.5 per cent during 2000 which demands the need for additional capacity of 60359 persons in Indian jails.

The occupancy rate has been recorded highest in Madhya Pradesh followed by Uttar Pradesh. Most of the revenue expenditure by states on different agencies on criminal system goes to police and courts and hardly funds are available for jails reforms and correctional systems. The national average of overcrowding in jails is 20 per cent in 1998 as against 9.33 per cent in 1996. The problem of over crowding is not uniformly prevailing in all the states. Delhi topped the list in overcrowding, followed by Haryana, Bihar, Madhya Pradesh, Orissa, Andman and Nikobar Islands, Goa, Andhra Pradesh, Karnataka. Over crowding is not big problem in Tamil Nadu, Kerala and West Bengal.

In the state of Uttar Pradesh, there are 82 jails. Out of total jails, most of the jails are district jails. Besides there are 5 central jails and one model jail in Lucknow. There has been 5.5 per cent compound annual growth rate of population increase in jails of U.P. during 1996 to 2001. During 1991 to 2001, average number of prisoners grew by 96.49 per cent. There has been increasing trend in the rates of convicted and under trials. During the year 2001, there were 54436 persons in jails against the effective capacity of 33802 prisoners. There are about 18 districts without jails.

More than 6170 prisoners were reported living in adjoining district jails. The occupancy rate in 2002 was recorded highest in Ballia, followed by Barabanki, Azamgarh, Varanasi, Lucknow and Sultanpur. While it was reported low in Lucknow Model Jail and Naini Central Jail. In U.P. Jails, 7889 posts are sanctioned while only 7069 persons were found employed and 820 posts are still vacant. Even the vacant Posts are mainly related to class one and class two. Studies demonstrate that prison personnel operate in an all round atmosphere of inefficiency, slackness, disinterest, poor discipline and lack of motivation. This causes demoralization and frustration among the prison staff.

This is attributed to low priority by government, poor pay scales, non payment of essential allowances, poor training, stagnation and poor promotional prospects, long hours of duty, restriction by courts in adequate resources etc. The jails also lack proper planning for human resources development and rehabilitation of prisoners due to lack of financial resources and political will.

CRIME AGAINST OLD WOMEN

The elder abuse as 'harm to an elder person caused by someone in a position of trust, who may have control over the victim. This includes material abuse such as financial exploitation, physical abuse, such as pushing, physical assault, psychological abuse, such as chronically threatening, swearing at or insulting the older person, and neglect or failing to provide necessary help such as meal preparation, housework or personal care.

In the past few years, the aged have frequently been the target of gang robberies or brutal killing by servants or outsiders. Old are attacked frequently due to their inability to put up a fight. Elders normally have to face up to the facts that, their energy and authority is eroding. To add to their woe is the death of any one of the spouse. Widows have to be dealt with specifically, as the death of a spouse for a woman in any age is a tragedy in itself, because of the norms and tradition and the manner in which she is treated after the death of her husband.

EXPLAINING WOMEN AND CRIME

The purpose at this stage is to re-consider the work of Dorie Klein and June Kress and Pat Carlen, during that early wave of feminist criminology. As

Klein and Kress observe women offenders have rarely been seen as either rational or willful: Women criminals have rarely been accorded even the grudging respect shown male criminals, who are at least seen as a threatening force with which to be reckoned. Instead, women have been the target of voyeuristic studies concerned only with their sexuality.

In a later review entitled the 'Etiology of Female Crime', Klein again makes reference, in her critique of authors who contribute to the 'legacy of sexism', to the way in which boys are 'instrumental' whilst girls are 'expressive' and that even; 'Economic offences such as shoplifting are explained as outlets for sexual frustration'. Men and boys have always been credited with committing crimes for a whole variety of reasons. In addition to being lead astray, being sick or evil, males have also been viewed as rational.

Male offenders have been credited with the faculty of reasoning, women offenders have not. As with the popular stereotypes of women in society generally women offenders are portrayed as hysterical, irrational and incapable of being fully responsible for her actions and crimes due to her biology and sex. In similar fashion to that of Klein and Kress in the mid 1970's Carlen's work also makes occasional reference to women offenders acting rationally. Carlen has identified four major characteristics belonging to female offenders. The first characteristic identified is economic rationality.

Carlen however, does little more than state the possibility that women are acting rationally and where her argument is more fully developed she concentrates on rationality as a form of escape from economic dependency and economic hardship. More importantly, Carlen's own analysis of rationality is one that is restricted to rationality born of a need to escape from poverty not one borne out of a vision of prosperity or the attraction and pull of material possessions. Yet one of her most renowned co-authors of Criminal Women, Jenny Hicks suggests she established her own criminal firm, defrauded a post office out of a quarter of a million pounds and used the profits from this to finance a lifestyle which included drugs. Similarly Chris Tchaikovsky '....my criminality was the result of a rational choice - nobody had coerced or cajoled me into it'. Daly has identified several pathways into criminality.

There are street women and those who enter through a relationship with a violent man and those whose friends/partners are involved in selling drugs. As suggested by Hicks and Tchaikovsky, it can be argued however, economic gain, the attraction of money and economic reward as a pull factor, is another. Shoplifting for example, may hold out the attraction of money and economic reward and is just one type of outlawed economic activity that may be an attractive earner to women. Carlen does occasionally suggest that escaping from poverty and abuse is not a generic and comprehensive explanation for women's involvement in crime. Similarly Klein and Kress acknowledge that rationality may not be an entirely male preserve. Although none of the develop this theme, they reiterate and acknowledge the possibility, that for some women who commit property crimes a different explanation may be appropriate. Clearly I suggest this could be an explanation that sees some forms of offending as a more purposely rational activity.

Doing Gender—Doing Difference

In line with a recent observation and recommendation offered by Steffensmeier and Allan, I would argue that it is productive to proceed following a gendered paradigm that 'acknowledges both the utility of traditional theory and the need to describe how the organization of gender specifies the impact of social forces suggested by traditional theory'. Some recently emerging literature is beginning to focus on the gendered nature of crime. This work is illuminating both gender difference, for example in the area of youth street gangs and gender similarity in crime.

Gender can now be viewed as a situated accomplishment; girls and boys 'do' masculinity and femininity. Crime is used as a resource for 'doing' gender, male youth crime is a resource used for accomplishing masculinity. Precisely what this means for women and girls is not yet clearly theorized but implies that women who 'do crimes for economic gain' would 'do' prostitution, shoplifting, cheque frauds and so on. To develop the idea of 'doing femininity', if we assume the 'doing gender - doing difference' approach, one consequence of this is that we never need to consider the 'generalisability problem' because of the separateness of the gendered explanations, women would simply be emphasizing their femininity. On the other hand we may choose to take on board the generalisability problem first which could reformulate the theorizing as follows, Generalisability and 'doing gender - doing difference':

- Take the rational choice perspective from mainstream criminology,
- Consider this perspective adopting a gendered position, with specific reference to women,
- Subject the outcome to the 'doing gender - doing difference' test

These are some of the complex and searching questions that can now begin to be addressed following developments within mainstream and feminist criminology's in the late 1980's.

Rational Choice

The rational choice perspective was used as an example of a development within mainstream criminology that emerged in the 1980's. Cornish and Clarke provide the most developed explanation for the viability of the rational choice perspective in the introduction to The Reasoning Criminal. Rational, Choice Perspectives on Offending.

John Carroll and Frances Weaver: 'Shoplifter's Perceptions of Crime Opportunities: A Process-Tracing Study', to this edited volume. This empirical study of shoplifting, uses verbal protocol procedure to find out what criminals 'really' think about when they are considering actual crime opportunities. The study, whilst it has limitations, is useful in two respects. First, it emphasizes the value of empirical and crime-specific analyses i.e. shoplifting.

Second, the findings suggest a fairly high degree of rationality in the decisions of both expert and novice shoplifters. Retrospective accounts through interviews were not carried out. In addition and significantly for the purposes of this stage, gender differences/similarities were not discussed in any depth although it is apparent that the data could have been further exploited on this subject.

In the early 1980's Steffensmeier also broached the question of rationality, but through a gendered lens. He looked at an organizations criminal enterprise in the context of 'sexsegregation in the underworld'. He suggested, 'rationality refers to the link of means to ends or the extent to which expeditious means are used to achieve goals' and with specific regards to women: if women are less into crime and are relatively less successful at it, this is less a result of single-mindedness in the rational pursuit of crime than because they lack access to organizations and social contacts that would enable them to pursue criminal enterprise more safely and profitably. It seems that the rational choice perspective may be called upon and further developed in respect of specific offences such as shoplifting, that the methods used to investigate this should be more pluralistic, and that the whole inquiry might usefully be conducted on women offenders. The concept of rationality needs to be subjected to the generalisability test.

SENTIMENTAL DEPICTIONS

Other writers also advocated for prisoners by noting how economic circumstances drive individuals to crime, the cruelty of particular punishments, and the poor prospects for released convicts. Lydia Maria Child advocated improvements in the criminal justice system in her journalism. In her story "The Irish Heart: A True Story," published in *Fact and Fiction* (1846), she tells of the young Irish immigrant James, unfairly sentenced as a forger to Sing Sing, which fails to provide him with adequate skills to earn a living; upon release he receives tools and other help from the New York Prison Association.

In the same anthology's "Rosenglory," Child describes Susan, a domestic servant corrupted by one employer's son who later steals money from another employer for not paying her wages. Susan is sent to prison and later receives assistance from a home for discharged women convicts. In Harriet Beecher Stowe's (1811–1896) *Uncle Tom's Cabin* (serialized in 1851–1852), Marie St. Clare sends her slave Rosa to be whipped in a New Orleans jail despite her sister-in-law Ophelia's protests that to put a girl under a man's lash degrades her body and soul.

Other writers represented more positive views of how the law protects the innocent, emphasizing the speedy, efficient resolution of crimes. Catharine Sedgwick was involved with the Women's Prison Association and the Isaac Hopper Home for discharged women prisoners. She alluded to the unfortunate situation of the innocent convict in her novel *Married or Single*? (1857), in which Alice Clifford visits her brother Max in the Tombs because he has been falsely indicted for forgery. After Alice spends a night in a jail cell adjacent to his, Max is acquitted because several individuals help Alice prove his innocence at trial. Horatio Alger's (1832–1899) prototypical rags-to-riches tale *Ragged Dick* (1868) contains a subplot detailing how a fellow boarder steals Dick's bankbook; tipped off by the victim, the police set a trap for the thief, who is arrested, convicted, and sentenced to nine months on Blackwell's Island.

SENSATIONALIZING CRIME

As Andie Tucher notes, American periodicals began printing crime news in 1820, shortly after certain London papers started columns reporting petty crimes. Economic fluctuations encouraged the editors James Gordon Bennett of the *New York Herald* and Horace Greeley of the *New York Tribune* to develop a newspaper readership among the working class by castigating greedy, fraudulent entrepreneurs and corrupt politicians as well as alleged murderers and thieves. Periodicals printed descriptions of jails and prisons based on reporters' visits and collected reports of domestic and foreign crimes. The *National Police Gazette* (published 1845 to 1933 and claiming a circulation of forty thousand readers in its first decade) described famous crimes in history and noted recent crimes reported in the popular press in the United States and abroad. The *Gazette* summarized criminal trials, editorialized about political crimes, and printed articles about historical and contemporary criminals; the editor, George Wilkes, also published the latter in pamphlet form some reprinted decades later. Patricia Cline Cohen argues that newspaper articles about the clerk Richard Robinson, acquitted for the alleged murder of his lover, the New York prostitute Helen Jewett, in 1836, increased sales of the papers and fueled competition in the 1840s by retailing obsessions about sex and death.

Sensational, dime, and western novels incorporated lurid details also used in newspaper crime stories. According to David Reynolds and Kimberly Gladman, the first American city novel was George Lippard's *The Quaker City; or, The Monks of Monk Hall: A Romance of Philadelphia Life* (1844–1845). Inspired by Eugène Sue's *Mystères de Paris, The Quaker City* describes upstanding citizens and criminals conspiring to seduce young women. Reynolds characterizes journalistic aspects of the prolific George Foster's *New York in Slices* (1849), *Fifteen Minutes around New York* (1854), and *New York Naked* (1854) as "realistic exposés" of everyday life in the city. George Thompson's many novels, including *Venus in Boston* (1849) and *City Crimes* (1849), lasciviously describe the degenerative effects of drinking and promiscuous sexual habits, unveiling seemingly virtuous individuals as deviants working closely with vicious criminal gangs. Dime novels, including some published in Erastus Beadle's series beginning in 1860, and some westerns were also criticized as morally pernicious. Bret Harte's "The Luck of Roaring Camp" (1868) more optimistically depicts the rehabilitation of those inclined toward transgression in plotting how a baby civilizes miners on the frontier.

REPRESENTING CRIME AND PUNISHMENT

In addition to the works already cited, images of incarceration and punishment appear in a number of other texts, including Indian captivity narratives and Revolution-era captivity narratives such as Thomas Dring's *Recollections of the Jersey Prison Ship* (1829); narratives of slavery, including Harriet Jacobs's *Incidents in the Life of a Slave Girl* (1861) and Harriet Wilson's novel *Our Nig* (1859); and anti-Catholic convent literature, such as Rebecca Reed's *Six Months in a Convent* (1835) and satires of the latter such as *Six Months in a House of Correction* (1835). After Henry David Thoreau resisted paying his poll tax in protest of the Mexican-American War, he described his night in the Concord jail in "Resistance to Civil Government" (1849).

Several American fiction writers refer to issues associated with historical and contemporary practices of crime and punishment, and some criticize contemporary reforms and reformers. Edgar Allan Poe's fictions represent transgressive anxieties and fears of incarceration; particularly chilling are depictions of murder in "The Tell-Tale Heart" (1843) and of an old man who "is the type and the genius of deep crime" (p. 272) in London, depicted in "The Man of the Crowd" (1840). In the first American detective stories, Poe describes Auguste Dupin's ratiocination in solving criminal cases in "The Murders in the Rue Morgue" (1841), "The Purloined Letter" (1844), and "The Mystery of Marie Roget" (1842–1843).

Nathaniel Hawthorne's works are more critical of criminal stereotypes and reform motivations. "Endicott and the Red Cross" (1838) and *The Scarlet Letter* (1850) characterize the cruelty of Puritan punishments directed at those who are different (Episcopalians, women, Indians).

The House of Seven Gables (1851) denounces social conventions falsely accusing Clifford Pyncheon, foreigners, deviants, women, and the poor of transgressive behaviours. *The Blithedale Romance* (1852) suggests that reforms focused on moral rehabilitation fail in representing Hollingsworth's "impracticable plan for the reformation of criminals through an appeal to their higher instincts".

Herman Melville mentions the prison reformer Elizabeth Fry in *The Confidence-Man* (1857) and François Eugéne Vidocq, the French criminal turned detective, in *White-Jacket* (1850) and *Moby-Dick* (1851). Melville's other fictions note the imprisoning aspects of civilizing society (*Typee,* 1846) and colonialism (*Omoo,* 1847; *Mardi,* 1849). Images of captivity recur in *Redburn* (1849), *The Piazza Tales* (1856), and *Israel Potter* (1855), as protagonists experience diverse forms of captivity on land and sea. The last scenes of "Bartleby, the Scrivener" (1853) and *Pierre* (1852) take place in the Tombs, a New York jail, and in *Billy Budd* (1924) the title character is summarily executed in a hasty trial at sea.

Foreshadowing naturalistic depictions of crime and punishment, *Life in the Iron Mills* (1861), by Rebecca Harding Davis (1831–1910), depicts the wretched circumstances endured by poor ironworkers, who labour like convicts in that their lives and work are constrained by those in authority.

In the novella, Deb picks the pocket of the rich observer who admires her cousin Hugh's ironwork, an action resulting in Hugh's conviction as a thief after he tries to return the money. Davis portrays the inevitable, cruel punishment heaped on the honest worker. Like Hawthorne and Melville, she suggests that Americans countenance social and economic inequalities as the byproduct of entrepreneurial spirit. Decades of investment in penitentiary programs and thousands of words endorsing moral rehabilitation in the antebellum period reflect and reconfigure reform ideals as inextricably tied to ideas of American progress.

ORGANIZED CRIME

We have looked at certain forms of professional, career crime in earlier parts of this stage but we have not discussed what is commonly referred to as 'organized crime'. This can be defined as that form of criminal activity that is organized as a business enterprise through the systematic use of administrative mechanisms, formal coordination, alliances, and joint ventures, and do so in relation to a range of markets for goods and services. Organized crime is criminal activity that goes beyond the relatively smallscale professional and gang activity considered so far. Like these, it has its roots in the specific subcultures of criminality that comprise the underworld, but it also has quite distinctive causes and conditions. Where organized crime exists, it affects the whole pattern of crime within a society. In this part as suggested, look at the common characteristics of organized crime in the United States, Russia, Japan, and Hong Kong, commonly seen as the foci of 'Mafia' style criminality in the world today.

Mafia and Cosa Nostra

Public recognition of something called the Mafia or Cosa Nostra in the United States dates largely from the 1950s and 1960s, when a series of Senate hearings brought the activities of a number of leading Italian-American criminals to public attention. The most influential model of 'Mafia' organization is that depicted by Donald Cressey, originally produced in association with a Presidential Task Force on organized crime. Cressey presented a picture of a huge national confederation involved in fraud, drugs, prostitution, corruption, gambling, and violence, but also using its funds in conventional business operations such as property, finance, clubs, and restaurants. Its methods had come to parallel those of other business enterprises and it was impossible to disentangle illegal from legal activities and profits. This type of organized crime may never have been quite as tight and centralized as they seemed to the public and as they were portrayed in such films as The Godfather, but it was, in many ways, a distinctive form of criminal activity.

Such organized crime became a prominent feature of major American cities in the 1920s and 1930s. It is often seen as a direct outgrowth of the rural networks of support and control that proliferated in Sicily and other isolated parts of Italian society in the nineteenth century and that were transplanted to the United States by migrants from these areas. These were loose networks of friends and relations, rather than secret societies, and were organized around the 'honour' of family and locality and were involved in a wide range of neighbourhood and regional activities. The true origins of organized crime are more recent and more complex.

It arose in its contemporary form after the great waves of European migration to New York, Chicago, and other American cities and was an outgrowth of the very specific conditions of the 1920s and 1930s. The urban slums gave rise to many loosely organized groups that were rooted in their distinctive subcultures. We have already shown how similar gangs also emerged in districts of London. The emergence of such gangs can be explained by the distinctive subcultures found in lowerclass areas of large cities and the corresponding differential association in which this results.

It depends also, however, on the attractiveness of an 'innovative' response to the anomie found in such areas. The gangs of the major US cities became especially involved in the production and sale of 'bootleg' alcohol, made profitable by the 'Prohibition' legislation of the American state. The central participants in the bootlegging of whiskey were European immigrants and the descendents of immigrants, and both Italians and Sicilians were prominent. They were actively involved in a range of criminal activities within their neighbourhoods and became drawn into intensive conflict for customers. An alliance of Sicilian and Italian gangs was forged in 1930–31 and came to be known by outsiders as the Mafia. Far from being a direct descendent of the rural neighbourhoods, then, the gang grouping of the 1930s was a new phenomenon and a distinctive product of American society. It is true, nevertheless, that many of the leading figures in the emerging criminal gangs were recent migrants who had fled the clampdown on the Italian mafia by Mussolini's Fascist regime in the late 1920s.

For all these reasons, Cressey rejected the 'mafia' label, holding that it is inaccurate and was not used by the participants themselves. Participants themselves preferred such impersonal terms as the 'organization', 'business', or 'firm', and sometimes 'Cosa Nostra'. The organization existed, Cressey argued, as a federation of separate and autonomous family-based gangs, each of which defended its particular territory and held that it had a legitimate claim on the support of its local population.

In acting 'honourably' towards 'their' people, providing them with the political influence and personal welfare they were denied by the city and national authorities, they earned the respect of people living in their neighbourhoods. This was reinforced by a structure of coercion that ensured that no one in the locality would challenge the right of the gang to monopolize its profitable ventures. Typical of such territorial groups was the Capone Mob of 1930s Chicago. By the 1960s, Cressey argued, there were over thirty such family mobs.

Each family boss—or 'Don'—had absolute authority in his territory. Through a series of cross-cutting alliances designed to protect the territorial claims of each of the gangs, a vast national organization had been built. The Organization itself had no single leader, but was run by a committee of major mobsters known as the 'Commission'.

Cressey held that, by the late 1960s, the Organization was dominated by nine powerful families: three from New York, three in the surrounding cities of Buffalo, Newark, and Boston, and one each in Philadelphia, Detroit, and Chicago. The various families recognized the role of the Commission in resolving disputes and coordinating activities at a national level. The criminal activities of a family were typically organized through a hierarchy of executive positions, running from the Don through his deputy and advisers to the 'Buffer', who acts as the interface or intermediary between the senior family members and the lower-level operatives. The Buffer had various 'Lieutenants' responsible for particular operating units, each of which had its to liaise with the 'Soldiers' who actually operate particular activities—money lending, lotteries, vending machine rackets, protection, and so on.

Beyond the level of the Soldiers, numerous non-Italians were employed or contracted for specific purposes at street level to take bets, answer telephones, sell narcotics, collect protection money, and so on. Cressey further claimed that the Organization and its families operated just as to a strict code of behaviour that governs all their activities.

This code comprises five principles:

- *Loyalty*: This is the basic injunction to respect the interests of other families and to keep silent about family activities.
- *Rationality*: This is the requirement to act coolly and calmly in pursuit of the family's business: not to take drugs, not to get into fights, and to follow orders as a good team player.
- *Honour*: This is tied to ideas of masculinity and patriarchalism, involving respect for women and for the senior members of the family.
- *Courage*: Family members are to withstand pressure and punishment without complaint. This is, again, tied to a strong ethos of masculinity.
- *Commitment:* Family members are to uphold their way of life without being drawn into the conventions of regular employment or social conformism.

Joseph Albini has warned that the Organization must be regarded not as a bureaucratic enterprise but as a looseknit system of patron–client or network relationships. As such, its structure is constantly in flux and no rigid model can describe its shape at any particular time. It is clear, nevertheless, that Cressey highlighted the ways in which such a loose-knit structure can coordinate and control the actions of its constituent gangs through both formal and informal mechanisms.

Other Organized Crime

Much discussion of organized crime in the United States has been concerned with that of Italian Americans, but a number of sociologists have pointed to the existence of many other forms of organized crime. Robert

Davidson has documented the rise of Asian-American gangs in Chicago and other cities. Those from China, the Philippines, India, Korea, and other parts of Asia now form a significant part of the US population. In a number of areas of Asian settlement, there has been a growth of criminal involvement in drug trafficking, especially the trade in heroin from South East Asia. Organized gangs in American cities use their connections with Chinese triads operating from Hong Kong to obtain heroin for re-sale in the United States.

Actual sales to users are handled by street gangs, but the bulk trade itself is a highly organized business. Outside the United States, evidence for strong organized criminal gangs has been found in Japan, Russia, and other parts of Eastern Europe. Organized crime had begun to develop in the final twenty years of Communism in Russia, when corrupt and self-serving politicians used illegal means to further their own interests, but it was the collapse of Communism that really stimulated its growth.

The disappearance of the strong, totalitarian state in Russia and the consequent privatization of state economic assets allowed many private individuals to amass considerable wealth through dealing in state assts. Many former Communist politicians were able to use their knowledge and connections to build up personal fortunes themselves and to join this emerging Russian 'mafia'. Organized crime has proliferated because of the economic dislocations that followed the ending of Communism, as this allowed the criminal syndicates to obtain and monopolize scarce resources from which they could benefit. Russian organized crime, like its American counterpart, is organized through loose 'syndicates' that operate on the basis of patron–client relationships.

In these relationships, a person of power or wealth helps or protects specific others, who, in return, perform services for their patron. The relationship is not a contractual, employment relationship but rests on informal patterns of trust and obligation. Hierarchies of patron–client relationships form networks of reciprocity and obligation centred on the most powerful individuals. Those involved in these networks are engaged in a range of illegal activities. Although Russia has virtually no bank robberies, bank fraud is rife and banks pay high levels of protection money to avoid becoming the targets of robberies. Forging of documents is widespread, as is illegal arms trading, including dealing in nuclear materials, prostitution, drug smuggling, money laundering, and illegal imports. Crime is so closely integrated with conventional business that it has been argued that there is a 'shadow economy' of marginal and unregulated business with its 'black market' for distributing goods.

There are high levels of political corruption, giving the criminal syndicates considerable influence over the state. Organized crime in Hong Kong and mainland China originated in the 'triad' secret societies, though it now reaches beyond them. Triads are a long-standing feature of traditional Chinese society and prospered in Hong Kong during its separation from the rest of China. A triad is a family- and neighbourhood-based grouping that provides support and services for its members and organizes its activities on the basis of secrecy and elaborate rituals of membership.

Acting outside, and often against, the central state, triads became involved in a range of legal and illegal activities. Triad activity in Hong Kong grew after the Communist revolution in China, when many prominent leaders were expelled from the mainland. The economic success of Hong Kong since the 1960s provided many opportunities for triads to expand their involvement in prostitution, gambling, and drugs. Thus, while there is continuity between the traditional triads and those of today, systematic involvement in organized crime is a recent and more specific phenomenon. Triads tend to be organized as loose networks of independent gangs that regard themselves as part of a larger 'family' or clan in which there is a decentralized structure of command. The various gangs are loosely ranked as 'Red Pole', 'Blue Lantern', and ordinary. Although they cooperate for common purposes, they are also involved in recurrent and intense conflict over the pursuit of their interests. Organized crime in Japan originated in gambling groups and itinerant dealers who banded together for mutual protection and were given official encouragement to organize markets at shrines and temples and to regulate the supply of labour for public works constriction.

By the early twentieth century, they were a strongly entrenched feature of Japanese society and had come to be known as Yakuza. They were used as government tools for strikebreaking and for fighting left-wing political groups and they had strong links with right-wing political leaders. The Yakuza took their present form, however, after the Second World War. Industrial reconstruction and slow political liberalization created opportunities for profitable enterprise in the black markets and in the supply of labour for construction and dock work.

They moved into the growing entertainment industry of bars, prostitution, and pachinko, and they extended their protection and extortion activities. Intense conflict among Yakuza led to the emergence of a small number of major syndicates, paralleling the structure of business groups that had developed in the conventional economy.

Despite a police clamp down in the 1960s, organized crime in Japan remains highly concentrated. Hill has established that there are currently about 90,000 men involved in organized crime in Japan and that about 40 per cent are involved in gangs affiliated to one of the three big syndicates: Yamaguchi-gumi, Iwagawa-kai, and Sumiyoshi-kai.

The syndicates have great similarities to Cressey's model of the Cosa Nostra and are organized in ways that draw on the idea of the traditional family household, with its paternalistic and authoritarian patterns of control by the 'father' over junior members. Formal administrative mechanisms are also used, however, and the syndicates are organized into series of ranks such as 'boss', executive, soldier, and trainee.

A Yakuza syndicate and its affiliated groupings are organized in relation to a tight discipline and obedience, embodied in a strict code of behaviour that is enforced, when necessary, through violence. Yakuza are currently involved in protection rackets, the supply of drugs, gambling, the sale of festival trinkets, prostitution, debt collection, loan sharking, rent collection, and the supply of labour through sub-contractors. In many of these areas they act under commission from conventional businesses and public authorities, which rely on the ability of the Yakuza to manage and manipulate their employees, shareholders, and voters through blackmail and coercion.

3

Sexual Harassment

SEXUAL HARASSMENT: WHAT ARE WE TALKING ABOUT?

One problem that occurs when discussing sexual harassment is that the experience is trivialized. Some have suggested that the prohibition against sexual harassment is like a code of civility for the workplace and complaints a matter of litigating bad manners. These suggestions miss two critical aspects of both the legal definition of sexual harassment and women's actual experience of it. To be legally actionable sexual harassment must be severe or pervasive. For many women, it is both severe and pervasive.

Sexual harassment can include instances of rape, forced oral copulation, and other sexual assaults. Some of the most egregious cases reported by those working with women complaining of sexual harassment involve women who "consented" to have sex with supervisors as a condition of employment. While it may seem absurd that a woman would feel compelled to have sex just to hold on to a job, the women targeted by some of the more predatory harassers are extremely vulnerable. Consider, for example, the case of a young woman in a position with insurance benefits, whose husband did not have insurance through his job, who had recently given birth to a child with a chronic and severe medical condition that was expensive to treat. Even the less dramatic case of a single mother with limited skills in "the best-paying job I've ever had" faces a difficult dilemma.

Documentation of sexual assault as part of sexual harassment is not limited to anecdotal report. Large surveys of women's experiences in a variety of workplaces have included reports of both demands for sexual favours and attempted or successful sexual assaults. A 1995 survey of women in the military found that 6 percent reported rapes or rape attempts as part of their military experience. The psychological consequences of these assaults are significant. For example, one study of women veterans seeking treatment for stress-related disorders found that for 43 percent of them, rape or attempted rape during their military service was a significant factor in their need for treatment.

Other forms of harassment not directly involving sexual activity but directed at women violating gender norms either in their own personal appearance or by working in stereotypically male jobs can also be severe. Studies of blue-collar workers find between 20 and 40 percent of respondents in traditionally male occupations report attempts by their male coworkers to cause them physical harm. Anecdotal reports and individual cases of women in traditionally male occupations such as neurosurgery and investment banking include attempts either to cause physical harm or to sabotage their work product—and thus their professional standing or employment.

Of course, some harassing behaviours are not particularly egregious in isolation. As Mary Rowe (1990) so eloquently describes, they are the micro-inequities and micro-aggressions that gain power, like water dripping on granite, through endless repetition. Much of the early research on sexual harassment focused on delineating the extensive contours of the harassment experience. The early surveys by the U.S. Merit Systems Protection Board (1981,1987) demonstrated that sexual harassment was a common and destructive phenomenon among federal employees.

In the late 1980s, Louise Fitzgerald and her colleagues introduced a measure that assessed almost thirty specific behaviours derived from theoretical constructs of sexual harassment. Their instrument, the Sexual Experiences Questionnaire (SEQ), with some modifications, is the most widely used and adapted instrument for the measurement of sexual harassment. Research using the SEQ and other instruments has established that the behaviours involved in sexual harassment occur with great frequency and that women generally report multiple forms of harassing experiences. Although the focus of sexual harassment research has shifted from documenting its existence to addressing antecedents and consequences, ongoing research continues to document the extensive nature of the experience.

In general, the behaviours comprising sexual harassment occur frequently. Some estimates suggest that as many as 50 percent of women will experience sexual harassment at some point in their life. Furthermore, although there is a range of behaviours starting with offensive verbal behavior, sexual harassment includes physical and sexual assaults and pressure for sexual favours. Although there is some evidence that individual psychological factors are significant for perpetrators of sexual assaults and attempts to coerce sexual favours as a condition of employment, the work environment and the gender stereotype of the work are the critical factors in determining the overall level of sexual harassment in a workplace. Women working outside the traditional female occupations have experienced the highest levels of sexual harassment, in both form of harassment and frequency of harassment. Their experiences can include daily occurrences of multiple forms of offensive conduct. In addition, the experiences of women working in stereotypically male occupations are more likely to include severe forms of nonsexual gender-based harassment. However, the data do not indicate that women in traditionally male jobs experience a differential rate of pressure for sexual favours as a condition of employment.

Feminist scholars and even the courts have recognized that sexual harassment is about power, not just about normal heterosexual behavior. At an almost axiomatic level, people cannot persist in unwanted behavior when those toward whom the behavior is directed have the power to make them stop. Conversely, research has found that structural changes that increase power inequities, such as the long-term use of temporary workers who lack standing as employees of the company, increase the likelihood that the less powerful workers will experience harassment. Other factors that have been shown to influence the amount of harassment that occurs in a particular work setting are the number of men in the setting, the gender stereotype of the job, the gender ratio of the job, and the tolerance of harassment by the organization.

SEXUAL HARASSMENT: A SPECIAL CASE

Sexual harassment is a somewhat complex issue, with discussion made more difficult by the fact that while the phenomenon is quite old, the term itself did not exist when the Civil Rights Act of 1964 was passed. From the fictional stories of female servants to the documented reports by female slaves and wage workers, the narrative of women being pressured or forced into sexual acts in the context of work is an all-too-common report. What is newer is the social recognition that such conduct is wrong and the legal apparatus for complaints about it. As late as the 1980s, male managers and supervisors, when challenged by a government agency in California about demanding sex from women as a condition of employment, were "surprised in many cases that such behavior was against the law".

The legal system, even after the passage of the Civil Rights Act, took some time to recognize sexual harassment as an unlawful act. Quite early in the legal interpretations of the Civil Rights Act, the Equal Employment Opportunity Commission (EEOC) recognized that Title VII prohibits harassment. The courts supported the EEOC position that Title VII creates an affirmative duty for employers to provide a work environment free from harassment. Court decisions, initially on race issues, recognized that harassment created a climate of discrimination *(Anderson v. Methodist Evangelical Hospital,* 1972). The prohibited conduct includes, but is certainly not limited to, berating employees for mistakes, imposing extra duties, restricting privileges, or suggesting that a woman does not belong in the job when these actions are based on the employees' sex/gender (or any other of the categories protected under Title VII). In other words, Title VII requires employers to create an atmosphere where employees are not insulted or demeaned because of their "race, sex, colour, religion, or national origin" (Equal Employment Opportunity Commission, 1992, sec. 615).

Although there was an early recognition that Title VII prohibited harassment, initially the courts did not view demands for sexual favours or other forms of sexual conduct as harassment. It was not until 1976 that a federal appellate court opined that a woman who had been fired because she refused the sexual advances of her male boss was the victim of sex discrimination. The lower court had ruled that such conduct was the private and arguably natural behavior of a man toward a woman rather than an issue covered by employment law. However, the appellate court accepted the argument, developed largely by feminist legal scholars, that this conduct was unlawful sex discrimination. The rationale is that the conduct is sex discrimination not because it involves sex but because it is conduct that is directed at a target because of her sex. In 1980, the EEOC developed and published guidelines on sexual harassment that continue to be in use. The EEOC guidance on sexual harassment states: Harassment on the basis of sex is a violation of Sec. 703 of Title VII (of the U.S. Civil Rights Act of 1964). Unwelcome advances, requests for sexual favours, and other verbal or physical conduct of a sexual nature constitute sexual harassment when:

1. submission to such conduct is made either explicitly or implicitly a term or condition of the individual's employment;
2. submission to or rejection of such conduct by an individual is used as the basis for employment decisions affecting such individual; or
3. such conduct has the purpose or effect of unreasonably interfering with an individual's work performance or creating an intimidating, hostile, or offensive work environment.

In 1986, the U.S. Supreme Court, in *Meritor Savings Bankv. Vin-son,* upheld the EEOC guidelines on sexual harassment. This case was particularly important because the Court upheld the concept of a hostile environment. In *Meritor,* the Court affirmed that the supervisor's demands for sexual favours created a hostile environment even though there was no direct threat of adverse job action. Several important psychological issues are presented by the Court decision in *Meritor.* First, the standard for what constitutes a legally actionable situation was articulated as when the discriminatory conduct is severe enough to alter the conditions of employment. Second, the Court asserted that what matters is not whether compliance with the sexual demands was voluntary but whether it was welcomed. The issue of what distinguishes "welcome" from "unwelcome" conduct continues to evolve through case law and interpretation.

In addition, the Court addressed the question of when an employer is liable for the action of a supervisor. One position on this issue, the strict liability position, is that the employer is always liable for the actions of supervisors. The other position is that the employer should be held liable for the action of the supervisor only if the employer was negligent, meaning the employer knew about the supervisor's conduct or should have known about it and failed to take appropriate action. For over a decade following the *Meritor* decision, the lower courts struggled with this issue. Finally, in 1998, the U.S. Supreme Court issued two opinions on the same day establishing clearer guidance on the issue of employer liability *(Burlington Industries, Inc.* v. *Ellerth,* 1998; *Fargherv. City of Boca Raton,* 1998). In these cases, the Court distinguished between situations where a tangible job action occurred and those where the issue was purely about the work environment or atmosphere. The Court stated:

An employer is subject to vicarious liability to a victimized employee for an actionable hostile environment created by a supervisor with immediate (or successively higher) authority over the employee. When no tangible employment action is taken, a defendant employer may raise an affirmative defense to liability or damages, subject to proof by a preponderance of evidence.... The defense comprises two necessary elements: (a) that the employer exercised reasonable care to prevent and correct promptly any sexually harassing behavior, and (b) that the plaintiff employee unreasonably failed to take advantage of any preventive or corrective opportunities provided by the employer or to avoid harm otherwise.... No affirmative defense is available, however, when the supervisor's harassment culminates in a tangible employment action such as discharge, demotion, or undesirable reassignment.

This decision appears to place employer liability for supervisors' actions when no adverse job action occurs in roughly the same category as the actions of coworkers.

Since these rulings, the issue of an affirmative defense has become a focus of considerable attention. Although there appears to be a tendency to equate the mere existence of a complaint procedure not used by the complaining party as evidence of an "unreasonable failure," psychological research may ultimately be important. In a recent article, psychologist Louise Fitzgerald and her colleagues present data that suggest reporting is often harmful to the complaining party.

Their data also suggest that the likelihood of reporting is influenced by the way in which the complaint will be handled. Furthermore, other research suggests that the response of management to issues around sexual harassment affects the likelihood that victims will complain, with positive efforts to stop or eradicate harassment leading to more reporting and negative responses leading to less reporting. Unless this issue is adequately addressed, the actual effect of the "unreasonable failure" provision may be to reward employers for dealing with complaints so badly that victims do not complain.

The legal issues surrounding sex discrimination and including sexual harassment will continue to evolve, as they have since 1964. Both congressional action and case law will undoubtedly mold the landscape in new ways. The hope is that these changes will incorporate and reflect the information that psychological research can provide. Without that inclusion, victims will be penalized. For example, it has been important for case law to acknowledge the ubiquitous psychological research finding that experience is not gender neutral. Men and women experience and interpret behaviours relating to social interactions differently. By emphasizing that the law's hypothetical "reasonable person" must be similarly situated (for example, of the same gender) as the actual victim, case law can incorporate the understandings that psychological research can provide.

LEGAL ISSUES: LEGAL CONTEXT

The psychological processes described above, operating in the historical context of women's limited and devalued role in the work world, provide the context for the various complaints of discrimination that find their way into the legal system. As was noted previously, Title VII of the Civil Rights Act of 1964 is the principal foundation for most claims of sex discrimination in the United States. Prior to the passage of the Civil Rights Act, it was not unlawful to discriminate in employment on the basis of sex. Although some of the actions that can fall under the rubric of workplace sexual harassment, for example, sexual assault, were crimes, they were not civil rights violations. Similarly, while pervasive or severe harassment may have been the basis for common law tort claims of negligent or intentional infliction of emotional distress, assault and battery, false imprisonment, or invasion of privacy, these did not fall under the banner of federal civil rights or employment law.

In the years since the passage of the Civil Rights Act of 1964, a number of changes have occurred. States and many local governments have passed employment rights laws that parallel and, in many cases, expand the federal protections against discrimination in the workplace. Legal actions have resulted in the abolition of various discriminatory practices such as sex-segregated employment advertisements, which provided formal barriers to women's full and equal participation in the workplace.

The legal actions brought under Title VII of the Civil Rights Act of 1964, as amended by the Civil Rights Act of 1991, can provide injunc-tive relief, forcing employers to rectify the discriminatory conduct. In addition, in some cases, monetary damages for lost wages and benefits, or even punitive damages, can also be awarded. However, monetary damages are generally awarded only when the discrimination has been intentional. Punitive damages are justified only when an employer acts with "malice or reckless indifference to the federally protected rights of an aggrieved individual".

One of the many legal controversies developing from Title VII has involved the issue of "mixed motives," that is, situations where an employer takes an action in part because of "legitimate" reasons and in part because of discriminatory reasons. This issue is critical for legal actions concerning discrimination in the workplace because employment decisions are rarely justified purely on the basis of discriminatory factors. Instead, it is the discriminatory results of the psychological processes, like stereotyping and prejudice, that cause employers to discipline women more or more harshly for certain actions than they would men. One could describe the cognitive effects of prejudice as the mental equivalents of flypaper and nonstick coatings. Thus, there is generally some legitimate basis for the employer's action: the woman did make a mistake, use a curse word, or behave rudely, even though the same behavior has not received the same punishment when performed by a male employee because all of the woman's past transgressions were both noticed and remembered.

This mixed-motive issue was addressed by the U.S. Supreme Court in *Price Waterhousev. Hopkins* (1989). In that case, evidence provided by psychologist Susan Fiske on sex stereotyping was cited by the Court in its decision supporting plaintiff Hopkins, who had been denied partnership because she was overly abrasive and advised by her employer to wear makeup and attend charm school. The Court recently affirmed and extended this decision in *Desert Palace, Inc.* v. *Costa* (2003). In that decision, the Court noted that the Congress, when it amended the Civil Rights Act in 1991, made it clear that it is unlawful for a company to use sex as a motivating factor in employment decisions even though other factors are also involved. This decision resolves almost twelve years of confusing case law concerning the proof a plaintiff must provide to establish that sex was a motivating factor. In *Desert Palace,* the Court stated that the plaintiff must establish only by a preponderance of evidence that sex was a factor in the decision. This was important because some courts had suggested that plaintiffs must present direct "smoking gun" proof in order to claim sex discrimination.

PREVENTION OF SEX DETERMINATION

In 1994, the Government of India passed the Pre-conception and Pre-natal Diagnostic Techniques (Prohibition of Sex Selection) Act with the aim of preventing female foeticide. The implementation of this Act was slow. It was later amended and replaced in 2002 by the Prenatal Diagnostic Techniques (Regulation and Prevention of Misuse) Act without ever having been properly implemented. The Act has a central and state level Supervisory Board, an Appropriate Authority, and supporting Advisory Committee.

The function of the Supervisory Board is to oversee, monitor, and make amendments to the provisions of the Act. Appropriate Authority provides registration, and conducts the administrative work involved in inspection, investigation, and the penalizing of defaulters. The Advisory Committee provides expert and technical support to the Appropriate Authority. Contravening the provisions of the Act can lead to a fine of Rs 10,000 and up to three years imprisonment for a first offence, with greater fines and longer terms of imprisonment for repeat offenders. The Appropriate Authority informs the central or state medical council to take action against medical professionals, leading to suspension or the striking off of practitioners found guilty of contravening the provisions of the Act.

Before conducting any prenatal diagnostic procedure, the medical practitioner must obtain a written consent from the pregnant woman in a local language that she understands. Prenatal tests may be performed in various specified circumstances, including risk of chromosomal abnormalities in the case of women over 35, and genetic diseases evident in the family history of the couple. Implementation of the 1994 Act. We conducted a study to assess the implementation of the 1994 Act in South Delhi and make recommendations for its improvement. This involved examining the organizational structure, observing 26 clinics, and distributing a questionnaire to patients.

The results showed up serious failures in management and implementation, lack of commitment and motivation, widespread corruption, and little knowledge in clinics of the provisions of the Act. The presence of individuals outside the medical profession, in particular those involved with human rights, would have helped to prevent fraternity bias-an unwillingness to bring medical colleagues to account. The survey of patient attitudes showed that only 40% of male patients and 30% of female patients were aware of the prohibition of sex determination. While 90% purported to agree with the principle of the Act, they nevertheless maintained that a male child was important for the strengthening of the family.

PREVENTING FEMALE FOETICIDE

The removal of this practice in Indian society is a serious challenge. It must involve

- A move away from religious teachings and the advocacy of a scientific, rational, and humanist approach.
- The empowerment of women and a strengthening of women's rights through campaigning against practices such as dowry, and ensuring strict implementation of existing legislation.
- Ensuring the development of and access to good health care services.
- Inculcating a strong ethical code of conduct among medical professionals, beginning with their training as undergraduates.
- Simple methods of complaint registration, accessible to the poorest and most vulnerable women.
- Wide publicization in the media of the scale and seriousness of the practice. NGOs should take a key role in educating the public on this matter.
- Regular assessment of indicators of status of women in society, such as sex ratio, and female mortality, literacy, and economic participation.

It is only by a combination of monitoring, education campaigns, and effective legal implementation that the deep-seated attitudes and practices against women and girls can be eroded.

- Chronic Hunger and the Status of Women in India
- How gender discrimination is the root cause of hunger.
- The historic opportunity of the 73rd amendment.
- Successful strategies to overcome patriarchy.

You can tell the condition of a nation by looking at the status of its women. — Jawaharlal Nehru

However much a mother may love her children, it is all but impossible for her to provide high-quality child care if she herself is poor and oppressed, illiterate and uninformed, anaemic and unhealthy, has five or six other children, lives in a slum or shanty, has neither clean water nor safe sanitation, and if she is without the necessary support either from health services, or from her society, or from the father of her childen. —Vulimiri Ramalingaswami, "The Asian Enigma" The women who participate in and lead ecology movements in countries like India are not speaking merely as victims. Their voices are the voices of liberation and transformation... The women's and ecology movements are therefore one, and are primarily counter-trends to a patriarchal maldevelopment. —Vandana Shiva

Amartya Sen-The Unheeded Conscience: We will lionise him, but will we ever listen to what he's saying? Sen points out that when he took up issues of women's welfare, he was accused in India of voicing "foreign concerns." "I was told Indian women don't think like that about equality. But I would like to argue that if they don't think like that they should be given a real opportunity to think like that." —Parmita Shastri, Outlook India, 1998

The persistence of hunger and abject poverty in India and other parts of the world is due in large measure to the subjugation, marginalization and disempowerment of women. Women suffer from hunger and poverty in greater numbers and to a great degree then men. At the same time, it is women who bear the primary responsibility for actions needed to end hunger: education, nutrition, health and family income. Looking through the lens of hunger and poverty, there are seven major areas of discrimination against women in India:

- *Malnutrition*: India has exceptionally high rates of child malnutrition, because tradition in India requires that women eat last and least throughout their lives, even when pregnant and lactating. Malnourished women give birth to malnourished children, perpetuating the cycle.
- *Poor Health*: Females receive less health care than males. Many women die in childbirth of easily prevented complications. Working conditions and environmental pollution further impairs women's health.
- *Lack of education*: Families are far less likely to educate girls than boys, and far more likely to pull them out of school, either to help out at home or from fear of violence.
- *Overwork*: Women work longer hours and their work is more arduous than men's, yet their work is unrecognized. Men report that "women, like children, eat and do nothing." Technological progress in agriculture has had a negative impact on women.
- *Unskilled*: In women's primary employment sector-agriculture-extension services overlook women.
- *Mistreatment*: In recent years, there has been an alarming rise in atrocities against women in India, in terms of rapes, assaults and dowry-related murders. Fear of violence suppresses the aspirations of all women. Female infanticide and sex-selective abortions are additional forms of violence that reflect the devaluing of females in Indian society.
- *Powerlessness*: While women are guaranteed equality under the constitution, legal protection has little effect in the face of prevailing patriarchal traditions. Women lack power to decide who they will marry,

and are often married off as children. Legal loopholes are used to deny women inheritance rights.

India has a long history of activism for women's welfare and rights, which has increasingly focused on women's economic rights. A range of government programs have been launched to increase economic opportunity for women, although there appear to be no existing programs to address the cultural and traditional discrimination against women that leads to her abject conditions.

The Inextricable Link

The greatest tragedy facing humanity today is the persistence of chronic hunger-an intolerable phenomenon that takes the lives of 24,000 of us every day. For fully one-fifth of humanity, life is a daily struggle to survive in conditions of relentless poverty. Day after day, the lives of one billion individuals are cut short or terribly diminished by chronic, persistent hunger. Day after day, one billion people are denied the opportunities they need to lead healthy and productive lives. People living with chronic hunger exist in conditions of severe poverty. What they lack is the chance to change their situation, to develop their own self-sufficiency. The most potent confirmation of this fact can be seen in the lives of women. They, along with their children, are the main victims of hunger, and they are also most lacking in opportunities to end their own and their families' hunger.

The Hunger Project has come to the recognition that the persistence of hunger in India-and elsewhere in the world where hunger is still an overriding social issue-is, to a large degree, due to the subjugation, marginalization and disempowerment of women. Furthermore, women's suppression is rooted in the very fabric of Indian society-in traditions, in religious doctrine and practices, within the educational and legal systems, and within families.

Ironically, much of the essential work of ending hunger rests in women's hands. Traditionally, women bear primary responsibility for the well-being of their families. Yet they are systematically denied access to the resources they need to fulfill their responsibility, which includes education, health care services, job training, and access and freedom to use family planning services.

In order to gain a shared understanding of the condition of the status of women in India and its impact on the persistence of hunger, this document surveys papers done by leading scholars in Indian development issues. It is organized in a framework of seven issues that characterize the plight of resource-poor women, with a focus on rural women, in India: malnutrition, poor health, lack of education, overwork, lack of skills, mistreatment and powerlessness. The link between these issues and the persistence of hunger in

India was underscored in a 1996 study: The Asian Enigma, by Vulimiri Ramalingaswami:

In short, the poor care that is afforded to girls and women by their husbands and by elders is the first major reason for levels of child malnutrition that are markedly higher in South Asia than anywhere else in the world. India, with a population of 989 million, is the world's second most populous country. Of that number, 120 million are women who live in poverty. India has 16 percent of the world's population, but only 2.4 percent of its land, resulting in great pressures on its natural resources.

Over 70 percent of India's population currently derive their livelihood from land resources, which includes 84 percent of the economically-active women. India is one of the few countries where males significantly outnumber females, and this imbalance has increased over time. India's maternal mortality rates in rural areas are among the world's highest. From a global perspective, Indian accounts for 19 percent of all lives births and 27 percent of all maternal deaths. "There seems to be a consensus that higher female mortality between ages one and five and high maternal mortality rates result in a deficit of females in the population. Chatterjee (1990) estimates that deaths of young girls in India exceed those of young boys by over 300,000 each year, and every sixth infant death is specifically due to gender discrimination." Of the 15 million baby girls born in India each year, nearly 25 percent will not live to see their 15th birthday.

"Although India was the first country to announce an official family planning program in 1952, its population grew from 361 million in 1951 to 844 million in 1991. India's total fertility rate of 3.8 births per woman can be considered moderate by world standards, but the sheer magnitude of population increase has resulted in such a feeling of urgency that containment of population growth is listed as one of the six most important objectives in the Eighth Five-Year Plan."

Since 1970, the use of modern contraceptive methods has risen from 10 percent to 40 percent, with great variance between northern and southern India. The most striking aspect of contraceptive use in India is the predominance of sterilization, which accounts for more than 85 percent of total modern contraception use, with female sterilization accounting for 90 percent of all sterilizations.

The Indian constitution grants women equal rights with men, but strong patriarchal traditions persist, with women's lives shaped by customs that are centuries old. In most Indian families, a daughter is viewed as a liability, and she is conditioned to believe that she is inferior and subordinate to men. Sons are idolized and celebrated. May you be the mother of a hundred sons is a common Hindu wedding blessing.

The origin of the Indian idea of appropriate female behavior can be traced to the rules laid down by Manu in 200 B.C.: "by a young girl, by a young woman, or even by an aged one, nothing must be done independently, even in her own house". "In childhood a female must be subject to her father, in youth to her husband, when her lord is dead to her sons; a woman must never be independent."

A study of women in the Swayam Shikshan Prayog (SSP), based in 20 villages in four districts in Maharashtra state was introduced in this way: The primary issue all women in the SSP were struggling with was that of everyday survival. Insufficient incomes and the lack of employment were reported to be their most pressing concerns. Survival is a constant preoccupation and at its most basic, survival means food.

The most common problems were the lack of basic amenities such as food, water, fuel, fodder and health facilities. In addition, the deterioration of the natural environment and the fact that many of their traditional occupations were no longer viable were conditions that were making it increasingly hard for women to continue sustaining their families, as they had done in the past. SSP is a loose, informal network of women's collectives, voluntary organizations, action groups and unions.

SEXUAL HARASSMENT INVESTIGATIONS AND THE ROLE OF HR EXPERTS

The universal issue that appears on both sides of sexual harassment lawsuits is the timeliness and quality of the sexual harassment investigation that should have been triggered by the sexual harassment complaint. My experience is that the quality and timeliness of the investigation are among the most pivotal issues that courts consider in assessing the conduct of the company accused of sexual harassment. A professionally executed sexual harassment investigation is the most effective deterrent against frivolous litigation and the best defense against liability when harassment has actually occurred.

Preparation for the Investigation

In preparing for the investigation, management should review the written sexual harassment complaint, which should have been solicited at the beginning of an investigation. This will avoid accusations of conveniently evolving stories and circumstances in addition to obtrusive measurement error. (Obtrusive measurement occurs when an investigator changes the facts and circumstances by the very process of the investigation—obviously not a desirable outcome.) Management should also determine whether the sexual harassment investigator has reasonably assessed the individuals privy to information about the alleged harassment before the actual investigation. They must be prepared to explain why any individual so identified might not have been interviewed for corroboration. Management may also need to comment about the nature of the investigation and interview team. A two-person team is ideal, though certainly not essential, for an internal investigation. If two interviewers are engaged, a male-female team is preferable.

Parties to the Investigation

Management should try to determine whether witnesses were told that there would be no retaliation for telling the truth or that their confidentiality could not be guaranteed. The experts should also be sensitive as to whether the complainant and witness information was shared only on a need-to-know basis. There is an obligation in an effective sexual harassment investigation to avoid defaming the accused harasser and unnecessarily embarrassing the complainant. It is always important to be aware that both parties have rights in a sexual harassment investigation.

Those conducting a sexual harassment investigation also have an obligation to protect the interests and reputations of all parties and should make no a priori assumptions as to motivation and fault. An HR management expert can be particularly effective in examining the facts and circumstances surrounding a sexual harassment investigation to make a determination as to whether the guidelines were followed. At trial, the expert may also be asked to comment about the wisdom of allowing the complainant to confront the accused harasser directly during the course of the investigation. In most circumstances, it is neither advisable nor necessary for the complainant to do this, although ideally, confrontation should have occurred prior to the initiation of a complaint.

The circumstances of any specific complaint may necessitate that the investigators interview other past or current employees who might have been exposed to harassment (if in fact it actually occurred). At trial, an HR management expert may be asked to second-guess the wisdom of those determinations (and the repercussions of the failure to do so).

Requirements of the Investigation

It is important that management understand that there is no single procedure that absolutely must be followed in conducting a professionally appropriate sexual harassment investigation. If, for example, a consultant has produced a guidebook outlining suggested steps for an investigation, it is unlikely that each step is an absolute requirement exactly as articulated. There is leeway in conducting appropriate sexual harassment investigations. Investigators must also consider whether an alleged incident is isolated or part of a pattern of harassment involving the complainant and possibly others. This may also be a legitimate area for expert inquiry in making a determination as to whether a pattern and practice exists.

Adverse Impact on Job Performance

A crucial issue in any employment situation is whether the conduct of the employer or its representatives had an adverse impact on job performance. That is a fundamental dimension of any assessment of harassment in the workplace. It is also understood to be an important motivating factor in the passage of antiharassment legislation. An expert should be prepared to comment about that issue and critique the measures used to make that determination.

Issues in the Investigation

An effective HR management expert needs to able to differentiate and explain to a jury the differences among insensitivity, tastelessness, and rudeness, which do not automatically reach the standard for determining that sexual harassment has occurred, unless other circumstances and conditions apply. An effective defense expert should be able to explain these differences to a jury.

The basic issues in most sexual harassment investigations boil down to whether the conduct in question was sexual in nature and whether the conduct was unwelcome in the sense that the complainant neither solicited nor incited it and also found it undesirable or offensive. These sensitive issues require care and finesse in understanding and interpreting. An expert may also be called on to determine whether the complainant or someone representing the complainant properly advised an alleged harasser in a hostile work environment situation that the behavior was unwelcome.

After a finding that sexual harassment has occurred, there are final issues in determining the appropriate discipline:

- Whether the complainant properly notified the alleged harasser
- The severity of harassment (obviously a judgment call, appropriate for expert testimony)
- The frequency of harassment
- Previous or concurrent harassment complaints

The conclusion of the investigation is also a subject for possible expert commentary, specifically with regard to sharing the response of the accused harasser as well as the outcome of the investigation with the complainant. An expert will be able to explain to the court that while the claimant should not be permitted to dictate disciplinary procedure or corrective action, if the claim is valid, the claimant's comfort with a particular outcome could be taken into consideration.

With regard to a sexual harassment complaint that is found to have merit, an expert may need to evaluate whether follow-up mechanisms were required or effective in ensuring that the harassment cease, with little or no probability of recurrence. Furthermore, an expert may be asked to assess whether corrective action was proper in order to stop the harassment, discipline the harasser, and reinforce that sexual harassment is neither acceptable nor tolerable.

Often the outcome of a sexual harassment investigation is inconclusive or disputed by one or another party. Management should be prepared to determine whether the investigation was concluded with any unresolved material inconsistencies between the parties. An expert may be asked to comment on whether actions taken within that investigation, such as separating the parties and minimizing their interaction, were appropriate. The expert may also be asked to provide an opinion as to whether such actions could have been accomplished with less detrimental impact on either party's position or reputation.

Liability in the Investigation

An expert's comments can be vital when reviewing the requirement of good faith and fair dealing that is entailed within a sexual harassment investigation, especially as it relates to the speed of such an investigation. When there is an attempt to achieve rapid resolution, an expert can determine whether greater speed might have compromised the integrity of the investigation, which is obviously not an acceptable outcome.

Retaliation

There is great sensitivity in HR to issues of retaliation or alleged retaliation. If that is part of the complaint, an expert may be asked to assess the behavior of the parties before and after the complaint to determine whether there was a change in conduct that might be reasonably determined to be retaliation or have the effect of retaliation. Management must assess who initiated the change in conduct (the complainant or the accused harasser) and then determine whether the change was in response to objective performance-related issues in the workplace. Nothing is more critical than precluding the possibility of retaliation after a sexual harassment complaint has been lodged. The HR management expert must be prepared to address any lapses at trial.

SEXUAL HARASSMENT AT WORK

According to Mac Kinnons sexual harassment of working women is primarily a problem faced by women, that men rarely face this problem and therefore it should be considered a form of sex discrimination. Sexual harassment as defined by the court stipulates:

- "Such unwelcome sexually determined behaviour as physical contact and advances,
- A demand or request for sexual favours, sexually coloured remarks,
- Showing pornography and any other unwelcome physical, verbal or non verbal conduct of sexual nature".

Burt says "unwanted sexual overtures", has the virtue of parsimony but necessarily concerns intentions and motivation, not just overt behaviour. Defining sexual harassment as unwanted sexual overtures has the same problem inherent in defining rape as unwanted sexual relations. In practise the woman has to prove that the sexual relations or the sexual overtures were unwanted. The male colleague will go out of the way to prove that the woman is of loose character. According to Quinn defining sexual harassment means setting boundaries on the term and differentiating sexual harassment from expressions of sexual interest.

Not all expressions of sexuality in the workplace could possibly be called sexual harassment. Men and women do meet dating partners and future spouses at work. Some people may even enjoy sexual jokes and flirting that can be ego enhancing and enrich their fantasy life. National Commission for Women has laid down the code of conduct at work place to prevent sexual harassment of women, which has been sent to all Government offices, Ministries, and Universities with the hope that employers would become more sensitive towards women.

The guidelines highlight that it shall be the duty of the employer to prevent or deter the commission of any act of sexual harassment at workplace would include unwelcome sexually determined behaviour by any person either individually or in association with other persons such as eve teasing, unsavoury remarks, jokes causing embarrassment, innuendo and taunts, gender based insults or sexist remarks and unwelcome sexual overtones in any manner, touching or brushing against any part of the body, molestation or displaying pornographic or other derogatory pictures or sayings.

Recommendations to the National Commission for Women based on the view that the definition of sexual harassment is deficient and that "sexual favours......sought by homosexual or lesbian employers of the same sex" also be included. The Court places an obligation on employers in both the public and private sector to "take appropriate steps to prevent sexual harassment" and "provide appropriate penalties" against the offender. The criminal law should be resorted to where the behaviour amounts to a specific offence under the Indian Penal Code. The Court also recommends that a complaint made by the victim and that such a committee should be headed by a woman, and not less than half its members should be women. However this guidelines does not specify any time limit for drafting the code.

The Court provides that the employer is responsible for drafting codes to prevent sexual harassment in the workplace. If the power to evolve these codes is to be in the hands of the employer, then given the conservative sexual climate in which we live, what is to prevent the employer from producing a code that encourages gender segregation in the workplace. The codes could be formulated so as to discourage gender interaction in the workplace, or encourage the establishment of same sex schools and universities instead of co-educational institutions. Perhaps more specific guidelines are required which provide that such sex segregation is not an appropriate response for dealing with sexual harassment. In many cases, it has been found that the committees within the organisations were set up only when there were serious allegations of sexual harassment. Many working women point out that, even if there is an enquiry committee, does anyone really bother to find out what happens to the victim when the enquiry is going on? She is an object of curiosity, sympathy, disdainful glances or simply isolated by her colleagues.

The situation at home is worse. Instead of sympathising with her plight or standing by her, the attitude is one of distrust and suspicion or often humiliation and shame. The work environment where sexual harassment occurs has hierarchy, norms, rules and constraints that profoundly affect the way people behave in that setting. In particular, the formal rules and informal norms of managers affect both the managers and their subordinates.

The top management has the power to influence the employee's work habits, style of dress, recreational interests and social behaviour. When the top management tolerates or condones sexual harassment of employees, the standard reverberates throughout the organization. Certain individuals use their positions of relative power to engage in sexual interactions. This type of behaviour clearly constitutes sex discrimination. Male ego problems, sexual perversion, sexual obsession, widow-hood, pornographic materials and media portrayal is said to be some of the reasons for their harassment.

Lawyers Facing Sexual Harassment at Work

A survey conducted by Sakshi, a Delhi based NGO, in a few major cities reported that 65 per cent of women lawyers interviewed were always or often subjected to, or had observed, verbal or physical sexual harassment from other lawyers. The harassment would take various forms according to the survey. They include use of stereo-typed role characterisation, sexual innuendo, devaluation of women's work, use of obscene or vulgar language, and comments on appearances and character. The bar report narrates two incidents. In one case, a woman lawyer was openly punched by a male colleague in the High Court premises for refusing to join him for a cup of coffee.

When she tried to report the incident, a senior member of the bar dissuaded the police from registering it, on the ground that "it would tarnish the reputation of the Bar". Forty-eight per cent of the women lawyers surveyed also stated that they had heard or experienced remarks or jokes that were demeaning to women. In a survey done by National Commission for Women of 1200 women, nearly 50 per cent complained of gender discrimination and physical and mental harassment at work.

While 40 per cent of the women said they "usually ignored" such provocation, 3.54 per cent said they reported these to their supervisors, 7.8 per cent to their colleagues and 1.24 per cent to the police. About 10 per cent said that they protested against such behaviour while 9 per cent said they warned the offenders. At least 20.17 per cent of the respondents said that no investigation was done on their complaints while 1.5 per cent said police harassed them again instead of making the enquiry. A majority of the respondents 84.97% were not aware of the supreme court judgement given in August 1997, for specific protection of women from sexual harassment at work.

4

Domestic Violence in Same-sex Relationships

Domestic violence also occurs in same-sex relationships. In an effort to be more inclusive, many organizations have made an effort to use gender-neutral terms when referring to perpetratorship and victimhood.

Historically domestic violence has been seen as a family issue and little interest has been directed at violence in same-sex relationships. It has not been until recently, as the gay rights movement has brought the issues of gay and lesbian people into public attention, when research has been conducted on same-sex relationships.

Studies have indicated that partner abuse among male same-sex couples is several times that of heterosexual couples. Gays and lesbians, however, face special obstacles in dealing with the issues that some researchers have labelled "the double closet". A recent Canadian study by Mark W. Lehman suggests similarities include frequency (approximately one in every four couples); manifestations (emotional, physical, financial, etc.); co-existent situations (unemployment, substance abuse, low self-esteem); victims' reactions (fear, feelings of helplessness, hypervigilance); and reasons for staying (love, can work it out, things will change, denial).

At the same time, significant differences, unique issues and deceptive myths are typically present. Lehman points to added discrimination and fear gays and lesbians can face; dismissal by police and some social services; a lack of support from peers who would rather keep quiet about the problem in order not to attract negative attention toward the gay community; the impacts of HIV status or AIDS in keeping partners together, due to health care insurance/access, or guilt; outing used as a weapon; and encountering supportive services that are targeted and/or structured for the needs of heterosexual women and which may not meet the needs of gay men or lesbians.

Diagnosis

The American Psychiatric Association planning and research committees for the forthcoming DSM-V (2012) have canvassed a series of new Relational disorders which include *Marital Conflict Disorder Without Violence* or *Marital Abuse Disorder (Marital Conflict Disorder With Violence).* Couples with marital disorders sometimes come to clinical attention because the couple recognize long-standing dissatisfaction with their marriage and come to the clinician on their own initiative or are referred by an astute health care professional. Secondly, there is serious violence in the marriage which is-"usually the husband battering the wife". In these cases the emergency room or a legal authority often is the first to notify the clinician. Most importantly, marital violence "is a major risk factor for serious injury and even death and women in violent marriages are at much greater risk of being seriously injured or killed (National Advisory Council on Violence Against Women 2000)."

The authors of this study add that "There is current considerable controversy over whether male-to-female marital violence is best regarded as a reflection of male psychopathology and control or whether there is an empirical base and clinical utility for conceptualizing these patterns as relational." Recommendations for clinicians making a diagnosis of *Marital Relational Disorder* should include the assessment of actual or "potential" male violence as regularly as they assess the potential for suicide in depressed patients.

Further, "clinicians should not relax their vigilance after a battered wife leaves her husband, because some data suggest that the period immediately following a marital separation is the period of greatest risk for the women. Many men will stalk and batter their wives in an effort to get them to return or punish them for leaving. Initial assessments of the potential for violence in a marriage can be supplemented by standardized interviews and questionnaires, which have been reliable and valid aids in exploring marital violence more systematically."

The authors conclude with what they call "very recent information" on the course of violent marriages which suggests that "over time a husband's battering may abate somewhat, but perhaps because he has successfully intimidated his wife. The risk of violence remains strong in a marriage in which it has been a feature in the past. Thus, treatment is essential here; the clinician cannot just wait and watch." The most urgent clinical priority is the protection of the wife because she is the one most frequently at risk, and clinicians must be aware that supporting assertiveness by a battered wife may lead to more beatings or even death.

Management

The response to domestic violence is typically a combined effort between law enforcement, social services, and health care. The role of each has evolved as domestic violence has been brought more into public view. Domestic violence historically has been viewed as a private family matter that need not involve the government or criminal justice. Police officers were often reluctant to intervene by making an arrest, and often chose instead to simply counsel the couple and/or ask one of the parties to leave the residence for a period of time. The courts were reluctant to impose any significant sanctions on those convicted of domestic violence, largely because it was viewed as a misdemeanor offence.

Medical Response

Medical professionals can make a difference in the lives of those who experience abuse. Many cases of spousal abuse are handled solely by physicians and do not involve the police. Sometimes cases of domestic violence are brought into the emergency room, while many other cases are handled by family physician or other primary care provider. Medical professionals are in position to empower people, give advice, and refer them to appropriate services. The health care professional has not always met this role, with uneven quality of care, and in some cases misunderstandings about domestic violence.

Washaw (1993) suggests that many doctors prefer not to get involved in people's "private" lives. Clifton, Jacobs, and Tulloch (1996) found that training for general practitioners in the United States about domestic violence was very limited or they had no training. Abbott and Williamson found that knowledge and understanding of domestic violence was very limited among health care professionals in a Midlands, United Kingdom county, and that they don't see themselves as being able to play a major role in helping women in regards to domestic violence.

Furthermore, in the biomedical model of health care, injuries are often just treated and diagnosed, without regard for the causes. As well, there is substantial reluctance for victims to come forward and broach the issue with their physicians. On average, women experience 35 incidents of domestic violence before seeking treatment. In the U. S., the Institute of Medicine recognized the shortcomings of the health care system in its 2002 report entitled Confronting Chronic Neglect and attributed some of the problems cited to a lack of adequate training among health professionals. Health professionals have an ethical responsibility to recognize and address exposure to abuse in their patients, in the health care setting. For example, the American Medical Association's code of medical ethics states that "Due to the prevalence and medical consequences of family violence, physicians should routinely inquire about physical, sexual, and psychological abuse as part of the medical history. Physicians must also consider abuse in the differential diagnosis for a number of medical complaints, particularly when treating women."

Duluth Model

In 1981, the Duluth Domestic Abuse Intervention Project became the first multi-disciplinary program designed to address the issue of domestic violence. This experiment, conducted in Duluth, Minnesota, frequently referred to as the "Duluth Project." It coordinated agencies dealing with domestic situations, drawing together diverse elements of the system, from police officers on the street, to shelters for battered women and probation officers supervising offenders. This program has become a model for other jurisdictions seeking to deal more effectively with domestic violence. Corrections/probation agencies in many areas are supervising domestic violence offenders more closely, and are also paying closer attention to the victim's needs and safety issues.

There has been controversy as the Duluth framework depends on a strict "patriarchal violence" model and presumes that all violence in the home and elsewhere has a male perpetrator and female victim. Also evidence of success of the model is limited, with scholarly analysis and critique. Many victims leave their abusers, only to return. Research has shown that a major factor in helping a victim to establish lasting independence from the abusive partner is her or his ability to get legal assistance. Economists at the Brennan Centre for Justice analysed Bureau of Justice Statistics data to determine what accounted for the nationwide reduction in reported abuse. Their findings revealed that one significant factor was the availability of legal services to assist abuse victims. Another major study by economists at Colgate University and the University of Arkansas flatly stated that the only public service that reduces domestic violence in the long term is legal aid. Legal assistance can provide essential safety planning, buttress a family's economic position through child or spousal support, allay fears planted by the batterer about loss of custody, and help victims to secure needed government benefits.

Law Enforcement

In the 1970s, it was widely believed that domestic disturbance calls were the most dangerous type for responding officers, who arrive to a highly emotionally charged situation. This belief was based on FBI statistics which turned out to be flawed, in that they grouped all types of disturbances together with domestic disturbances, such as brawls at a bar. Subsequent statistics and analysis have shown this belief to be false.

Statistics on incidents of domestic violence, published in the late 1970s, helped raise public awareness of the problem and increase activism. A study published in 1976 by the Police Foundation found that the police had intervened at least once in the previous two years in 85% of spouse homicides. In the late 1970s and early 1980s, feminists and battered women's advocacy groups were calling on police to take domestic violence more seriously and change intervention strategies. In some instances, these groups took legal action against police departments, including in Oakland, California and New York City, to get them to make arrests in domestic violence cases. They claimed that police assigned low priority to domestic disturbance calls.

The Minneapolis Domestic Violence Experiment was a study done in 1981-1982, led by Lawrence W. Sherman, to evaluate the effectiveness of various police responses to domestic violence calls in Minneapolis, Minnesota, including sending the abuser away for eight hours, giving advice and mediation for disputes, and making an arrest. Arrest was found to be the most effective police response. The study found that arrest reduced the rate by half of re-offending against the same victim within the following six months. The results of the study received a great deal of attention from the news media, including *The New York Times* and prime-time news coverage on television.

Many U. S. police departments responded to the study, adopting a mandatory arrest policy for spousal violence cases with probable cause. By 2005, 23 states and the District of Columbia had enacted mandatory arrest for domestic assault, without warrant, given that the officer has probable cause and regardless of whether or not the officer witnessed the crime. The Minneapolis study also influenced policy in other countries, including New Zealand, which adopted a pro-arrest policy for domestic violence cases.

However, the study was subject of much criticism, with concerns about its methodology, as well as its conclusions. The Minneapolis study was replicated in several other cities, beginning in 1986, with some of these studies having different results; one of which being the fact that the deterrent effect observed in the Minneapolis experiment was largely localized. In the replication studies which were far more broad and methodologically sound in both size and scope, arrest seemed to help in the short run in certain cases, but those arrested experienced double the rate of violence over the course of one year.

Criminologists do not fully understand the reasons why deterrent effects do not last over time. But they suggest that abusers who are employed and have ties to the community may initially fear punishment, though many cases do not make it all the way through the criminal justice process. If the victim is uncooperative during investigation, the prosecutor may choose not to pursue the case. If the case is pursued through the criminal justice system, sometimes the resulting sentence is minor. Subsequently, any fear that the abuser has of punishment may have diminished.

Each agency and jurisdiction within the United States has its own Standard Operating Procedures (SOP) when it comes to responding and handling domestic calls. Generally, it has been accepted that if the understood victim has visible (and recent) marks of abuse, the suspect is arrested and charged with the appropriate crime. However, that is a guideline and not a rule. Like any other call, domestic abuse lies in a gray area. Law enforcement officers have several things to consider when making a warrantless arrest:

- Are there signs of physical abuse?
- Were there witnesses?
- Is it recent?
- Was the victim assaulted by the alleged suspect?
- Who is the primary aggressor?
- Could the victim be lying?
- Could the suspect be lying?

Along with protecting the victim, law enforcement officers have to ensure that the alleged abusers' rights are not violated. Many times in cases of mutual combatants, it is departmental policy that both parties be arrested and the court system can establish truth at a later date. In some areas of the nation, this mutual combatant philosophy is being replaced by the primary abuser philosophy in which case if both parties have physical injuries, the law enforcement officer determines who the primary aggressor is and only arrests that one. This philosophy started gaining momentum when different government/private agencies started researching the effects. It was found that when both parties are arrested, it had an adverse affect on the victim. The victims were less likely to call or trust law enforcement during the next incident of domestic abuse.

DOMESTIC VIOLENCE

Violence against women in the family occurs in developed and developing countries alike. It has long been considered a private matter by bystanders — including neighbours, the community and government. But such private matters have a tendency to become public tragedies. In the United States, a woman is beaten every 18 minutes. Indeed, domestic violence is the leading cause of injury among women of reproductive age in the United States. Between 22 and 35 per cent of women who visit emergency rooms are there for that reason.

The highly publicized trial of O. J. Simpson, the retired United States football player acquitted of the murder of his former wife and a male friend of hers, helped focus international media attention on the issue of domestic violence and spousal abuse. In Peru, 70 per cent of all crimes reported to the police involve women beaten by their husbands. In Pakistan, Prime Minister Benazir Bhutto strongly defended a 35-year-old mother of two who was severely burned by her husband in a domestic dispute.

"There is no excuse for such a behaviour", the Prime Minister declared after visiting the hospitalized victim. "My presence here is to send a message to all those who violate Islamic teachings and defy laws of the land with their inhuman treatment of women. This will not be tolerated."

According to the Human Rights Commission of Pakistan, in the 400 cases of domestic violence reported in 1993 in the province of Punjab, nearly half ended with the death of the wife. According to the Special Rapporteur's report, many Governments now recognize the importance of protecting victims of domestic abuse and taking action to punish perpetrators. The establishment of structures allowing officials to deal with cases of domestic violence and its consequences is a significant step towards the elimination of violence against women in the family. The Special Rapporteur's report highlights the importance of adopting legislation that provides for prosecution of the offender. It also stresses the importance of specialized training for law enforcement authorities as well as medical and legal professionals, and of the establishment of community support services for victims, including access to information and shelters.

Traditional Practices

In many countries, women fall victim to traditional practices that violate their human rights. The persistence of the problem has much to do with the fact that most of these physically and psychologically harmful customs are deeply rooted in the tradition and culture of society.

Female Genital Mutilation

According to the World Health Organization, 85 million to 115 million girls and women in the population have undergone some form of female genital mutilation and suffer from its adverse health effects. Every year an estimated 2 million young girls undergo this procedure. Most live in Africa and Asia — but an increasing number can be found among immigrant and refugee families in Western Europe and North America. Indeed, the practice has been outlawed in some European countries.

In France, a Malian was convicted in a criminal court after his baby girl died of a female circumcision-related infection. The procedure had been performed on the infant at home. In Canada, fear of being forced to undergo circumcision can be grounds for asylum. A Nigerian woman was granted refugee status since she felt that she might be persecuted in her home country because of her refusal to inflict genital mutilation on her baby daughter.

There is a growing consensus that the best way to eliminate these practices is through educational campaigns that emphasize their dangerous health consequences. Several Governments have been actively promoting such campaigns in their countries.

Son Preference

Son preference affects women in many countries, particularly in Asia. Its consequences can be anything from foetal or female infanticide to neglect of the girl child over her brother in terms of such essential needs as nutrition, basic health care and education.

In China and India, some women choose to terminate their pregnancies when expecting daughters but carry their pregnancies to term when expecting sons. According to reports from India, genetic testing for sex selection has become a booming business, especially in the country's northern regions. Indian gender-detection clinics drew protests from women's groups after the appearance of advertisements suggesting that it was better to spend $38 now to terminate a female foetus than $3,800 later on her dowry.

A study of amniocentesis procedures conducted in a large Bombay hospital found that 95.5 per cent of foetuses identified as female were aborted, compared with a far smaller percentage of male foetuses. The problem of son preference is present in many other countries as well. Asked how many children he had fathered, the former United States boxing champion Muhammad Ali told an interviewer: "One boy and seven mistakes."

Dowry-related Violence and Early Marriage

In some countries, weddings are preceded by the payment of an agreed-upon dowry by the bride's family. Failure to pay the dowry can lead to violence. In Bangladesh, a bride whose dowry was deemed too small was disfigured after her husband threw acid on her face. In India, an average of five women a day are burned in dowry-related disputes — and many more cases are never reported.

Early marriage, especially without the consent of the girl, is another form of human rights violation. Early marriage followed by multiple pregnancies can affect the health of women for life. The report of the Special Rapporteur has documented the destructive effects of marriage of female children under 18 and has urged Governments to adopt relevant legislation.

CAUSES OF DOMESTIC VIOLENCE

There is no one single factor to account for violence perpetrated against women. Increasingly, research has focused on the inter-relatedness of various factors that should improve our understanding of the problem within different cultural contexts. Several complex and interconnected institutionalized social and cultural factors have kept women particularly vulnerable to the violence directed at them, all of them manifestations of historically unequal power relations between men and women.

Factors contributing to these unequal power relations include: socioeconomic forces, the family institution where power relations are enforced, fear of and control over female sexuality, belief in the inherent superiority of males, and legislation and cultural sanctions that have traditionally denied women and children an independent legal and social status. Lack of economic resources underpins women's vulnerability to violence and their difficulty in extricating themselves from a violent relationship. The link between violence and lack of economic resources and dependence is circular. On the one hand, the threat and fear of violence keeps women from seeking employment, or, at best, compels them to accept low-paid, home-based exploitative labour. And on the other, without economic independence, women have no power to escape from an abusive relationship. The reverse of this argument also holds true in some countries; that is, women's increasing economic activity and independence is viewed as a threat which leads to increased male violence. This is particularly true when the male partner is unemployed, and feels his power undermined in the household.

Studies have also linked a rise in violence to the destabilization of economic patterns in society. Macro-economic policies such as structural adjustment programmes, globalization, and the growing inequalities they have created, have been linked to increasing levels of violence in several regions, including Latin America, Africa and Asia. The transition period in the countries of Central and Eastern Europe and the former Soviet Union – with increases in poverty, unemployment, hardship, income inequality, stress, and alcohol abuse – has led to increased violence in society in general, including violence against women.

These factors also act indirectly to raise women's vulnerability by encouraging more risk-taking behaviour, more alcohol and drug abuse, the breakdown of social support networks, and the economic dependence of women on their partners. Cultural ideologies – both in industrialized and developing countries – provide 'legitimacy' for violence against women in certain circumstances. Religious and historical traditions in the past have sanctioned the chastising and beating of wives.

The physical punishment of wives has been particularly sanctioned under the notion of entitlement and ownership of women. Male control of family wealth inevitably places decision-making authority in male hands, leading to male dominance and proprietary rights over women and girls. The concept of ownership, in turn, legitimizes control over women's sexuality, which in many law codes has been deemed essential to ensure patrilineal inheritance. Women's sexuality is also tied to the concept of family honour in many societies.

Traditional norms in these societies allow the killing of 'errant' daughters, sisters and wives suspected of defiling the honour of the family by indulging in forbidden sex, or marrying and divorcing without the consent of the family. By the same logic, the honour of a rival ethnic group or society can be defiled by acts of sexual violence against its women. Experiences during childhood, such as witnessing domestic violence and experiencing physical and sexual abuse, have been identified as factors that put children at risk. Violence may be learnt as a means of resolving conflict and asserting manhood by children who have witnessed such patterns of conflict resolution.

Excessive consumption of alcohol and other drugs has also been noted as a factor in provoking aggressive and violent male behaviour towards women and children. A survey of domestic violence in Moscow revealed that half the cases of physical abuse are associated with the husband's excessive alcohol consumption.

The isolation of women in their families and communities is known to contribute to increased violence, particularly if those women have little access to family or local organizations. On the other hand, women's participation in social networks has been noted as a critical factor in lessening their vulnerability to violence and in their ability to resolve domestic violence.

These networks could be informal (family and neighbours) or formal (community organizations, women's self-help groups, or affiliated to political parties). Lack of legal protection, particularly within the sanctity of the home, is a strong factor in perpetuating violence against women. Until recently, the public/ private distinction that has ruled most legal systems has been a major obstacle to women's rights. Increasingly, however, States are seen as responsible for protecting the rights of women even in connection with offences committed within the home.

In many countries violence against women is exacerbated by legislation, law enforcement and judicial systems that do not recognize domestic violence as a crime. The challenge is to end impunity for the perpetrators as one means of preventing future abuse.

Investigations by Human Rights Watch have found that in cases of domestic violence, law enforcement officials frequently reinforce the batterers' attempts to control and demean their victims. Even though several countries now have laws that condemn domestic violence, "when committed against a woman in an intimate relationship, these attacks are more often tolerated as the norm than prosecuted as laws....In many places, those who commit domestic violence are prosecuted less vigorously and punished more leniently than perpetrators of similarly violent crimes.

PROSECUTING DOMESTIC VIOLENCE

In Scotland, the decision to prosecute is made by the procurator fiscal, and is based on two key factors-whether there is a sufficiency of evidence, and whether it is in the public interest to proceed to trial. Two independent sources of corroborative evidence are required-in cases of assault, the statement of the complainer is one source of evidence. Other sources might include forensic evidence, medical reports, photographs of the injuries sustained or the scene of crime, or the testimony of other witnesses who saw or heard the assault. Taken together, the evidence must demonstrate beyond reasonable doubt that an offence was committed, and that the accused person was the perpetrator of that offence.

In cases of assault by a partner, as in other cases of violence against women, the presumption has been that the woman herself is the main witness in the Crown case. The nature of the crime means that eye witnesses are rare, or reluctant to come forward. Children and young people are often the main witnesses to assaults on their mothers, but it may not be considered appropriate to call them as witnesses in court. Corroboration may therefore be difficult to find. Even where women have welcomed the arrest and charging of their abuser, they may be unwilling or unable to co-operate with the prosecution. The time delay between arrest and trial can mean that they have reconciled with their partner in the hope that things will now change; or they may be pressured to 'withdraw the charges' by the accused or his family. Whatever the reason, the procurator fiscal must then decide whether to proceed to trial with a 'hostile' chief witness (Barry, 2000).

In other jurisdictions, prosecution may proceed without the woman's co-operation. In Canada, a 'pro-prosecution' policy has applied in all provinces since 1986, i.e. cases will be prosecuted where there is sufficient evidence, regardless of the wishes of the individual complainer. In practice, this means that the Crown must consider whether to lead the case without the woman's testimony, taking into account the strength of any other available evidence. It is not generally considered appropriate to compel her to testify, or to charge her with contempt if she doesn't.

By reducing the number of withdrawals of charges, the pro-prosecution policy aimed to reduce the attrition rate. Early studies suggested that it was successful. 38.4% of charges were dismissed or withdrawn prior to the introduction, in 1981, of the pro-prosecution policy in London, Ontario. By 1990, this rate had decreased to 10.9%. The policy also aimed to improve the co-operation of women survivors with the criminal justice process. The non-co-operation of survivors of domestic violence continues to be a source of frustration for prosecutors but there are ongoing developments to improve this position. A recent study identified the availability of witness support and the use of video taped evidence as the two most influential elements in determining the cooperation of women. In the U.S.A. the use of 'no-drop' policies has a similar history, with different jurisdictions adopting variations on this theme since the 1980s. The most rigidly applied policies include the option of arresting and jailing women who do not co-operate with the prosecution of their abusive partner. More flexible approaches are similar to the Canadian model, intent on prosecution where there is sufficient evidence, but acknowledging the difficulties some complainers may have in testifying (Ford, 2003).

As with mandatory arrest policies, pro-prosecution or 'no-drop' policies can be contentious. Although predicated on the assumption that prosecution protects women, Ford (2003) suggests that there is a lack of empirical evidence to support this. Where there is evidence, as in a 2001 study which found that 'no-drop' policies did increase convictions, he notes that further analysis identified a significant degree of 'screening out' of cases which were unlikely to gain convictions. Overall, he argues, 'coerced victim participation' in domestic violence prosecutions has no demonstrable impact on the safety of women in the wider community, and may actively jeopardise the safety of the individual woman it seeks to protect (Ford, 2003).

Work with Domestic Violence Offenders

It is not within the scope of this report to review the substantial body of literature on offenders. However, in the context of domestic abuse, it is important to acknowledge that 'making men visible' 22 is central to the effectiveness of the multi-agency initiatives which are recognized as examples of best practice. How far domestic violence offender programmes actually improve the safety of women and children continues to be the subject of debate. Research suggests that a significant number of men attending probation programmes refrain from violence in the short term but that this impact diminishes over time. Attrition is high and sanctions for breaching probation orders are not always implemented, although where they are, the completion rate improves and recidivism appears to reduce.

The content and ethos of domestic abuse offender programmes may vary considerably. Some programmes take a therapeutic focus, others an educational focus. Most involve a combination of inidividual work and groupwork. In the U.K., most programmes are psycho-educational, and make use of cognitive behavioural techniques combined with an analysis of the gendered nature of domestic abuse (Mullender and Burton, 2000). Minimum standards of practice have been adopted by RESPECT, the National Association for Domestic Violence Perpetrator Programmes and Associated Support Services. Key principles for RESPECT would include work with the partners of abusive men as an essential part of any programme, and the need for programmes to be linked to the overall community response to domestic abuse (RESPECT, 2000).

Men's programmes in the U.K. are almost exclusively court-mandated probation programmes. An exception is 'Working with Men', a project based in north Edinburgh and initially funded by DAPHNE 23 to carry out a feasibility study into the development of a voluntary intervention for men who have assaulted their partners, or are at risk of doing so. A model of good practice was developed as part of the initial study. This involved practitioner training programmes on how to recognise and respond to abusive men, the adaptation of an existing men's programme, and the design of a suggested referral pathway for a men's service. An overarching theme was the integration of any voluntary men's programme into a multi agency response to domestic abuse. The project is now funded by DASDF 24 to develop the model further.

DOMESTIC VIOLENCE IN THE MARITAL RELATIONSHIP

Ahuja (1998) and Visaria (1999) have recently conducted studies on 'domestic violence' within marital relationship. The findings of their study have been discussed below. Domestic violence has been defined as " all actions by the family against one of its members that threaten the life, body, psychological integrity or liberty of the member.

In identifying factors leading to wife beating, both Visaria and Ahuja, in their survey, have tested the co-relationship between wife beating and education. According to Visaria's (1999) survey in Gujarat, illiterate women face more violence than literate women. Relationship between abusive behaviour and level of education has been found to be statistically significant (Visaria 1999:12). Illiterate women and those with education up to primary level (class 4) tend to be more subjected to violence as compared to those who had received education beyond the primary level. However, one has to keep in mind that the percentage of literate women in Gujarat is overall only between 20% to 50%. In one district, Banas Kantha in Kutch, the total percentage of literate women is even lesser than 20%. In contrast a study by Ahuja (1998) shows that there is no significant relationship between beating and educational level of the couple. Educated women are beaten as much by their husbands as those who are illiterate or less educated.

About one-fourth of the batterers (24%) in Ahuja's study were those who were moderately educated and about one-fourth (26%) were highly educated. However, he added that men whose educational attainment is low, are more likely to beat their wife than men who are better educated. Study findings of Ahuja shows that although women of all ages are victims of wife-battering, a larger number of victims (72%) are among those with an age difference of unto 10 years between spouses. According to the survey findings of Visaria (1999), women who experience domestic violence early in their marriage, continue to be subjected to it even with increase in age. His findings point out that family structure, the presence or absence of children, and the size of the family have little co-relation with wife battering (Ibid.:157). The study also points out that family income, husband's occupation and employment of women are not co-related with wifebattering.

According to survey findings of Visaria (1999) joint family tends to offer women some protection or acts as a deterrent to husbands using physical force to subdue them. The forms of violence commonly found by Ahuja (1998) were slapping, kicking, tearing hair, pushing and pulling, hitting with an object, attempting to strangulate and threatening. Forms of psychological abuse were also found to exist, for instance, verbal abuse, sarcastic remarks in the presence of outsiders, imposing severe restrictions on freedom of movement, totally ignoring the wife in decision-making processes, making frequent complaints against her to her parents, friends, neighbours, and kin much to the embarrassment of the wife. Some of the reasons given by the women were financial matters, behaviour with in-laws, back-biting, talking to any male without the liking of the husband, asking for money, preventing him from drinking and husbands personality traits.

Some of the worse forms of violence has been reported by Visaria in her study (1999), for instance, beating with sticks or iron rod, knives, utensils, blades and ladles, throwing women against objects or bashing their heads against the walls, burning of breasts and vagina. In addition, sexual assaults in the form of both hitting women in the vagina by kicking or forcing her into sexual intercourse were reported by nearly 10% of the women. Some of the women who had become victim of this form of violence indicated that injury in their private parts cannot be noticed by anyone and they would be too ashamed to talk about it to others. A couple of women also hinted that men know that their wives cannot report such punishment even to their own parents or seek medical treatment due to a sense of shame. Some of the reasons given by women, in the survey done by Visaria is, meals not served properly, economic constraints, financial matters, men wasting money at tea stalls, drinking of alcohol, men feeling that women are paying less attention to the children and vis-à-vis, men feel women have a lot of free time and so on. One of the main cause why domestic violence prevails and continues is the lack of alternatives among the victims. Women and children may be economically dependent on abusers. Elderly people and children may feel too powerless to escape. Language or cultural barriers may isolate victims from seeking help.

Victims generally feel, it is better to suffer in silence than to be separated from loved ones. They keep hoping for improvement, but it is normally observed that, without help, violence gets worse.

Victims may also feel helpless, guilty or worthless. They may feel ashamed of the poor quality of the relationship. Abusers may fear the consequences of seeking help, unaware that continuing as before may be even more dangerous. Family members may be unaware of the help that is available from the local agencies. They may also be unaware of their legal rights. In India we have no provision for protection of a complainant, not even under the Prevention of Dowry Act. A woman who has complained of harassment goes back to the very people against whom she has complained. What security can she possibly feel in such a situation, and how can she continue to act on her complaint? She obviously continues to be victimised often paying the ultimate price (Bedi K, 1999).

Many complainants are faced with eviction from the family home, are cut off without maintenance, and are unable to follow the complaint precisely because they have no means to do so.

Frequent, unexplained injuries, reluctance to seek medical treatment for injuries or denial of their existence, fear in the presence of certain family member/s, social isolation, disorientation or grogginess, especially in elders indicating misuse of medication and decline in physical appearance and personal hygiene indicating increased isolation and a lack of desire to continue living are some of the indicators of violence (Aravamudan G, 1995)

Dowry Harassment and Bride Burning

Dowry is a transfer of property from the bride's family to that of the bridegroom, at the time of marriage (Negi,1997: 14). According to the present practice, dowry usually subsumes material gifts and cash paid to the bridegroom and his kin. This practise continues even after marriage (Paul; 1993). The dowry given at the time of marriage is not the only transaction as far as the daughters marriage is concerned.

There is a series of ceremonies associated with the girls in the family. The practice of giving gifts to the husband's family in cash and kind and rituals connected with pregnancy, childbirth and ceremonies for piercing the ear of the girl and so on (Negi; 1997: 15). The gifts are no longer a token of affection from parents to the daughter, but instead an elaborate demand from the marital family (Negi; 1997: 16).

The commonest elements of dowry in India include gifts for the bride such as clothes, jewels and other house-hold and luxury goods like a refrigerator and kitchen utensils and so on. These are ideally treated as the bride's streedan (wife's property) and form the nucleus of the conjugal estate. Dowry also includes gifts for the son-in-law and other luxury items like scooter, VCR, VCP, and such other gifts for the bridegrooms' parents and other relatives.

Over and above, it includes hard cash paid as contribution towards the marriage expenses. In some cases, dowry is also paid as compensation for the expenditure incurred on the education and other training of the groom. The bridegroom's parents usually keep this money. Some state that this is kept by the parents as security against the bridegroom staying separately after marriage.

According to Chatterji, the practice was a means of giving gifts to the daughter during the marriage, so that the couple can start a life on their own and to compensate her share of the property, as she is otherwise excluded from inheriting parental property (Chatterji; 1992: 7).

The Dowry Prohibition Act 1961 was amended in 1984, 1985 and 1986. Dowry deaths constitute a special category of death that was for the first time defined in a section introduced into the Indian Penal Code (IPC) In 1986, Section 304(B) stipulates that death of a woman within seven years of her marriage by burns or bodily injury with evidence of cruelty or harassment by her husband or his relatives in connection with a demand for dowry is 'dowry death' and punishable with imprisonment for not less than seven years.

Three years prior to this, Section 498(A) was introduced in the IPC. This states that 'any form of cruelty, whether it is from a husband or the relative of a husband, to a woman is an offence that is punishable with imprisonment up to three years'. Cruelty, as defined in this section, includes 'any wilful conduct that could cause mental torture, physical injury, or drive the woman to commit suicide, whether in connection with any unlawful demand for property or not'.

The first part of Chapter XVI of the IPC (Sections 299 to 311, which are offences affecting life) can also be invoked in case of dowry death or suicide. Under sections 299, 300, 301 and 304(A), culpable homicide, murder and death by negligence are crimes. Section 302 lays down punishment for murder: death sentence or imprisonment for life. Sections 113(A) (presumption as to abetment of suicide of a married woman) and 113(B) (presumption as to dowry death) were added to the Indian Evidence Act and can be invoked in cases of dowry murder or suicide. The Code of Criminal Procedure (mainly sections 174 and 175) lays down the procedure and principles of investigation into a crime (Menon; 1999).

Despite a list of legislation protecting the rights of women, most importantly the prohibition of giving and taking of dowry under the Dowry Prohibition Act 1961, women in India are tortured physically and mentally and even killed or driven to suicide by their husbands and in-laws for not bringing sufficient dowry. Dowry related violence against married women by the families they marry into is a phenomenon that is on the increase in the country. The following table gives an indication of the increase in dowry related violence against women. However this data is only a tip of the iceberg, as most of these cases do not get reported unless it reaches an extreme case of death.

In an investigation done by Vimochana, (a Bangalore based NGO), the category of dowry deaths in a technical sense only include those cases that had been booked by the police under the relevant sections of law. The accident cases that have been closed for want of evidence, however are largely due to stove-bursts or kitchen accidents (Menon; 1999: 66). There are rarely any eyewitnesses who are prepared to give evidence against the murderers as the crime is committed within the four walls of a home and those who are present inside are those who are committing the crime. According to Menon (1999), the large number of these deaths is an indication that the law is not a sufficient deterrent for those who commit these crimes. The following are some of the reasons why these gruesome murders are registered under accidents. There are pressures on the woman to conceal the truth about the reality even if they are on the verge of dying. Her husband's family often threatens to harm her natal family or her children if she does not declare that it was an accident. Relatives and family members of her natal family also sometimes remain silent, as they fear the husband's family. The victim's dying declaration, which is supposed to be taken in private by the policeman in the presence of a doctor, is invariably a public procedure. While on one hand the family does not want to get involved in the time-staking and laborious process of legal proceedings, on the other hand the police do not take interest to penetrate this community resistance to look for evidence of what really could have happened (Menon, 1999:69). According to Damodaran, exposure to the media has resulted in an increasing trend towards consumerism. People cannot afford the luxuries that are thrust upon them through advertisements targeted at the urban population. They see dowry as an avenue to fulfil their otherwise impossible dreams (Negi; 1997: 15).

The interplay of pre-capitalist values and modern forces with the accentuation of the free market economy and the consumer culture in the era of unequal development have thus become a part of the complex and contradictory fabric of our present-day society. The traditional values of the necessity of marrying a girl for spiritual merit and the modern system of calculation and other considerations of the groom's family in a milieu of inequality and insecurity have brought to the surface a sense of competition and manipulation to the advantage of the bridegroom (Paul; 1993:37).

According to Paul the treatment of a daughter-in-law depends very much upon the quantum of dowry she brings along with her before, during and after the marriage ceremony (Paul; 1986: 26). However there have been cases when the status of the girl's parents has reduced after the marriage, or there is a loss in the business and the girl is illtreated in the husband's house thereafter. The dowry normally continues for many years after the marriage. Often, the dowry brought by her is taken away after marriage. In times of financial problems in the husband's house, her jewellery and dowry items are normally the first to be sold.

For some people, paying dowry at their daughter's marriage is an investment for fetching high dowry through their son's marriage. Some others, including women discuss on 'marriage with high dowry', with pride. Generally, marriages with pomp and show is preferred.

The girls too think it is their right to take dowry with them when they go to the husband's house. People believe that the effective way of equipping women is to resort to dowry in arranging a marital alliance. Another feeling among the mothers-in-law is that when she herself brought dowry from her house at the time of her marriage, why shouldn't she take dowry for her son. According to Menon (1999), dowry related crime is motivated mainly by greed.

Sale of Wife

In traditional farming communities, women helped in farming and bridegrooms paid a bride price to her parents. In the past this used to be a token amount. If a widow or a married woman chose to enter into a live-in relationship with another man, the latter in turn paid the first husband the amount he had spent at the time of the marriage. This system has, in the last decade become completely distorted with women being sold and resold for astronomical sums and the panchayats and police turning a blind eye to these goings on. With the bride price sometimes running into a lakh or more, 'nata' brokers have mushroomed around Kotah, Bundi, Deoli, Ajmer and Tonk districts of Rajasthan, whose only job is to keep an eye on prospective women and force them to enter into a nata because the local brokers earned a hefty commission out of this deal. The kind of money at stake can be gauged from the fact that one of the fathers admits to having spent Rs 62,000 in bringing her back.

Realising the selling and reselling of girls had reached rampant proportions, a Deoli based NGO, 'Women's Rights Committee Against Atrocity' conducted a survey in Sandla and Bhanvarthala villages in Tonk District of Rajasthan and came up with some disturbing conclusions. Of the 517 households surveyed, the survival rate of marriages in the backward classes during the last five years was less than 50 per cent and in some cases as high as 70 per cent. Nata exits also in Rajgarh district of Madhya Pradesh. It is the practise of the sale of the women to men in return for a handsome price. The largest beneficiary is the father of the girl who uses her to gain a neat sum. Closely connected to the issue of sale and resale of women is the custom of child marriage. Unless a boy is committed to child marriage, he cannot indulge in nata. Men are prepared to pawn their goats, cows and buffaloes and in well-to-do households, even gold and silver to get a woman. In all these transactions the woman is never in the picture-she accepts the deal as part of her womanhood (Chandrasekhar, 1996).

Indira Pancholi, the Co-ordinator of the committee believes, "no household has remained unaffected, there is an unsuccessful marriage in every household here."

The Panchayats have turned a blind eye to this jostling around. They are accused more often than not, of siding with the husbands and are blamed for pushing up the nata rates. The jhagda money is decided upon in presence of the Panchayat with the amount being written on a document called Kagli. "Husbands are selling their wives to get more money and the Panchayats are doing nothing to protect these women", points out the Jaipur based women's rights activist, Kavita Srivastava. She cites an instance of Lalibai, an anganwadi worker, who was harassed to enter into a nata after her husband's death. She refused and had to seek intervention of social activists to escape harassment. According to a Jaipur based DIG (CID), Sudhir Pratap Singh " lack of education and total ignorance of inheritance rights amongst women are the reasons why this practice has continued."

Indira Pancholi, the Co-ordinator of the committee believes, "the inability of a bride to return to her marital home would be a triggering factor, especially in cases of atta satta agreement where two families exchange children in marriage when they are quite young. After marriage, the boy's family reciprocate by not sending their son to bring the bride. Entire villages are at war with each other." For instance, Simla Ram, from the village Nappa Ke Kheda of Rajasthan is facing rejection from her college going husband who does not want an illiterate wife. Village custom demands that the husband either comes down himself or sends someone to fetch her. Four years into the marriage, Simla is still waiting to be escorted to her husband's home. Simla is completely against nata. She says she would like to settle down only with her husband. Marriages in villages have come under pressure for other reasons as well. Dowry and modern lifestyle demands, including incompatibility, are reasons cited for marital breakdowns and consequently the sale of women.

Eve Teasing

Eve teasing is an act of terror that violates a woman's body, space and self-respect. It is one of the many ways through which a woman is systematically made to feel inferior, weak and afraid. Whether it is an obscene word whispered into a woman's ear; offensive remarks on her appearance; an intrusive way of touching any part of a woman's body; a gesture which is perceived and intended to be vulgar: all these acts represent a violation of a woman's person, her bodily integrity. Eve teasing denies a woman's fundamental right to move freely and carry herself with dignity, solely on the basis of her sex (Hindu, August 2, 1998).

Some acts of eve-teasing mentioned by girl students interviewed are; indecent remarks, singing obscene songs, hitting, touching or pinching in crowded places, snatching dupatta and in some cases even forced kissing, mailing anonymous love letters and exhibiting male genital in front of women. (Ashraf, 1997 : 89).

Eve teasing by itself is not an offence under any law, but Sections 294 and 349 of the Indian Penal Code cover substance of eve teasing. Sections 294 punishes "whoever, to the annoyance of others (a) does any obscene act in any public place, or (b) sings, recites or utters any obscene song, ballads or words in or near any public place" is liable to be punished with imprisonment or with fine. The section is very wide in nature and a person can be hauled up even if the acts forming part of the substance of the offence are addressed to the public at large, provided this cause annoyance. Clearly a girl or a woman who feels annoyed by any obscene song or words can take recourse to the provision of the section and put up a complaint before a police station. The offence is cognisable, i.e. a police officer can arrest the offender without a warrant but it is bailable (Ashraf;1997) A graver form of eve teasing is accompanied by the use of gesture indicating threat or use of force. 'Criminal force' has been defined under Section 349 of Indian Penal Code.

According to this section 'a person is said to use force to another if he causes motion, change or cessation of motion to that other person'. In such a case also, action can be taken against the person using it. The punishment is such cases are imprisonment for two years or fine or both. The offence is cognisable. Thus, simple eve teasing accompanied with gesture to use force are punishable under the existing provisions of the Indian Penal Code. (Ashraf; 1997: 89).

A graver form of eve teasing is accompanied by the use of gesture indicating threat or use of force. In such a case also, action can be taken against the person using it Stereotypically, men are conceived of as natural prey to uncontrollable lust.

Women therefore have to protect themselves at any costs. In an ironic twist of responsibility, women then bear the burden of guilt for an act of violence against themselves. This is the basis for the second typical response to a violation of women's bodily integrity: to exhort women to censor their movements and appearance.

Another misconception believes that men who abuse women are rowdy lower class elements. In fact, men who violate a woman's space and body do not belong to any particular social group or class. Eve teasers are there in the family, the neighbourhood, in one's classroom and place of work.

What is perceived as male lust in our culture represents a desperate and frantic inability to communicate with women. This inability often translates into acts that hurt and terrorise. Consider the fact that popular representations of romance, as in film, clearly link up eve teasing to love. This not only naturalises abuse as love, but also legitimises male power over women. In the larger cultural context the man-woman relationships is simply not open to free, unfettered discussions of romance and sexuality. In such a context, communication between the sexes necessarily suffers.

There is an influence of the cinema and cheap literature in which sex permeates. The current advertisements trying to promote sale of under garments, towels bed-sheets, etc. by indecently exposing the female anatomy also lead to degeneration of women as a commercial commodity in the mind of man.

There is a rush to the urban area in search of adventure and employment. Away from the restraining influence of the families, the youngsters look for excitement and thrills which they seem to get in acts of eve teasing. Infliction of pain on the eve acts as a stimulant to their sex desires (Hindu; 1998).

There is also a lack of fear of punishment or adverse publicity or social disgrace. The police with its insufficient strength and preoccupation with other problems of law and order and courts with their proverbial delays and intricate legal procedures fail to bring most of the perpetrators to book (Ashraf, 1997: 93).

There are no particular places where eve teasers congregate. In this sense, no place is really "safe" and inviolate for women. Roads, buses, train, cinema halls, parks, beaches, even a woman's home and neighbourhood may be sites where her self-worth is abused. It does not matter if a woman is alone, with a friend, in a group, or sometimes even with another man. Segregating the spaces that men and women occupy only compounds, not solves the problem (Hindu; 1998).

Magnitude Of The Problem

The extent, validity and reliability of the data available are critical in determining the magnitude of the problem and in identifying priority areas for intervention. Prevalence studies with samples of representative populations are relatively new in developing countries. Such studies were initially conducted in industrialized countries – the United States, Canada, and Europe. For example, one very influential survey conducted in Canada in 1993 under the auspices of the Canadian government was developed in consultation with women's organizations and ensured adequate support and services for women participating in the survey.

When designing research on violence against women, it is important that the research itself does not put women at risk. The World Health Organization (WHO) has developed specific ethical and safety recommendations that take into account, among other issues, the safety of respondents and the research team, protecting confidentiality to ensure both women's safety and data quality, and specialized training of interviewers.

Most of the data available on violence against women are believed to be not only conservative, but unreliable. Studies vary in the sample size of women chosen, and the ways in which questions have been posed.

It is difficult to compare these studies because of inconsistency in the definition of domestic violence and in the parameters used, which can range from physical abuse alone, to physical, sexual and psychological abuse. Debate regarding the magnitude of the problem is also clouded by the fact that domestic violence is a crime that is underrecorded and under-reported.

When women file a report or seek treatment, they may have to contend with police and health care officials who have not been trained to respond adequately or to keep consistent records. On the other hand, shame, fear of reprisal, lack of information about legal rights, lack of confidence in, or fear of, the legal system, and the legal costs involved make women reluctant to report incidents of violence.

Physical abuse

A growing body of research studies confirms the prevalence of physical violence in all parts of the globe, including the estimates of 20 to 50 per cent of women from country to country who have experienced domestic violence. Statistics are grim no matter where in the world one looks. Data from industrialized and developing countries as well as from transitional countries provide an overview of the global problem. The data focus only on physical assault. There are few comparable statistics on psychological violence, sexual abuse, and murder of women at the hands of intimate partners and other family members. Physical violence is usually accompanied by psychological abuse, and in many cases by sexual assault.

CYCLE OF VIOLENCE

Frequently, domestic violence is used to describe specific violent and overtly abusive incidents, and legal definitions will tend to take this perspective. However, when violent and abusive behaviours happen within a relationship, the effects of those behaviours continue after these overt incidents are over. Advocates and counsellors will refer to domestic violence as a pattern of behaviours, including those listed above. Lenore Walker presented the model of a Cycle of violence which consists of three basic phases:

Tension Building Phase

Characterized by poor communication, tension, fear of causing outbursts. During this stage the victims try to calm the abuser down, to avoid any major violent confrontations.

Violent Episode

Characterized by outbursts of violent, abusive incidents. During this stage the abuser attempts to dominate his/her partner (victim), with the use of domestic violence.

Honeymoon Phase

Characterized by affection, apology, and apparent end of violence. During this stage the abuser feels overwhelming feelings of remorse and sadness. Some abusers walk away from the situation, while others shower their victims with love and affection.

Although it is easy to see the outbursts of the Acting-out Phase as abuse, even the more pleasant behaviours of the Honeymoon Phase serve to perpetuate the abuse. Many domestic violence advocates believe that the cycle of violence theory is limited and does not reflect the realities of many men and women experiencing domestic violence.

Cause

There are many different theories as to the causes of domestic violence. These include psychological theories that consider personality traits and mental characteristics of the offender, as well as social theories which consider external factors in the offender's environment, such as family structure, stress, social learning. As with many phenomena regarding human experience, no single approach appears to cover all cases.

Psychological

In general, about 80% of both court-referred and self-referred men in these domestic violence studies exhibited diagnosable psychopathology, typically personality disorders.

Estimates of personality disorder in the general population would be more in the 15-20% range [...] As violence becomes more severe and chronic, the likelihood of psychopathology in these men approaches 100%." Psychological theories focus on personality traits and mental characteristics of the offender.

Personality traits include sudden bursts of anger, poor impulse control, and poor self-esteem. Various theories suggest that psychopathology and other personality disorders are factors, and that abuse experienced as a child leads some people to be more violent as adults. Studies have found high incidence of psychopathy among abusers.

Dutton has suggested a psychological profile of men who abuse their wives, arguing that they have borderline personalities that are developed early in life. Gelles suggests that psychological theories are limited, and points out that other researchers have found that only 10% (or less) fit this psychological profile. He argues that social factors are important, while personality traits, mental illness, or psychopathy are lesser factors.

Social Theories

Looks at external factors in the offender's environment, such as family structure, stress, social learning, and includes rational choice theories.

Resource Theory

Resource theory was suggested by William Goode (1971). Women who are most dependent on the spouse for economic well being. Having children to take care of, should they leave the marriage, increases the financial burden and makes it all the more difficult for them to leave. Dependency means that they have fewer options and few resources to help them cope with or change their spouse's behaviour.

Couples that share power equally experience lower incidence of conflict, and when conflict does arise, are less likely to resort to violence. If one spouse desires control and power in the relationship, the spouse may resort to abuse. This may include coercion and threats, intimidation, emotional abuse, economic abuse, isolation, making light of the situation and blaming the spouse, using children (threatening to take them away), and behaving as "master of the castle".

Social Stress

Stress may be increased when a person is living in a family situation, with increased pressures. Social stresses, due to inadequate finances or other such problems in a family may further increase tensions. Violence is not always caused by stress, but may be one way that some (but not all) people respond to stress.

Families and couples in poverty may be more likely to experience domestic violence, due to increased stress and conflicts about finances and other aspects. Some speculate that poverty may hinder a man's ability to live up to his idea of "successful manhood", thus he fears losing honour and respect. Theory suggests that when he is unable to economically support his wife, and maintain control, he may turn to misogyny, substance abuse, and crime as ways to express masculinity.

Social Learning Theory

Social learning theory suggests that people learn from observing and modelling after others' behaviour. With positive reinforcement, the behaviour continues. If one observes violent behaviour, one is more likely to imitate it. If there are no negative consequences (e.g. victim accepts the violence, with submission), then the behaviour will likely continue. Often, violence is transmitted from generation to generation in a cyclical manner.

Power and Control

In some relationships, violence is posited to arise out of a perceived need for power and control, a form of bullying and social learning of abuse.

Abusers' efforts to dominate their partners have been attributed to low self-esteem or feelings of inadequacy, unresolved childhood conflicts, the stress of poverty, hostility and resentment toward women (misogyny), hostility and resentment toward men (misandry), personality disorders, genetic tendencies and sociocultural influences, among other possible causative factors. Most authorities seem to agree that abusive personalities result from a combination of several factors, to varying degrees.

A causalist view of domestic violence is that it is a strategy to gain or maintain power and control over the victim. This view is in alignment with Bancroft's "cost-benefit" theory that abuse rewards the perpetrator in ways other than, or in addition to, simply exercising power over his or her target(s). He cites evidence in support of his argument that, in most cases, abusers are quite capable of exercising control over themselves, but choose not to do so for various reasons.

An alternative view is that abuse arises from powerlessness and externalizing/projecting this and attempting to exercise control of the victim. It is an attempt to 'gain or maintain power and control over the victim' but even in achieving this it cannot resolve the powerlessness driving it. Such behaviours have addictive aspects leading to a cycle of abuse or violence. Mutual cycles develop when each party attempts to resolve their own powerlessness in attempting to assert control.

Questions of power and control are integral to the widely utilized Duluth Domestic Abuse Intervention Project. They developed "Power and Control Wheel" to illustrate this: it has power and control at the centre, surrounded by spokes , the titles of which include: Coercion and threats, Intimidation, Emotional abuse, Isolation, Minimizing, denying and blaming, Using children, Economic abuse, Male privilege.

The model attempts to address abuse by one-sidedly challenging the misuse of power by the 'perpetrator'. The power wheel model is not intended to assign personal responsibility, enhance respect for mutual purpose or assist victims and perpetrators in resolving their differences. It is an informational tool designed to help individuals understand the dynamics of power operating in abusive situations and identify various methods of abuse. Critics of this model suggest that the one-sided focus, which presumes men are to blame for all domestic violence, is problematic.

Mental Illness

Psychiatric disorders are sometimes associated with domestic violence, like Borderline personality disorder, Antisocial personality disorder, Bipolar disorder, Schizophrenia, Drug abuse and Alcoholism. In past medical knowledge, untreated Attention Deficit Hyperactive Disorder and Conduct disorders in childhood was associated with domestic violence in adulthood.

Gender Aspects of Abuse

The role of gender is a controversial topic related to the discussion of domestic violence. Among the persons killed by an intimate partner, about three quarters are female, and about a quarter are male: in 1999, in the US, 1,218 women and 424 men were killed by an intimate partner, regardless of which partner started the violence and of the gender of the partner. In the US, in 2005, 1181 females and 329 males were killed by their intimate partners.

The UN Declaration on the Elimination of Violence against Women (1993) states that "violence against women is a manifestation of historically unequal power relations between men and women, which have led to domination over and discrimination against women by men and to the prevention of the full advancement of women, and that violence against women is one of the crucial social mechanisms by which women are forced into a subordinate position compared with men."

Erin Pizzey, the founder of an early women's shelter in Chiswick, London, has expressed her dismay at how domestic abuse has become a gender-political football, and expressed an unpopular view in her book *Prone to Violence* that roughly two-thirds of women in the refuge system had a predisposition to seek abusive relationships, and to inflict violence. Pizzey also expressed the view that domestic violence can occur against any vulnerable intimates, regardless of their gender.

A Freudian concept, repetition compulsion, has been cited as a possible cause of a woman who was abused in childhood seeking an abusive man (or vice versa), theoretically as a misguided way to "master" their traumatic experience. There continues to be discussion about whether men or women are more abusive, whether women's abuse of men or men's abuse of women is typically more severe, and whether abused men should be provided the same resources and shelters that exist for women victims seka Carney (2007).

A problem in conducting studies that seek to describe violence in terms of gender is the amount of silence, fear and shame that results from abuse within families and relationships. Another is that abusive patterns can tend to seem normal to those who have lived in them for a length of time. Similarly, subtle forms of abuse can be quite transparent even as they set the stage for further abuse seeming normal. Finally, inconsistent definition of what domestic violence is makes definite conclusions difficult to reach when compiling the available studies.

Martin S. Fiebert of the Department of Psychology at California State University, Long Beach, provides an annotated bibliography of over two hundred scholarly works which demonstrate that women and men often exhibit comparable levels of IPV violence. In a Los Angeles Times article about male victims of domestic violence, Fiebert suggests that "...consensus in the field is that women are as likely as men to strike their partner but that—as expected—women are more likely to be injured than men. However, he noted, men are seriously injured in 38% of the cases in which "extreme aggression" is used. Fiebert additionally noted that his work was not meant to minimize the serious effects of men who abuse women.

In a Meta-analysis, John Archer, Ph. D., from the Department of Psychology, University of Central Lancashire, UK, writes: The present analyses indicate that men are among those who are likely to be on the receiving end of acts of physical aggression. The extent to which this involves mutual combat or the male equivalent to "battered women" is at present unresolved. Both situations are causes for concern. Straus (1997) has warned of the dangers involved—especially for women—when physical aggression becomes a routine response to relationship conflict. "Battered men"—those subjected to systematic and prolonged violence—are likely to suffer physical and psychological consequences, together with specific problems associated with a lack of recognition of their plight. Seeking to address these problems need not detract from continuing to address the problem of "battered women."

Donald G. Dutton and Tonia L. Nicholls, from the Department of Psychology at the University of British Columbia also undertook a meta-analysis of data in 2005. They concluded: Clearly, shelter houses full of battered women demonstrate the need for their continued existence. Moreover, outside of North American and Northern Europe, gender inequality is still the norm (Archer, in press). However, within those countries that have been most progressive about women's equality, female violence has increased as male violence has decreased (Archer, in press). There is not one solution for every domestically violent situation; some require incarceration of a terrorist perpetrator, others can be dealt with through court-mandated treatment, still others may benefit from couples therapy. However, feminist inspired intervention standards that preclude therapists in many states from doing effective therapy with male batterers are one outcome of this paradigm. The failure to recognize female threat to husbands, female partners, or children is another (Straus et al., 1980 found 10% higher rates of child abuse reported by mothers than by fathers).

The one size fits all policy driven by a simplistic notion that intimate violence is a recapitulation of class war does not most effectively deal with this serious problem or represent the variety of spousal violence patterns revealed by research. At some point, one has to ask whether feminists are more interested in diminishing violence within a population or promoting a political ideology. If they are interested in diminishing violence, it should be diminished for all members of a population and by the most effective and utilitarian means possible. This would mean an intervention/treatment approach based on other successful approaches from criminology and psychology.

Theories that women are as violent as men have been dubbed "Gender Symmetry" theories. In the most serious violence the men do dominate for example in 1999 in the US, 1,218 women and 424 men were killed by an intimate partner, regardless of which partner started the violence and of the gender of the partner. On the other hand, Michael Kimmel of the State University of New York at Stony Brook found that men are more violent inside and outside of the home than women.

Both men and women have been arrested and convicted of assaulting their partners in both heterosexual and homosexual relationships. The bulk of these arrests have been men being arrested for assaulting women. However, in the case of reciprocal violence, frequently only the male perpetrator is arrested. Determining how many instances of domestic violence actually involve male victims is difficult. Male domestic violence victims may be reluctant to get help for a number of reasons. Another study has demonstrated a high degree of acceptance by women of aggression against men,

Murders of female intimate partners by men have dropped, but not nearly as dramatically. Men kill their female intimate partners at about four times the rate that women kill their male intimate partners. Research by Jacquelyn Campbell, PhD RN FAAN has found that at least two thirds of women killed by their intimate partners were battered by those men prior to the murder. She also found that when males are killed by female intimates, the women in those relationships had been abused by their male partner about 75% of the time.

Some researchers have found a relationship between the availability of domestic violence services, improved laws and enforcement regarding domestic violence and increased access to divorce, and higher earnings for women with declines in intimate partner homicide. However, both men and women are far less likely to be abused when married to each other. The bulk of injuries from domestic violence involves co-habitation or the distresses of relationship breakups. Gender roles and expectations can and do play a role in abusive situations, and exploring these roles and expectations can be helpful in addressing abusive situations, as do factors like race, class, religion, sexuality and philosophy. None of these factors cause one to abuse or another to be abused. In 1997, the Canadian Advertising Foundation ruled that a national ad campaign that featured Nicole Brown Simpson's sister Denise with the slogan "Stop violence against women" was in fact portraying only men as aggressors, that it was not providing a balanced message and was, in fact, contributing to gender stereotyping. (The murder of Nicole Simpson also included the murder of Ronald Goldman.)

VIOLENCE AGAINST WIDOWS

Closely linked with Sati and harassment of widows, is the custom of child marriage producing number of child widows, but not child widowers. Widow remarriage is not common and not sanctioned by society, however men were allowed to remarry. Sati idealised as sitting on the funeral pyre of the deceased husband; and those widows who did not go through this had to make themselves physically unattractive and absent from public functions. Widows are called inauspicious and are avoided, whenever possible. Sati according to Giri was recommended after 500 AD in the dharmashastras and spread across the country around 1000 AD. There are three kinds of widows. One is a young girl with no children, a woman who becomes a widow after some years of marital span and has children. The third is case of a woman who is widow of 50 years and above of age. Giri mentions three options for a widow woman according to orthodox tradition; sati, ascetic widowhood or remarriage. Widows are expected to lead an ascetic life by the society with restrictive codes of dress, diet and demeanour and of social ostracism from the religious and social life of the community.

She is expected to remain in perpetual mourning, and give up eating 'spicy food', in order to cool her sexual energy, and remain celibate, devout and loyal to her husband's memory. According to Dreze J. the well being of widow is not just a question of economic security, but also one of dignity, self-respect and participation in society. Many widows in the Chen sample suffered from different forms of social isolation, psychological abuse or emotional distress.

According to Dreze J., the social marginalised of widows was frequently found to take one or more of the following forms: Rumours and accusations: Widows are often accused of being responsible for their husband's deaths, regarded as sexually threatening, and generally considered as inauspicious by the society. Widows are also accused often of immoral realtions Enforced dress and behaviour codes: Many widows are under strong pressure to observe restriction in codes of dress, appearance and behaviour.

Some of the traditional restrictions have become quite rare, even among the upper castes, but others remain widespread. Social ostracism: A widow is often excluded from the religious and social life of the community, due to her perceived in auspiciousness. Physical violence: violence against widows primarily takes the form of sexual harassment or property related violence. Emotional harassment: Sarcastic remarks in the presence of others, verbal abuse, beating and illtreatment of her children are some of the forms of emotional harassment. There have also been reports of houseowners sexually abusing widows who are living alone and cannot pay rent. Not all widows, according to Dreze J. face these type of mistreatment. Many older widows who live with their sons enjoy their respect and love.

Some older widows are happily integrated in their daughters households. If is young widows who are most vulnerable to mistreatment, unless they have the support of their parents or brother. Percentage of total widows to total female population is 6.5 for women and 1.94 for men. The percentage of women widows is much more than men from age group 40 onwards to 80+. The highest male female difference is in the age group 70 to 74, where the percentage of female widows is 66.51 and male widows is 18.70%.

Some of the essential factors that account for high levels of deprivation among Indian widows include limited freedom to remarry, insecure property rights, social restrictions, on living arrangements, restricted employment opportunities and lack of social support. Patrilocal Residence: The system of patrilocal residence, which has the effect of isolating women, is a fundamental source of gender inequalities in many parts of rural India and also plays a crucial part in the deprivation of widows. Patrilocality in the narrow sense refers to the norm, prevalent in most Hindu communities of India, according to which a woman has to leave her parents home at the time of marriage to join her husband in his home.

In a broader sense, especially in most Hindu communities of North India where marriage rules dictate marriage outside the clan and village. If could also result in drastic alienation from her parental family. In North India, widows are expected to remain in their husband's village, and most of them do so. At the same time they are unlikely to receive much support from their inlaws. On the contrary, the relationship between a widow and her in-laws is typically quite tense. Widows are thus denied both the freedom to leave their husband's village, and the support they need to live there happily. Limited freedom to remarry, in some communities, particularly in northwest India, ascriptive leviratic unions remain quite common. Elsewhere, the standard pattern is that most childless widows remarry, but only a small proportion of widowed mothers does so. Out of 562 respondents in the Chen sample of widows. 510

women had lost their husbands and did not remarry; 35 women, who had lost their husbands, remarried and then became widowed again by losing their second husbands, and 17 women who had lost their husbands, remarried, and were still married at the time of the survey.

In the Chen sample of 562 ever-widowed women, 13% in North India had remarried compared with only 6% in South India. The lower probability of remarriage in South is due in part to the practice of levirate in the North. The issue of remarriage, according to Srivastava is linked to property issue. Widow remarriage is not allowed so that part of the property does not pass into another family's hands. Some part of the population encourage leviratic relationships to ensure that the property stays with the family.

In cases where she gets into a 'nata', the relationship is formalised by the village community and she loses right to her first husband's property. She has a lower status in a 'nata' than a remarriage. Employment restrictions: Aside from these general restrictions, widows face specific difficulties in seeking gainful employment opportunities. These include: lack of access to indivisible productive assets owned by the deceased husband's family: weak bargaining power vis-à-vis male partners in economic transactions, frequent absence of a literate member in the household: limited access to institutional credit, and, particularly in the case of widows with young children, the burden of domestic work. Social restriction of living arrangements: One of the clearest and most important findings of Chen's and other studies is the overwhelming dependence of widows on themselves and their own sons. The proportion of widows who live in households headed either themselves or by one of their sons are well over 85% in the Chen sample. The proportion of widows who live in a household headed by a brother-in-law or parent-in-law is below 3% and the number of widows who live in a household headed by a brother of the father is also below 3%. Legal inheritance rights: Formally according to contemporary Indian law, a widow has an unequivocal right to a share of her husband's property, including his land. This is in addition to the legal rights she has irrespective of her marital status to a share of her parents' property.

Field studies, however, indicate that these legal rights are comprehensively violated, and that a large majority of widows have very limited and insecure property rights. This deprivation of property rights not only represents the loss of a potential source of independent income, but also diminishes the bargaining power of a widow vis-à-vis her in-laws, sons and other potential supporters. Modernisation: Singh has mentioned urbanisation and modernisation and consequently the erosion of the traditional form of care of the elderly people, which was prevalent in India like joint family. There is an emotional estrangement between the young and the old in nuclear family.

Lack of loyal servants: Even if the old has money to fend for themselves, many are unable to do so due to the lack of loyal domestic servants. Indicators: Some of the other indicators of violence against the old and widow could be symptoms of withdrawal. Mental deterioration, cessation of activities, felling of inferiority, inadequacy and frustration. Old and widows are victimised by relatives, informal care providers, house-owners, friends or formal care-givers in institutional settings. They are abused almost by anybody who has power over them.

EXAMINING THE CAUSES OF VIOLENCE AGAINST WOMEN

Many perspectives try to explain the causes of violence against women. Here is an overview of some of the major ones; bear in mind that many researchers who study violence against women have concluded that no one approach adequately explains the phenomenon.

The perspectives are divided into two categories: individual, focusing on causes of violent behaviour unique to individuals; and sociocultural, focusing on the influences of society and culture. A combination of multiple factors, from both of these types of perspectives, actually best explains what is known about the causes of violence against women.

Individual Perspectives

The most popular individual-focused perspectives are the *social learning theories,* which explain violent behaviour as learned from one's environment. These theories, individuals learn how to behave from their exposure to and experiences of violence. When they observe or imitate behaviour, they learn what those around them consider appropriate. Boys are most likely to imitate fathers, and girls to imitate mothers, through the socialization processes that take place in families. When their behaviour is responded to and reinforced, they become conditioned to continue the behaviour.

This process is responsible for the *intergenerational transmission of violence,* in which violence against women is learned from one generation to the next. Violence is learned as a tactic for getting what one wants or expressing emotions. Social learning theories have provided a valuable perspective on the complex issue of the influence on children of exposure to violence in the community and in the media as well as in the family.

This exposure—along with other factors, but not by itself—is recognized to have had a significant impact on the behaviour of people who later use violence. But critics of social learning theories say that they don't explain much of the phenomenon of violence against women.

The notion of children as passive learners who do what they see and respond only to conditioning is not supported by child development research.

It is also too simplistic a view of the many kinds of dynamics within families that influence children's learning and behaviour. Although studies of people who perpetrate violence or abuse indicate that witnessing violence is an important risk factor—in other words, people who use violent behaviour are more likely than those who don't to have been exposed to violence during childhood—most people who were abused or who witnessed violence as a child do not grow up to be violent, nor do they become victims of violence.

Also, the correlation between witnessing violence and becoming a victim of it is low—it is estimated that about 30 per cent of adult female victims witnessed violence or abuse as children. Intergenerational patterns of violence can also be attributed to other kinds of environmental influences on children and their later behaviour as adults. Recent studies have identified the transmission of attitudes from parents to children as significant: for example, attitudes about how men treat women or about circumstances in which aggressive behaviour is justified.

One of the most important explanations for violence that stems from childhood exposure to violence in the home comes from studies that focus on *trauma*—specifically, the traumatic effects on children of witnessing abuse or violence. Rather than experiencing a cognitive, learning process, children may respond to violence by undergoing a series of physical and emotional changes in the process of attempting to cope with overactive stress responses and ongoing traumatic stress reactions.

They may manifest hypervigilance, hypersensitivity, increased startle responses, dissociation, nightmares, and serious distractability; most relevantly, they may too easily perceive danger and threat in situations that most others do not view the same way. Post- traumatic stress is identified in the histories of many people who use violent behaviour. It is commonly believed that individuals who are violent towards women are not solely influenced by their childhood environments but have *mental disorders or personality disorders*, and so they don't have normal inhibitions that stop them from using violence.

Some violence is committed by people with antisocial disorders, who have no sense of conscience, remorse, or empathy with the victim or concern about the consequences of their actions. There is evidence that some people who use violent behaviour may be depressed, bipolar, obsessive, or narcissistic.

Donald Dutton, who has counseled and studied men who abuse their intimate partners, identifies in these men patterns of what he calls "borderline personality organization," which has some of the features of borderline personality disorder but occurs only in the intimate relationship and not in other arenas of the batterer's life. Men who assault women have been found to have greater needs for power than men who do not assault women. It is possible that men who have low self-esteem or who feel little control over others or the events in their lives are more likely to feel powerless, which may lead them to attempt to control or punish women. Critics of these psychopathological explanations of violence against women are concerned that psychological problems are often used as an excuse for violent behaviour, minimizing the deliberate nature of abusive behaviour and the perpetrator's responsibility for his actions. Also, there is no consistent pattern of psychopathology in studies of batterers or rapists.

Psychological patterns such as obsessiveness or borderline personality organization may be difficult to distinguish from intentional emotional manipulation and control. The overwhelming majority of people who have the psychological problems suspected of causing violence against women do not abuse or rape women. Therefore, some factor or factors must combine with these problems or disorders to cause violence against women.

Biological and physiological explanations consider men's use of aggressive or violent behaviour towards women as part of the process of natural selection. In one example of this thinking, since the goal for males is to reproduce as much as possible to increase the chance of passing on their genes, rape can be seen as an extreme response to natural selection pressure. The use of *alcohol,* commonly associated with violent behaviour, is consistently found in many of the profiles of abusive men and is linked to rape. There is also a link between drug abuse and violence. Although victims, abusers, and rapists often believe that alcohol or drugs cause the violence, experts believe that people use alcohol and drugs to reduce their inhibitions about hurting others and are very likely to become violent with or without getting drunk or high.

Sociocultural Perspectives

Sociocultural theories explain violence against women as stemming from social structures or cultural conditions. Advocates of these theories say that men abuse women "because they can." They mean that in our society men who are inclined to abuse women for any number of personal reasons find it easy to justify it and get away with it without being punished or stopped. *Family structure perspectives* focus on family violence in particular, arguing that women are as violent as men in relationships and families. Well-known family violence researcher Murray Straus, the origin of the problem is in the nature of the family structure. Violence in U.S. families is often considered legitimate: many parents spank their children or accept sibling violence as inevitable.

Aggressive, abusive, and violent behaviour is defended as within the range of normal in all relationships in the family. Solutions to the problem of family violence lie in challenging these attitudes about violence as normal and identifying them as harmful and unacceptable. Critics believe that this perspective ignores the power and status differences between men and women, arguing that men's use of violence is not the same as women's. Family structure perspectives do not make distinctions among the patterns, contexts, or motivations for use of violence, and therefore they may not present an accurate picture of the effects of violence.

They also approach violence as resulting from conflict between family members, which ignores commonly seen patterns of coercive control. The value of this perspective, however, is that it addresses social norms that tolerate and therefore allow violent and aggressive behaviour within the family and in intimate relationships. *Cultural acceptance of violence* is high in the United States.

Societies that reinforce the use of violence as a legitimate means to achieve desired ends support violence against women. Although this does address cultural tolerance for and glorification of violence, this explanation, however, is criticized as not explaining why only some men use violent behaviour against women. Some see *stress* as a risk factor for family violence.

When individuals or groups face stressors they cannot manage—for instance, poverty, discrimination, immigration problems, community crises, personal difficulties, or medical problems—the resulting stress has the potential to lead to violent behaviour. *Feminist theory* focuses on power, on gender, and on the structure of relationships in a male-dominated, patriarchal culture.

Feminist theory, the main factors that contribute to violence against women include historically male-dominated social structures and socialization practices teaching men and women gender-specific roles. Feminists have analysed dynamics of oppression and the intersection of gender, race, and class to explain that the institutionalization of violence against women in political, legal, and economic systems makes it invisible and acceptable.

Feminist research has focused on women's stories of their own survival, victimization, and fears as the major source of information about gendered violence, and it has confronted gender bias in research that reflects patriarchal social attitudes. Feminist theories have been criticized for an exclusive, toosimplistic focus on gender.

Violence against women is too complex to be understood only as a problem of gender. Gender roles—and sexism and racism embedded in social structures—are powerful components of male violence towards women, but other factors contribute as well, and multiple dimensions interact with one another to make it complex, difficult to explain, and difficult to eradicate. This book emphasizes the complexity of these interacting factors and uses the analysis of social structural power dynamics related to gender, race, and class inherent in feminist theory as a guiding principle—not to oversimplify, but rather to account for complex social environments that perpetuate and influence individual acts of violence.

Multidimensional Perspectives

Multidimensional explanations of violence against women integrate social factors, such as class, gender, and culture, with individual characteristics, such as family history, psychopathology, and alcohol or drug use. Reluctance of institutions to intervene, cultural approval of violence, and social constructions of " masculinity" contribute additional dimensions. These theories view violence against women as complex, with individual and social factors combining to cause and perpetuate the problem.

Violence as a Manifestation of Institutionalized Sexism

Many feminists attribute the pervasiveness of violence against women to *institutionalized sexism*—cultural norms and expectations that accept women as " legitimate victims" of male violence. In general, cultural norms and expectations prescribe and proscribe the rights and responsibilities of all people in a particular social status or category. They are learned and transmitted from one generation to the next in the home, workplace, and in peer groups.

In most societies, norms related to gender and violence support female subordination and justify male violence. They pervade legal systems, literature, media, and everyday discourse. Nilda Rimonte, founder of the Center for the Pacific Asian Family in Los Angeles, defines " legitimate victims" as individuals seen as having little or no reason to complain about their victimization because they belong to an inferior social class. Their social status justifies their victimization—they deserve punishment.

Although most men do not maintain these attitudes or use aggressive behaviours towards women, the cultural norms in the United States and worldwide create a remarkable social tolerance for violent behaviour in the family or towards certain women. What makes this clear is that beating, emotional torture, and sexual violation are unquestionably intolerable and unacceptable if committed by a stranger or by one man towards another.

A well-known study simulated a scene of a man yelling at and hitting a woman on a public walkway with many people passing by. When anyone approached to help, the man said, "She's my wife," and passersby backed away and did nothing to help. Teenage girls have reported that fights between boys in school or in public get an immediate response from authorities, whereas violent incidents against girls, occurring in view of others, get no response at all.

A small per centage of cases of rape and battering are actually prosecuted, and convictions are rare compared to the numbers of reports made to law enforcement and compared to the consequences for stranger assault in the United States and worldwide. Several specific societal dynamics operate together to enforce the legitimacy and acceptability of violence against women as a means to control women as a class.

Cultural myths blame victims for their victimization, view domestic violence as a private matter, eroticize and excuse male violence, fail to hold men accountable, and trivialize the real consequences of violence for women, whether directly victimized or not. Sexual scripts, a concept introduced by psychologist Sandra Bem, reflect androcentric heterosexuality, eroticize sexual inequality, and support male domination as normal and natural. In these "scripts," men objectify women, emphasizing their physical attractiveness and ability to stimulate and satisfy men's desires, rather than seeing women as human beings like themselves. *Gender and gender-related social roles* define masculinity and femininity as clusters of traits that depend on what is considered masculine in societies and cultural groups.

An example is the belief that men are dominant, strong, and "in charge," and that women are passive, irrational, weak, and submissive—traits that are not naturally exclusive to men or women, but that vary with culture, class, ethnicity, and other social statuses. Views of *women as property* are prevalent globally. In Western societies, rape was originally seen as a property crime against the father or husband of the victim, resulting in diminished value of the woman. This view of women as property has been established historically as being at the root of social attitudes about rape and domestic violence.

It can be found in Western laws, customs, and religious beliefs. Early marriage laws gave men the legal right to hit their wives. Laws in the United States were modeled after English common law, which expected men to be responsible for and physically "discipline" wives, who had no legal status separate from husbands or fathers and, after marriage, were owned and controlled by their husbands. Early British rape law similarly required that restitution for rape be paid to the victim's husband or, if the victim was not married, to her father.

While early U.S. criminal laws against rape and domestic violence did not completely conform to British common law, and were reformed during the

1980s, remnants of the early laws persist in attitudes and actual practices within justice systems. Twenty years ago, researcher Murray Straus called the marriage license a "hitting license," and some violence researchers believe the husband's ownership and control of the wife is embedded in the marriage contract. This ownership extends to dating and other intimate relationships and continues after a marriage ends. Men's entitlement to women's bodies and exclusive attention, and to intrude upon women's physical space without thought, stem from these assumptions and attitudes, even though women's rights to be autonomous from men have gradually changed during the past century.

Pervasive beliefs that women are responsible for men's emotional and sexual well-being, without regard to any harmful consequences for women, are often openly stated by men when they justify rape and abuse. Abusers often express their "right" to take out their frustrations, insecurities, and anger on certain women, such as their wives or girlfriends, or to punish them for not being exclusively available whenever they want or need them. They do not target others at random; they target those they feel entitled to control. *Rape culture* refers to a set of values and beliefs that create an environment conducive to rape, based on assumptions that men are aggressive and women are passive and acquiescent.

These assumptions about gender contain a double standard in which men who are sexually aggressive are viewed positively as manly and successful, whereas women who enjoy sex or engage in premarital sex are seen as "sluts" and demeaned. These attitudes are the basis for myths about rape such as "She wanted it," "Girls say no when they mean yes," or "Women lead men on." *Male bonding* in peer groups contributes to a dynamic seen in hypermasculine settings, such as the military, athletics, gangs, and fraternities, in which men bond in brotherhood, and prove their masculinity to one another, by objectifying or sexually coercing or assaulting women.

In these circumstances, men who might not rape individually do so in a group that pressures men to fit the distorted and stereotyped ideal of the sexually aggressive, masculine man. The group attacks a woman who represents the faceless "other," the object of their fear and hatred that men must avoid resembling at all costs—the distorted feminine stereotype of a woman. Carole Sheffield writes, "Sexual Terrorism," that "the right to control the female body is the cornerstone of patriarchy."

Patriarchy is a system of social structures and practices, in which men dominate, oppress, and exploit women. Whether we conceptualize this social phenomenon as patriarchy or as *male supremacy* or *male domination,* feminists view it as a consistent pattern of ideological and structural practices that serve to justify and perpetuate men's oppression of women. Susan Brownmiller, in her groundbreaking 1975 book *Against Our Will: Men, Women and Rape,* wrote that rape is the "enforcer of male supremacy, the use of the penis as weapon" and "the conscious process of intimidation by which all men keep all women in a state of fear." Sheffield defines sexual terrorism as the system by which men frighten women to control and dominate them, a system with the same characteristics as other forms of terrorism.

This includes nonviolent sexual intimidation and the threat of violence as well as overt sexual violence. Its institutionalization is reflected in laws, in rape during war, and in slavery worldwide. As Lisa Price writes in *Feminist Frameworks: Building Theory on Violence Against Women,* her excellent analysis of feminist theory on violence against women, "Experience with political terrorism has shown that its strength lies largely in its unpredictability, targeting a whole population but selecting individual victims randomly." Unlike other crimes, crimes of violence against females cut across socioeconomic lines. These are the crimes least likely to be reported, and when reported, they are the crimes least likely to be brought to trial or to result in conviction. They are often blamed on the victim; they are generally not taken seriously; and they fuse dominance and sexuality. As British researcher Elizabeth Stanko wrote, "All women have some experience of male violation.... *To walk the streets warily at night is how we actually feel our femininity.*"

In their daily work, lawyers, advocates, and counselors who see men and/or boys charged with acquaintance rape, intimate partner violence, or other violence against women observe perpetrators' shock and disbelief that anyone thinks they have done something illegal or wrong. Rapists are often genuinely surprised to learn that the victim has called the police or is seriously injured, thinking, "She wanted it!" One young man told a police officer when he was arrested for assault and battery, "What do you mean this is illegal?! She's my girlfriend!" Any female can be a victim. The perpetrators—child molesters, batterers, wife beaters, rapists—often do not understand they have done anything wrong, views that are often shared by judges, police, and others. Sexual violence is rarely punished; an estimated 5 per cent of reported rape cases result in convictions. Several studies of complaints by women abused by intimate partners found that none had resulted in convictions.

There are many ways that the fear of violence affects women: for example, how we dress, where and when we go out, where we work, and the kinds of work and other activities we do. Think about the ways we judge women who have been raped. Women are often asked what they did to bring it upon themselves, how they dressed, what they were doing that provoked it, and so on. Class makes a difference in the degree of choice women have about where they go, what hours they work, how vulnerable they are to rape. Therefore, violence against women functions as a means of social control in the same way that justifying and threatening violence enforces oppression against any group.

VIOLENCE IN THE COMMUNITY

Rape

Rape can occur anywhere, even in the family, where it can take the form of marital rape or incest. It occurs in the community, where a woman can fall prey to any abuser. It also occurs in situations of armed conflict and in refugee camps. In the United States, national statistics indicate that a women is raped every six minutes. In 1995, the case of a Brazilian jogger raped and murdered in New York City's Central Park drew international attention once again to the problem. The incident occurred only a few years after an earlier sensational jogger-assault case in which the victim -- an American assaulted in the same general area of the park — barely survived after her assailants left her for dead.

Relations between residents of the Japanese island of Okinawa and American GIs were thrown into turmoil in 1995 after two marines and a sailor allegedly kidnapped and raped a 12-year-old girl. The Special Rapporteur's report underlines the importance of education to sensitize the public about the special horrors of rape, and of sensitivity training for the police and hospital staff who work with victims.

Sexual Assault within Marriage

In many countries sexual assault by a husband on his wife is not considered to be a crime: a wife is expected to submit. It is thus very difficult in practice for a woman to prove that sexual assault has occurred unless she can demonstrate serious injury. The report of the Special Rapporteur noted that light sentences in sexual assault cases send the wrong message to perpetrators and to the public at large: that female sexual victimization is unimportant.

Sexual Harassment

Sexual harassment in the workplace is a growing concern for women. Employers abuse their authority to seek sexual favours from their female co-workers or subordinates, sometimes promising promotions or other forms of career advancement or simply creating an untenable and hostile work environment. Women who refuse to give in to such unwanted sexual advances often run the risk of anything from demotion to dismissal. But in recent years more women have been coming forward to report such practices — some taking their cases to court. In her report, the Special Rapporteur stressed that sexual harassment constitutes a form of sex discrimination. "It not only degrades the woman", the report noted, "but reinforces and reflects the idea of non-professionalism on the part of women workers, who are consequently regarded as less able to perform their duties than their male colleagues."

Prostitution and Trafficking

Many women are forced into prostitution either by their parents, husbands or boyfriends — or as a result of the difficult economic and social conditions in which they find themselves. They are also lured into prostitution, sometimes by "mail-order bride" agencies that promise to find them a husband or a job in a foreign country. As a result, they very often find themselves illegally confined in brothels in slavery-like conditions where they are physically abused and their passports withheld.

Most women initially victimized by sexual traffickers have little inkling of what awaits them. They generally get a very small percentage of what the customer pays to the pimp or the brothel owner. Once they are caught up in the system there is practically no way out, and they find themselves in a very vulnerable situation.

Since prostitution is illegal in many countries, it is difficult for prostitutes to come forward and ask for protection if they become victims of rape or want to escape from brothels. Customers, on the other hand, are rarely the object of penal laws. In Thailand, prostitutes who complain to the police are often arrested and sent back to the brothels upon payment of a fine.

The extent of trafficking in women and girl children has reached alarming proportions, especially in Asian countries. Many women and girl children are trafficked across borders, often with the complicity of border guards. In one incident, five young prostitutes burned to death in a brothel fire because they had been chained to their beds. At the same time, sex tours of developing countries are a well-organized industry in several European and other industrialized countries.

The Special Rapporteur has called on Governments to take action to protect young girls from being recruited as prostitutes and to closely monitor recruiting agencies.

VIOLENCE AGAINST WOMEN MIGRANT WORKERS

Female migrant workers typically leave their countries for better living conditions and better pay — but the real benefits accrue to both the host countries and the countries of origin. For home countries, money sent home by migrant workers is an important source of hard currency, while receiving countries are able to find workers for low-paying jobs that might otherwise go unfilled.

But migrant workers themselves fare badly, and sometimes tragically. Many become virtual slaves, subject to abuse and rape by their employers. In the Middle East and Persian Gulf region, there are an estimated 1.2 million women, mainly Asians, who are employed as domestic servants. According to the independent human rights group Middle East Watch, female migrant workers in Kuwait often suffer beatings and sexual assaults at the hands of their employers.

The police are often of little help. In many cases, women who report being raped by their employers are sent back to the employer — or are even assaulted at the police station. Working conditions are often appalling, and employers prevent women from escaping by seizing their passports or identity papers.

The report of the Special Rapporteur draws attention to the fact that there are many international instruments that can be used to prevent abuse against migrant women and suggests some measures to protect the human rights of migrant women.

Pornography

Another concern highlighted in the Special Rapporteur's report is pornography, which represents a form of violence against women that "glamorizes the degradation and maltreatment of women and asserts their subordinate function as mere receptacles for male lust".

5

Discrimination against Women

Underpinning discrimination against women in the workplace is a set of attitudes and beliefs about gender and work. People have stereotyped views about both the characteristics of women and the characteristics of particular jobs or job duties. They often have difficulty accepting that women can do work that requires the attributes normally ascribed to men, such as intelligence, decisiveness, strength, or aggressiveness. In addition, at least some people respond with hostility when individuals fail to conform to the standards expected for their gender. Finally, in many instances, the work environment does not eliminate, and may enhance, the general social power men have over women.

In an extensive review of the literature on stereotyping, prejudice, and discrimination, psychologist Susan Fiske (1998) describes a number of ways in which the cognitive properties of stereotyping create problems for women and other devalued groups. Psychological research has demonstrated that stereotypes, or preconceived expectations, affect the information that is sought and the degree to which it is remembered. Thus, an evaluator, supervisor, or hiring manager may fail to identify the stereotype-inconsistent abilities of women to perform "male" tasks and may forget about the evidence of effective performance that women demonstrate. Furthermore, the filtering effects of prejudice also affect the interpretation of information. For example, on "masculine tasks," men's successful performance tends to be attributed to ability, while women's positive performance is attributed to effort or luck.

Stereotyping and prejudice also constrain the way that behavior is interpreted. The finding that the same conduct, especially involving traditionally masculine characteristics such as strength, assertiveness, decisiveness, or goal rather than process orientation, is interpreted positively when performed by men and negatively when performed by women has been confirmed by multiple studies. Thus, when women perform their workplace duties in the same manner that men perform them, the women tend to be negatively evaluated, creating quite a double-bind for women performing tasks where those "male" behaviours are necessary or desirable.

What makes the actions of stereotyping and prejudice even more problematic is that they can operate without conscious awareness. Furthermore, social psychologists have repeatedly demonstrated that stereotypes and prejudices become self-fulfilling prophecies, with the beliefs of the perceiver influencing the behavior of the actor in a manner consistent with the perceiver's original bias. Finally, calling attention to the stereotype or prejudice does not necessarily inhibit the effect and can make matters worse.

Discrimination toward women in the workplace is and has been manifested in a wide variety of actions. Some of those manifestations involve direct discriminatory action, like being denied positions, opportunities, or training. Other manifestations include gender-based hostility and unwanted sexual attention. Many of the instances of discriminatory conduct that women, or members of other devalued and stigmatized groups, experience are not dramatic like the "men only" job signs of earlier years. They are instead what have been called micro-inequities and micro-aggressions, seemingly minor slights, insults, and hostilities that form what has been labelled the mi-nutia of sexism. Because these events are, each by itself, almost trivial, it is difficult for an individual to protest them without seeming thin-skinned or petty. Yet in their cumulative weight, these small acts of omission and commission provide the fabric of a hostile or unwelcoming environment, creating barriers to women's participation and success in the workplace.

One common manifestation of discrimination, whether based on unconscious stereotype or conscious plan, is the perpetuation of the gender segregation of work. Davison and Burke (2000), in a meta-analysis of studies that examined sex discrimination in employment over a thirty-year period, generally found that applicants applying for "opposite-sex" jobs received discriminatory evaluations. Although women now participate in many more than the seventeen job categories that accounted for most of women's work in 1960, numerous studies have found systematic differences in the work assignments of men and women even when their formal job titles were the same. As many have pointed out, one frequent pattern is for men rather than women to be assigned to the tasks and duties that improve their skills and prepare them for career advancement. This pattern of discrimination can be particularly difficult to address because the actual discriminatory effect can take years to accumulate. Furthermore, job assignment within a job classification is generally considered the purview of management rights, protected from intervention by union grievance or court scrutiny. Thus, all women and minority men are unable to effectively challenge the discriminatory practice until it has resulted in real differences of skills and experience, differences that can then be offered as a justification for differential rates of promotion or pay.

Some theorists have attempted to separate the discriminatory conduct by whether it is based on an overt endorsement of male superiority and female inferiority or on a more superficially benign endorsement of male and female difference. They label as hostile sexism the attitudes based on an endorsement of male superiority. A second set of attitudes, based on an endorsement of female superiority in such stereotypical female attributes as nurturance, congeniality, and patience, are labelled benevolent sexism. One problem with such distinctions is that although it is possible to develop scales that distinguish between the two attitudes, both are rooted in acceptance of categorical difference between males and females. All such beliefs overemphasize the stereotypical differences between males and females while ignoring the degree to which individual men or women frequently do not differ in the stereotyped direction on any particular attribute.

Other scholars have attempted to distinguish between behavior based on gender hostility and behavior based on sexual desire. Unfortunately, this is not as easy or clear a distinction as it might initially appear because of the intertwining of sex and sexuality with power, dominance, and hostility. As psychologist Kay Deaux (1998) notes, "Sexual harassment can be primarily sexual or primarily hostile, that is, its goal could be to secure a sexual liaison or to make life uncomfortable for a woman". Furthermore, as those working in the area of sexual assault frequently report, even acts that are designed to obtain sexual liaisons can be as much about power, dominance, and submission as about genital stimulation.

LIFE BEFORE THE PREGNANCY DISCRIMINATION ACT

The history of the treatment of pregnant women, or even women who may become pregnant, in the workplace is not a pleasant one. Based on the idea that women, especially mothers, did not belong in the workplace, as well as the desire to reserve jobs for men, protective legislation for women was passed in the early part of the twentieth century. This protective legislation is typified in the famous 1908 Supreme Court case of *Muller* v. *Oregon.* The state of Oregon had limited the number of hours per day that women could work but had passed no such limitation for men. The Court upheld this law, reasoning that it was women's "performance of maternal functions" that placed them at a natural disadvantage in life compared to men and that long working hours could injure women's fragile health, yet women needed to remain healthy in order to have healthy children. While a limitation of working hours today might be considered a reasonable and humane law, in the exploitative labour conditions at the turn of the twentieth century, legislation such as this deprived women of employment opportunities, which was its intended result.

This treatment was not just a phenomenon of the early twentieth century. Strikingly unequal treatment of pregnant women persisted into the 1970s, and during the 1950s and 1960s, some states even adopted new legislation that prohibited women from being hired for a specified period of time before and after childbirth. Employers routinely denied women disability benefits for pregnancy while providing coverage for many other temporarily disabling conditions. In some cases, employers forced pregnant women to take leave without assurance that their jobs would be there upon their return to work.

The women's movement of the 1970s aimed to change these practices, as well as other forms of discrimination against women. To address pregnancy discrimination in employment, women's advocates thought they already had the necessary legal tools. In *Reed* v. *Reed* in 1971, the Supreme Court first adopted the view that the equal protection clause of the Fourteenth Amendment prohibited differential treatment by the government based on sex. Feminists then argued that based on the clear connection between women's reproductive capabilities and societal discrimination, pregnancy discrimination was part and parcel of sex discrimination, and thus was covered by the equal protection clause. In 1974, the Court decided *Cleveland Board of Education* v. *LaFleur.* In *LaFleur,* the Supreme Court addressed two public school district polices that required teachers to take mandatory maternity leave for four or five months before the expected childbirth, which is long before most pregnant women would prefer to stop working. The lower courts that had previously heard these cases based their decisions on the equal protection clause, but the Supreme Court held that these polices violated the due process clause of the Fourteenth Amendment due to the burden they imposed on the fundamental right to bear children. Although this case advanced the rights of pregnant workers by invalidating these discriminatory policies, the rationale for the case focused on women in relation to reproduction, not sex discrimination. The Court also later used this due process rationale to invalidate a Utah unemployment compensation statute, which had provided that women would get no benefits during unemployment in the third trimester of pregnancy or six weeks after childbirth because the state presumed a woman could not work then *(Turnerv. Department of Employment Security,* 1975).

In addition, there was a federal statute protecting women in the workplace. Title VII of the Civil Rights Act of 1964, the foundation of modern employment antidiscrimination law, prohibited sex discrimination in employment, and it provided simply that discrimination based on sex was forbidden. But Title VII itself did not provide a definition of the term *sex,* and due to the unusual way in which the word was included in the act, the legislative history behind the inclusion of this term or what Congress considered it to cover was scant. The EEOC stepped into this breach and began addressing to what extent the prohibition of discrimination based on sex applied to the treatment of pregnancy. Though it took eight years, the EEOC produced administrative guidelines by 1972 that clearly stated that Title VII prohibited differential treatment of pregnancy, including in disability and other benefits policies. This was at a time when the exclusion of pregnancy from such policies was routine. Thus, when women challenged policies that denied disability benefits for disability from pregnancy but not from other sources, including ones that primarily affected men, they met with success. Many federal district courts and several courts of appeals agreed that differential treatment based on pregnancy violated Title VII.

However, this initial success was short-lived. The issue of whether pregnancy was included within the meaning of sex under the equal protection clause reached the Supreme Court in 1974 in *Geduldig v. Aiello.* At issue in *Geduldig* was the California State Disability Insurance Program, which provided disability payments to workers who were temporarily disabled by an illness but not eligible for workers' compensation funds. This plan specifically excluded disability based on pregnancy from coverage, while covering disability from almost every other cause. The Court examined this plan as it traditionally did other social insurance schemes, which meant it gave a wide berth to the policy choices of the state. The Court defined the policy of the state as excluding a benefit that would be expensive so as to keep employee contributions low and still keep the system solvent. The Court refused to see the exclusion of benefits for pregnancy as discrimination based on gender and stated in a line that later became famous (though it was relegated to a footnote in the opinion itself), "While it is true that only women can become pregnant... the program divides potential recipients into two groups—pregnant women and nonpregnant persons. While the first group is exclusively female, the second group includes members of both sexes. The fiscal and actuarial benefits of the program thus accrue to members of both sexes".

This seductively simple statement masks the reality of pregnancy discrimination, which feminists of the 1970s and today argue is that pregnant women are discriminated against because they are engaging in the reproductive role of women and that women are discriminated against in large part because they are the gender that is capable of bearing children. Justice William Brennan wrote a strong dissent to the *Geduldig* decision in which he examined pregnancy discrimination in a more thorough manner and concluded, "Such dissimilar treatment of men and women, on the basis of physical characteristics inextricably linked to one's sex, inevitably constitutes sex discrimination". Today, the *Geduldig* decision remains much criticized but valid law.

Geduldig was a constitutional decision, but Title VII was statutory law that reached beyond the Constitution to regulate private employment and was not necessarily subject to the same analysis. So even after *Geduldig,* women continued to challenge the exclusion of coverage of pregnancy from disability policies under Title VII against private employers. And the lower courts hearing those cases found that the analysis in *Geduldig* did not necessarily apply in the context of Title VII and that pregnancy was included in the prohibition of sex discrimination in Title VII.

The issue of whether pregnancy was included within the meaning of "sex" under Title VII reached the Supreme Court in 1976 in *General Electric Co.* v. *Gilbert.* Gilbert challenged a disability plan that was almost identical to the one in *Geduldig,* though offered through her employer, and the Court proceeded to analyse her challenge almost identically as well. The Court found that its analysis under the equal protection clause was applicable to Title VII and this time emphasized the "nonpregnant persons" language to state that the reason *Geduldig* rejected the feminist argument about the nature of pregnancy discrimination, and the Court was doing so again, was that neither plan in itself discriminated based on sex, since both men and women were the nonpregnant comparison group. However, Title VII also has a second avenue of liability that is not available under the equal protection clause: liability based on disparate impact. The theory of disparate impact liability is that a practice by an employer, even if neutral on its face, may be discriminatory if its negative effects fall disproportionately on a protected group. The Supreme Court in *Gilbert* recognized the possibility of applying this theory to the disability policy challenged, but it found the disparate impact theory not applicable to the case, reasoning that overall, the plan did not discriminate against women in that it covered them for many causes of disability. In so doing, the Court did not consider that the particular practice of excluding pregnancy, not the plan itself, was having the negative effect and that its sole effect was on women.

Justice Brennan also wrote a dissenting opinion in this case, and in that opinion he explored the context of sex discrimination at the company that provided the challenged plan. The company sued had "a history of... practices that have served to undercut the employment opportunities of women who become pregnant while employed", including scaling women's wages at two-thirds of men's and forcing employees to take maternity leave while not providing them with disability payments. That is, of course, the better way to see pregnancy discrimination: as part of a larger pattern of discrimination.

The reaction to the *Gilbert* decision in the feminist, union, and civil rights communities can be fairly described as livid. Critical discussions of the case immediately surfaced in legal articles, and feminists and others began a campaign to have Congress overrule the Court's decision, which it could do, since the Court's decision was interpreting a statute, not the Constitution. It was called the Campaign to End Discrimination Against Pregnant Workers, and it offered, among other strategies, the testimony of prominent feminists to Congress.

A year later, however, the Supreme Court issued a ruling that appeared to back off its stand in *Geduldig* and *Gilbert*. In *Nashville Gas Co.* v. *Satty (1977)*, the Court found that a policy of forcing pregnant women to both take leave and forfeit their accrued seniority when they returned from leave, requiring them to compete with less senior people for their old jobs back, did violate Title VII. In distinguishing this situation from that in *Gilbert,* the Court used a benefit-versus-burden analysis to find that although employers did not have to extend maternity disability benefits to women that were inapplicable to men, they could not punish a woman by imposing on her the "substantial burden" of losing her seniority. This benefit-versus-burden analysis was briefly the law under Title VII, and at least two courts applied it to invalidate employer policies that did burden pregnant workers *(Zuniga* v. *Kleburg County Hospital,* 1982; *Mitchell* v. *Board of Trustees,* 1979).

PSYCHOLOGY AND THE LAW

The courts must make decisions about cases before them in a timely manner. The U.S. Constitution guarantees a "fair and speedy trial" to criminal defendants. The courts do not have to rely on the most current research on gender, but they do have to provide decisions that are consistent with past legal decisions (that is, precedent). Court decisions tend to reflect well-established social norms and conservative interpretations of the law, because the obligation to follow precedent tends to prevent dramatic changes in legal decision making. In examining legal cases related to women, we can see how the judges are viewing women and their role in society, and we can see how that role is then expanded or constricted as a result of their decisions. The courts give power to enforce gender roles when they define what is acceptable and not acceptable (not constitutional) treatment of women by employers, insurers, or the government itself. Scholars analysing legal cases must spend as much time reading between the lines as they do reading the words of Supreme Court justices, since much of what affects women is in the unspoken assumptions made by those in power.

PHYSICAL STRENGTH OF PSYCHOLOGISTS

While psychologists theorized about the nature of gender identity for the individual, the law was required to make concrete decisions about the importance of gender in employment and other social relationships. Early legal decisions purported to want to protect women from the strains of the industrialized workplace by limiting hours (*Muller v. Oregon,* 1908). Making assumptions about the physical characteristics of women, these early decisions also helped promote stereotypes. It was now a legal fact that women were not as strong as men, and it was a legal value to protect women. More specifically, this was a value to protect women's bodies.

Consider the comments of Gloria Steinem (1994) about the history of the treatment of women's bodies: Though cultural differences were many, there were political similarities in the way women's bodies were treated that went as deep as patriarchy itself. Whether achieved through law and social policy, as in this and other industrialized countries, or by way of tribal practice and religious ritual, as in older cultures, an individual woman's body was far more subject to other people's rules than was that of her male counterpart. Women always seemed to be owned to some degree as the means of reproduction. And as possessions, women's bodies then became symbols of men's status, with a value that was often determined by what was rare. Thus, rich cultures valued thin women, and poor cultures valued fat women. Yet all patriarchal cultures valued weakness in women. How else could male dominance survive? In my own country, for example, women who "belong" to rich white men are often thinner (as in "You can never be too rich or too thin") than those who "belong" to poor men of colour; yet those very different groups of males tend to come together in their belief that women are supposed to be weaker than men; that muscles and strength aren't "feminine."...

If I had any doubts about the psychological importance of cultural emphasis on male/female strength difference, listening to arguments about equality put them to rest. Sooner or later, even the most intellectual discussion came down to men's supposed superior strength as a justification for inequality, whether the person arguing regretted or celebrated it. What no one seemed to explore, however, was the inadequacy of physical strength as a way of explaining oppression in other cases. Men of European origin hadn't ruled in South Africa because they were stronger than African men, and blacks hadn't been kept in slavery or bad jobs in the United States because whites had more muscles. On the contrary, males of the "wrong" class or colour were often confined to labouring positions precisely because of their supposedly greater strength, just as the lower pay females received was often rationalized by their supposedly lesser strength. Oppression has no logic—just a self-fulfilling prophecy, justified by a self-perpetuating system....

The more I learned, the more I realized that belief in great strength differences between women and men was itself part of the gender mind-game. In fact, we can't really know what those differences might be, because they are so enshrined, perpetuated, and exaggerated by culture. They seem to be greatest during the childbearing years (when men as a group have more speed and upper-body strength, and women have better balance, endurance, and flexibility) but only marginal during early childhood and old age (when females and males seem to have about the same degree of physical strength). Even during those middle years, the range of difference among men and among women is far greater than the generalized difference between males and females as groups. In multiracial societies like ours, where males of some races are smaller than females of others, judgments based on sex make even less sense. Yet we go right on assuming and praising female weakness and male strength....

But there is a problem about keeping women weak, even in a patriarchy. Women are workers, as well as the means of reproduction. Lower-class women are especially likely to do hard physical labour. So the problem becomes: How to make sure female strength is used for work but not for rebellion. The answer is: make women ashamed of it. Tough hard work requires lower-class women to be stronger than their upper-class sisters, for example, those strong women are made to envy and imitate the weakness of women who "belong" to, and are the means of reproduction for, upper-class men—and so must be kept even more physically restricted if the lines of race and inheritance are to be kept "pure." That's why restrictive dress, from the chadors, or full-body veils, of the Middle East to metal ankle and neck rings in Africa, from nineteenth-century hoop skirts in Europe to corsets and high heels here, started among upper-class women and then sifted downward as poor women were encouraged to envy or imitate them. So did such bodily restrictions as bound feet in China, or clitoridectomies and infibulations in much of the Middle East and Africa, both of which practices began with women whose bodies were the means of reproduction for the powerful and gradually became generalized symbols of femininity. In this country, the self-starvation known as anorexia nervosa is mostly a white, upper-middle-class, young-female phenomenon, but all women are encouraged to envy a white and impossibly thin ideal.

STATE-SPONSORED DISCRIMINATION

In many countries, statutory restrictions curtailed women's freedom of movement, prevented women from inheriting property, limited their ability to divorce, restricted their access to education, and barred them from the workplace. Guarantees of equal protection under law, due process, and equal rights and equal opportunities for all citizens did not protect women from discrimination. In many cases, this discrimination was encouraged and enforced by state actors.

Despite constitutional guarantees of equality, the Moroccan family code continued to subject women to discriminatory treatment in 1998. Under the family law, women's autonomy remained subject to male guardianship and authority. Discriminatory laws governing the dissolution of marriage, for example, severely restricted women's access to divorce, even in cases of domestic violence. Magistrates' hostility to divorce proceedings initiated by women severely curtailed women's ability to exercise their rights under law. Battered women filing for divorce lived in fear of retaliation without hope of state intervention or prevention of further violence.

The opposition's victory in November 1997 elections and the new government's pledge to address the plight of Moroccan women raised hopes among activists for a more egalitarian reform of the family code. At this writing, however, the new government had taken no significant steps to eliminate discrimination against women in law or in practice.

Perhaps the year's most glaring attacks on women's human rights were seen in Afghanistan, where the Taliban stripped women of their rights to work, travel, and attend school. The Taliban further barred women from obtaining health care unless they were accompanied by a male family member, the treating doctor was a woman, and the medical facility maintained segregated services for women. These policies drastically limited women's access to health care even in emergency situations with deadly results; for example, women turned away from doctors and clinics died from obstetric complications. Throughout 1998, the Taliban countered any attempts to protect women's basic rights with more restrictive policies. In June, for example, the Taliban closed down scores of home schools for both girls and boys. Nongovernmental organizations (NGOs) providing relief for Afghans tried with little success to protect their ability to deliver food, health care, and education to women as well as men and to hire local female staff.

In a disturbing development, Afghan women refugees in Pakistan providing services to Afghans inside Afghanistan and in refugee camps and working to monitor and expose violations of women's rights received threats from Taliban representatives directing them to cease their activities and return to Afghanistan. In Iran, despite women's increasing visibility in public life and open discussions of women's rights, the government continued to enforce discriminatory civil and criminal laws that subordinate women's status in Iranian society and restrict their personal freedom. In addition, new laws drastically restricted the scope of public debate on women's rights and threatened women's access to adequate health care, while activists were subject to intimidation and arbitrary arrest.

In August 1998, the Iranian Islamic Consultative Assembly, or Majles, attempted to silence the proponents of women's human rights by amending the press law to prohibit discussion of "issues that entail opposition between men and women by defending their rights outside the framework of the Shari'a. " On June 30, the Iranian government arrested Hojatoleslam Mohsen Saeid-Zadeh, an outspoken women's rights advocate who questioned the religious legitimacy of state imposition of the Shari'a.

At this writing, no charges had been filed. Restrictions on women's access to employment also continued in 1998. The government of Bangladesh imposed a total ban on women traveling abroad to work as housemaids and nurses. Authorities passed the discriminatory act in response to growing reports of abuse of Bangladeshi women working abroad.

Women's rights organizations protested the ban as an inadequate and inappropriate state response to the problem. Rather than address the abuse through education, warnings, and diplomatic relations, the government instead curtailed the rights of women to travel and to seek employment.

Rwandan women faced discriminatory inheritance laws. After the devastating genocide that left more than half a million people dead, many widows were unable to return to their property because of discriminatory customary laws denying them the right to inherit from their husbands. Government initiatives to reform the law crawled through the legislative process; as of November 1998, the draft law was stalled in parliament.

Some women whose husbands were arrested and imprisoned for the genocide were forced off their property. Many refugee women returning to Rwanda from Burundi and Tanzania found their homes occupied. No legal recourse was available to them. In a few cases, women's activism bore fruit, if belatedly.

Women's Rights Organizations

Nigerian women's rights organizations celebrated a landmark court decision in February 1998 which invalidated the customary practice of denying inheritance rights to widows. Caroline Mojekwu challenged her uncle-in-law for denying her the right to inherit her late husband's estate. The decision, after thirty-nine years of legal wrangling, was seen as a victory for women's human rights in the region. Some activists questioned whether the decision wasenforceable in rural areas of Nigeria, but many viewed it as a first step in eliminating discriminatory customary and religious practices harmful to women.

Meanwhile, women continued to suffer under Pakistan's discriminatory Hudood Ordinances. These penal laws, which criminalize adultery but not domestic violence, remained a stark example of the gender bias built into the legal system. One well-publicized case involved Kanwar Ahson and Riffat Afridi, a man and woman from two different ethnic groups who chose to marry without their families' consent.

The Afridi family initially charged Ahson with kidnapping, which both he and Ms. Afridi denied. The family then charged the couple with adultery, a crime under the Hudood Ordinances. Ms. Afridi's elders sentenced her to death for dishonoring her family.

Ahson was arrested and charged with adultery, then later critically wounded by a group of his wife's kinsmen, including her father and brother. Afridi turned herself in to the police to face charges of illicit sex. After Ahsan was acquitted of the charges, the couple sought asylum abroad.

In Turkey, Women and Family Affairs Minister Isilay Saygin provoked the fury of women's human rights organizations internationally when she defended the practice of virginity exams for young women.

After five girls who were forced by the director of their state foster home to go through the exams attempted suicide, the minister stated, "If girls commit suicide because of the virginity tests, they would have committed suicide anyway. It is not that important." Women's groups immediately demanded Saygin's resignation. Saygin refused to resign and claimed that she had been "misunderstood."

STATE-TOLERATED DISCRIMINATION

Elsewhere, states continued to tolerate discrimination against women by private actors, failing to live up to the commitment to "end all forms of discrimination" mandated in CEDAW. Instead, states turned a blind eye to evidence of discrimination or actively encouraged such discrimination.

Sex discrimination had a particularly egregious impact on women displaced by war. Bosnian women, for example, faced discrimination in the reconstruction period. Micro-credit programs aimed at women provided significantly smaller loan amounts, in sorne cases only one-third of the amount, offered to male entrepreneurs under similar programs. Women found themselves ghettoized in training programs developed to prepare them for gender-stereotyped, low-paying occupations, including secretarial positions and hairdressing.

According to a World Bank official in Republika Srpska, public works jobs went solely to male applicants. The World Bank and USAID insisted that their programs included women as beneficiaries, but in general, these and other aid agencies failed to maintain reliable statistics on women's participation in employment, training, and loan programs. Women remained the vast majority of the displaced, eking out an existence and served by disproportionately limited programs. Many displaced women found themselves stuck in collective centers where deplorable conditions, poverty, hopelessness, and health concerns plagued all of the occupants. Many hoped to return home but feared reprisals.

In other instances, employers' discrimination against women based on their reproductive capacity-practices tolerated by many governments-undermined women's attempts to participate fully in the labor market. The assumption that women would become pregnant, and therefore were a "bad investment," perpetuated de facto discrimination. The Mexican government, for example, continued to allow transnational corporations to discriminate against women in the export processing (maquiladora) sector there.

Human Rights Watch research in 1997 and 1998 found that women applying for work as assemblers were required to reveal their pregnancy status as a condition for employment. Women were required to undergo pregnancy testing through analysis of urine samples, revelation of birth control use, the provision of information regarding sexual activity, and by submitting to abdominal examinations. Those found to be pregnant were not hired.

Factories also discriminated against women after they were hired. Some maquiladoras required women workers to submit urine samples for pregnancy analysis after they had been hired as a condition for maintaining their employment. Moreover, factories practiced more invasive types of pregnancy checks, such as requiring women workers to prove that they were still menstruating, and therefore not pregnant, by showing factory medical personnel their used sanitary napkins.

The government of Mexico did nothing to remedy hiring-process sex discrimination and made only token gestures to condemn and investigate on-the-job pregnancy discrimination, failures that violated Mexico's domestic labor law and its international human rights obligations.

In fact, the government argued that pregnancy testing in the hiring process was permissible under Mexican law. With regard to on-the-job pregnancy discrimination, the government's sole remedial effort was to reiterate that such practices are illegal in Mexico. In the face of Mexican refusal to enforce its own domestic laws, human rights organizations sought redress through the North American Agreement on Labour Cooperation, commonly referred to as the labour rights side agreement of the North American Free Trade Agreement, (NAFTA). Human Rights Watch, the International Labour Rights Fund, and the National Association of Democratic Lawyers (Asociación Nacional de Abogados Democráticos) submitted a petition against Mexico to the United States National Administrative Office (U.S. NAO, the body charged with hearing cases of alleged violations by Canada or Mexico of the labour rights side agreement) that charged unremedied sex discrimination.

Prohibit Discrimination

In January 1998 the U.S. NAO found that Mexico's constitution and labour code prohibit discrimination based on sex; pre-employment pregnancy testing did occur in Mexico; there were contradictory interpretations of Mexico's law regarding the illegality of this practice; and while on-the-job pregnancy-based sex discrimination was clearly illegal under Mexican labour law, greater efforts needed to be made toward awareness programs for women workers. This was the first case heard by the U.S. NAO that dealt explicitly with the right to gender equality in the workforce.

Discrimination against women in labour markets in their own countries only increased the likelihood that women and girls would be trafficked into forced labour abroad. Unable to find work at home, women from virtually every region of the globe acceptedseemingly lucrative opportunities to work as domestic servants, dancers, waitresses, or sex workers abroad. Others accepted apparently legitimate offers of marriage, only to find themselves caught in situations of battery and extreme cruelty, forced labour, and sexual abuse.

Young girls tricked into migrating or sold by their families to traffickers found themselves trapped in brothels or sweatshops, unable to return home. The United States government estimated that one to two million women and girls were being trafficked annually around the world for the purposes of forced labour, forced prostitution, servile domestic labour, or involuntary marriage.

Women trafficked into forced labour experienced human rights abuses such as debt bondage, slave-like conditions, illegal confinement, enforced isolation, wage withholding, deprivation of identity documents, rape, and sexual and other physical abuse. Trafficked women's status as illegal migrants and their complete isolation left them at risk for exploitation by traffickers. Women interviewed by Human Rights Watch in several countries expressed reluctance to approach police or state officials, fearing traffickers' reprisals against themselves or their families, imprisonment and prosecution for illegal entry or employment by the state, and deportation. In many countries, women forced into prostitution feared even greater penalties for engaging in an illegal occupation. While many officials in countries such as Thailand, India and Israel considered the arrest and deportation of the women and girls a form of "rescue," this impression did not reflect the reality of the experience. For trafficked Burmese women detained in Thai prisons, for example, "rescue" meant potential rape by police and the possibility of sale back to the same or another brothel owner.

Traffickers worldwide operated with near-impunity, as corrupt officials, economic crisis, and states' failure to prosecute this modern form of slavery coalesced to guarantee high profits and low risk. In Cambodia, economic and political crisis led to a surge in domestic trafficking of women and girls, as families desperate for money sold their children into the sex trade. With the spread of HIV and AIDS, the demand for younger and younger girls increased. According to local press reports, traffickers in Phnom Penh commanded prices of up to U.S.$1,000 for a virgin. Thai NGOs reported that corrupt police officers received bribes from brothel owners and free sexual services from the trafficked women as pay-offs to guarantee their turning a blind eye. Such extortion on the part of officials was not uncommon. In Macau, local press reported that police arrested a police constable for allegedly leading a racket which blackmailed women overstaying their visas.

In policy terms, states focused on trafficking as an issue of illegal migration and prostitution, but crackdowns and criminalization of prostitution often led to incarceration and further abuse of the trafficked women. Due to corruption among officials and police, enhanced enforcement measures led to higher bribes by traffickers resulting in higher debts for the women and girls. When arrests were made, it was the women, not the traffickers, who were detained. In Israel, for example, the government arrested and deported over 1,000 women back to Eastern Europe and the former Soviet Union from 1994 through 1998, according to an Israeli women's NGO. Law enforcement officials blamed the women themselves for the lack of prosecutions of traffickers, despite the complete absence of witness protection for the women.

WOMEN VICTIMS OF TRAFFICKING

Across the globe, women victims of trafficking were by and large unable to bring civil cases for lost wages, violations of civil rights, and violations of labour codes against traffickers and others engaged in the buying and selling of human beings. Few states offered support services such as safe shelter, legal aid, psychological assistance, and medical aid. The Netherlands and Belgium continued to provide funding to women's organizations offering some of these services. Dutch, Italian, and Belgian legislation provided for stays of deportation while women decided whether or not to participate as witnesses in criminal proceedings. During that period, women received temporary work permits, psychological counseling, shelter, social security benefits, and medical care.

In an effort to set standards for the protection of the human rights of trafficked women, the Global Alliance Against Trafficking in Women drafted a set of standard minimum rules concerning the treatment of trafficked persons. These draft rules included the right to freedom from persecution or harassment from authorities, access to competent translators during legal proceedings, access to free legal assistance and representation, access to legal possibilities of compensation and redress, legal permission to stay in the country of destination if unsafe to return home, and protection against reprisals from authorities or perpetrators.

6

Psychological Effects on Abortion

In 1969, the American Psychological Association (APA) Council of Representatives adopted a resolution that identified termination of unwanted pregnancies as a mental health and child welfare issue. It resolved that termination of pregnancy be considered a civil right of pregnant women, to be handled like other medical and surgical procedures in consultation with her physician. In 1980, in response to governmental attempts to suppress research on abortion, the APA Council of Representatives passed a resolution supporting the right to conduct scientific research on abortion and reproductive health, stating that the APA "affirms the right of qualified researchers to conduct appropriate research in all areas of fertility regulation".

In February 1989, the APA, wishing to improve the accuracy of the debate, convened a panel of experts to review the best scientific studies of abortion outcome. In August 1989, the APA Council of Representatives, concerned about the distortions of the research findings in the press, passed its third abortion resolution. This resolution, which cited the work of the panel, initiated a public awareness effort to correct the record on the scientific findings of abortion research.

Psychological Research on the Effects of Abortion

The psychological research on abortion has focused on postabortion emotional responses.

Stress and coping

From the stress and coping perspective, an unwanted pregnancy is seen as an event that can be challenging or stressful. Stress has been defined as emerging from an interaction of the individual and the environment in a situation that the person appraises as "taxing or exceeding his or her resources and endangering his or her well-being". Termination of an unwanted pregnancy may reduce the stress engendered by the occurrence of the pregnancy and the associated events. At the same time, the abortion itself may be experienced as stressful.

Research on the psychological effects of abortion has found that most women do not show any long-term harm after having had an abortion. According to Cozzarelli, Sumer, and Major (1998), "Although most women do not appear to experience severe, negative, postabor-tion psychological responses, abortion is perceived as an acute stres-sor by a large number of women." In general, individuals who feel efficacious have been found to handle stressful life events, including abortion, more effectively. Furthermore, self-efficacy beliefs have been found to mediate the positive effects of more global personal resources such as self-esteem, optimism, and locus of control on adjustment.

Adler et al. (1992) note the methodological difficulties in the psychological research literature on abortion, including researcher bias, too narrow a focus on pathological or negative outcomes of abortion, and questionable validity and reliability of outcome measures such as interviews.

The varied quality of these studies makes it difficult to draw conclusions from the entire body of existing research literature. Many reports are clinical observations of small numbers of women. Some provide no data, or data are inappropriately or inadequately analysed. Some studies report responses of women having illegal or therapeutic abortions rather than legal, elective procedures. Some studies, particularly those that are retrospective, may have a mix of women who had illegal, therapeutic, and elective abortions that are not analysed separately.

In order to try to draw some conclusions from existing research, Adler et al. (1992) reviewed research that met the following minimum criteria: the study must be empirical (involving the collection of data subjected to statistical analysis) and use a definable sample. The studies used only samples of women who had abortions under legal, non-restrictive conditions in the United States. The studies involved a range of medical settings, and the subjects covered a range of ethnicities and ages.

The weight of the evidence was that legal abortion, as a resolution to an unwanted pregnancy, particularly in the first trimester, does not create psychological hazards for most women undergoing the procedure. In fact, psychological distress has generally been found to drop from before the procedure to immediately after and from preabortion or immediately postabortion to several weeks afterward.

Self-esteem

Russo and Zierk (1992) examined the relationship of abortion and childbearing to self-esteem in a national sample of 5,295 U.S. women interviewed annually from 1979 to 1987 in the National Longitudinal Study of Youth. Controlling for preexisting self-esteem, employment, income, and education, neither having one abortion nor having repeat abortions in the period from 1980 to 1987 was related to self-esteem. This study demonstrates that up to eight years following an abortion, no negative associations occur with self-esteem.

Demographic and social factors

Younger and unmarried women without children were relatively more likely than those who were older and who had already given birth to experience negative responses. So too were women whose culture or religion prohibits abortions and those who attended church more frequently.

The decision process

A number of studies have examined the relationship between aspects of the woman's decision process regarding abortion and her emotional response afterward. Most women do not have difficulty with the abortion decision. Osofsky, Osofsky, and Rajan (1973) found that 12 percent of 100 first-trimester patients stated the decision to have an abortion was difficult, and 7 percent reported initial indecision regarding continuation or termination of the pregnancy. Among 200 second-trimester patients in the study, 51 percent reported difficulty in deciding, and 36 percent reported initial indecision. Other correlates of difficult decisions or ambivalent feelings are being married and being Catholic.

Studies examining satisfaction with the abortion decision and post-abortion emotional response consistently found that women who were satisfied with their choice or reported little difficulty in making the decision showed more positive postabortion responses. Greater difficulty in making the decision has been associated with higher negative postabortion reactions, including feelings of guilt, anxiety, and internally based negative emotions, such as regret and depression. Women who initially want to be pregnant may react more negatively to abortion. Shusterman (1979) found an association between a woman's immediate affective response to learning that she was pregnant and her response to abortion. Women who reported the pregnancy as "highly meaningful" to them reported more physical complaints immediately after and anticipated more negative consequences from the abortion than did women who reported their pregnancy to be less meaningful.

Abortion in the Context of Culture

Catherine MacKinnon (1987) describes the aspect of abortion that the legal decision makers have chosen to overlook: that abortion is "inextricable from sexuality" and that men's and women's lives are very different for that reason: I first situate abortion and the abortion right in the experience of women. The argument is that abortion is inextricable from sexuality....

Most women who seek abortions became pregnant while having sexual intercourse with men. Most did not mean or wish to conceive. In contrast to this fact of women's experience, which converges sexuality with reproduction with gender, the abortion debate has centered on separating control over sexuality from control over reproduction, and on separating both from gender and the life options of the sexes.... Sexual intercourse, still the most common cause of pregnancy, cannot simply be presumed coequally determined. Sex doesn't look a whole lot like freedom when it appears normatively less costly for women to risk an undesired, often painful, traumatic, dangerous, sometime illegal, and potentially life-threatening procedure than to protect themselves in advance.

In the context of a sexual critique of gender inequality, abortion promises to women sex with men on the same reproductive terms as men have sex with women.

Kathleen M. Sullivan and Susan R. Estrich (1989) noted, Abortion restrictions, like the most classic gender-based restrictions on women seeking to participate in the worlds of work and ideas, have historically rested on archaic stereotypes of women as persons whose "paramount destiny and mission... [is] to fulfill the noble and benign office of wife and mother".... Legislation prohibiting abortion, largely a product of the years between 1860 and 1880, reflected precisely the same ideas about the natural and proper role of women as did the legislation of the same period—long-since discredited—that prohibited women from serving on juries or participating in the professions, including the practice of law.

Abortion as an International Health Concern

The World Health Organization defined reproductive health as "complete physical, mental and social well-being in all matters related to the reproductive system". It defined sexual health as "a part of reproductive health that includes healthy sexual development, equitable and responsible relationships and sexual fulfilment, and freedom from illness, disease, disability, violence and other harmful practices related to sexuality". Henry David (1994) noted that the most significant development in reproductive behavior over the past few decades has been the political commitment to the worldwide expansion of more effective contraceptive practice:

Historically, the human rights rationale emerged when women began to assert their rights as equal partners. A woman who lacks control over her fertility has considerable difficulty completing her education, maintaining gainful employment, and making independent marital decisions. The demographic rationale evolved in response to concerns about the negative effects of rapid population growth on socio-economic development and environmental degradation. The health rationale became the basis for advocating that pregnancy be delayed until the most appropriate time and for preventing high-risk unintended pregnancies. The human rights rationale is inextricably intertwined with a woman's role in decision making, cultural traditions, and access to education. In societies in which a woman's value is based on the number of children she has, her ability to regulate and control her fertility will be limited. Women in developing countries with seven or more years of education tend to marry, on average, four years later and have two or three fewer children than women with no schooling.

LAW OF ABORTION

Until relatively recently, abortion was treated like one of many methods of birth control and was not viewed as morally distinct from other methods. Law professors Sylvia Law, Jane E. Larson, and Clyde Spil-lenger reviewed the history of abortion in the United States in their amicus curiae brief submitted to the Supreme Court in *Planned Parenthood of Southeastern Pennsylvaniav. Casey* (1992). They noted that at the time of the drafting of the federal constitution in the late eighteenth century, abortion was known and not illegal. In the nineteenth century, it became even more widely accepted.

Through the nineteenth century, American common law decisions uniformly reaffirmed that women committed no offence in seeking abortions. Both common law and popular American understanding drew distinctions depending upon whether the fetus was "quick," i.e. whether the woman perceived signs of independent life. There was some dispute whether a common law misdemeanor occurred when a third party destroyed a fetus, after quickening, without the woman's consent. But early common law recognition of this crime against a pregnant woman did not diminish the woman's liberty to end a pregnancy herself in its early stages. Abortion was not a pressing social issue in colonial America, but as a social practice, it was far from unknown. Herbal abortifacients were widely known, and cookbooks and women's diaries of the era contained recipes for such medicines. Recent studies of the work of mid-wives in the 1700s report cases in which the midwives appeared to have provided women abortifacient compounds. Such treatments do not appear to have been regarded as extraordinary or illicit by those administering them....

In the late eighteenth century, strictures on sexual behavior loosened considerably. The incidence of premarital pregnancy rose sharply; by the late eighteenth century, one third of all New England brides were pregnant when they married, compared to less than ten percent in the seventeenth century. Falling birth rates in the 1780s suggest that, at the time of the drafting of the Constitution, the use of birth control and abortion was increasing....

Through the nineteenth century and well into the twentieth, abortion remained a widely accepted practice, despite growing efforts after 1860 to prohibit it....... The most common methods of abortion in the nineteenth century involved self administered herbs and devices available from pharmacists. Nonetheless, women also relied on professional abortionists: in 1871, New York City, with a population of less than one million, supported two hundred full-time abortionists, not including doctors who also sometimes performed abortions. The late nineteenth century saw a movement toward professionalization across disciplines. This was a time when industrial and scientific developments were rapid, and meaningful progress was being made in the understanding of the basic sciences and their applications to medicine. At the same time, many workers perceived economic competition from both increased immigration and the increased levels of education (including professional education) becoming available to blacks and to women. The late 1800s saw the opening of the first women's colleges and the first black colleges, as well as some progress toward allowing these previously excluded groups to attend state universities. As occupations such as medicine and law developed professional associations, they also created standards of training and licensure that were narrowly drawn and inevitably excluded women, minorities, and recently arrived immigrants. Law et al. (1992) note that between 1850 and 1880, the American Medical Association became the "single most important factor in altering the legal policies toward abortion in the country":

The doctors found an audience for their effort to restrict abortion because they appealed to specific social concerns and anxieties: maternal health, consumer protection, discriminatory ideas about the properly subordinate status of women, and racist/nativist fears generated by the fact the elite Protestant women often sought abortions. Some of these doctors also sought to attribute moral status to the fetus. Abortion regulation became a tool in the political and economics-driven process of defining who should be allowed to practice medicine and a means of excluding groups such as midwives and abortion providers who were not medical doctors. Law et al. (1992) note, Physicians were the principal nineteenth-century proponents of laws to restrict abortion. A core purpose of the nineteenth-century laws, and the doctors in supporting them, was to control medical practice in the interest of public safety.... Anti-abortion laws would weaken the appeal of the competition and take the pressure off the more marginal members of the regulars' [regular physicians] own sect.

While physicians at the time argued that abortion regulation was for the purpose of protecting the safety and health of women, there is ample evidence of a general resistance to the increasing independence and self-determination of women. Similar arguments were waged at the idea of women receiving college educations, and women seeking education were warned that college would be both physically and socially damaging to them. Specifically, it would damage their ability to bear children and would certainly make them less attractive to potential husbands argue that the enforcement of sharply differentiated concepts of the roles of men and women underlay efforts to regulate abortion and contraception in the nineteenth century:

Physicians persuaded political leaders (who were, of course, uniformly male) that "abortion constituted a threat to social order" and to male authority. Since the 1840s, a growing movement for women's suffrage and equality had generated popular fears that women were departing from a purely maternal role—fears fueled by the decline in family size during the nineteenth century. A central rhetorical focus of the woman's movement was framed by a new perception of women as the rightful possessors of their own bodies.

Opposition to abortion and contraception were closely linked, and can only be understood as a reaction to the uncertainties generated by changes in family function and anxieties created by women's challenges to their historic roles of silence and subservience. These challenges were critical factors motivating the all-male state legislatures that adopted restraints on women, including restrictions on abortion. In opposition to the feminist demand for control of reproduction, the federal government in 1873 took the lead in banning access to information about both contraception and abortion. Law et al. (1992) argue that contraception and abortion regulation also reflected ethnocentric fears about relative birthrates of immigrant and white Protestants during a period of intense immigration at the end of the nineteenth century:

Beginning in the 1890s, and continuing through the first decades of the twentieth century, nativist fears coalesced into a drive against what was then called "race suicide." The "race suicide" alarmists worried that women of "good stock"—prosperous, white, and Protestant—were not having enough children to maintain the political and social supremacy of their group. Anxiety over the falling birth rates of Protestant whites in comparison with other groups helped shape policy governing both birth control and abortion.

Abortion became a focal point in the debate about women's lives. Interestingly, during the post-Civil War period, when the women's suffrage movement was gaining momentum and the first wave of feminism was attempting to redefine women's roles, there were feminists opposed to abortion. Mary Krane Derr, in a 1991 amicus curiae brief, notes:

Early feminist opposition to abortion was deep-seated, and addressed the causes of abortion, not just the practice. In this way, it was distinguished from other anti-abortion efforts including those of the American Medical Association. Feminists documented that abortion was caused by, among other things, culturally enforced ignorance about sexual and reproductive physiology, especially family planning and fetal development; cultural construction of pregnancy as a pathological condition; a sexual double standard which permitted men to be sexually and parentally irresponsible; the social valuing of "legitimacy" over children's lives and women's well-being; and lack of social and economic support for mothers, especially single ones.

For women, the choices were never simple or free of stigma, but before 1973, upper-and middle-class patients with the right health care resources could obtain "therapeutic abortions" if they declared themselves suicidal and received the appropriate documentation from one or two psychiatrists. In 1970, more than 98 percent of the legal therapeutic abortions were for mental health reasons.

FETAL RIGHTS OF ABORTION

The question of whether a fetus has rights independent of its mother has been the subject of political debate and has presented challenges to well-established rights of privacy, opportunities for valuable stem cell research, and the basic concept that a woman should have control over her own body. Issues of gender, race, and poverty discrimination are all raised in reference to the populations immediately affected by these policies. In what has been referred to as a frontal assault on abortion rights, legislators at the state and federal levels have sought to define life as starting at conception, thus making abortion illegal as a form of murder. Congressman Duncan Hunter (R-CA) introduced a bill titled the "Life at Conception Act of 2003." Hunter's bill asserts that life begins at conception, and the California congressman hopes that if it ever becomes law, abortion supporters will have no legal leg on which to stand: "The only way that we're going to legislatively overturn Roe v. Wade is to establish personhood early on—and that is at conception," Hunter said. Beyond abortion access, this type of legislation has implications for a woman to be held criminally accountable for the outcome of her pregnancy.

Ferguson v. *City of Charleston* (2001) accentuates the distinct problems behind conceptually separating a woman from her fetus for the purpose of law. Heard by the Supreme Court, *Ferguson* v. *City of Charleston* addressed matters of self-incrimination, right to privacy, and discrimination.

In 1989, in response to concern over the apparent increase in the use of cocaine by pregnant patients and "crack babies," the Medical University of South Carolina (MUSC) implemented a policy ordering drug screening to be performed on urine samples of pregnant women suspected of using cocaine. MUSC developed and implemented this policy in conjunction with local law enforcement officials. Police could be involved in one of two ways: identification of drug use during pregnancy and the identification of drug use after delivery. In the first way, the patient faced arrest only if she tested positive a second time or refused to enter and complete a substance abuse program. In the second way, the police promptly arrested the patient. Ten women who received care at MUSC were arrested after testing positive for cocaine. In *Ferguson* v. *City of Charleston,* they challenged the policy, stating that warrantless and nonconsensual drug tests conducted for criminal investigatory purposes were unconstitutional searches.

The Supreme Court found that the state hospital's policy violated the constitutional rights of the women who were tested. It held that "a state hospital's performance of a diagnostic test to obtain evidence of a patient's criminal conduct for law enforcement purposes is an unreasonable search if the patient has not consented to the procedure".

The Court described the invasion of privacy in *Ferguson* as far more substantial than similar cases in that the hospital did not provide these pregnant women with an understanding about the purpose of the test, the potential use of the test results, or protections against the unauthorized distribution of the results to third parties. The Court noted that it was apparent that "the focus of the policy was on the arrest and prosecution of the drug-abusing mothers." While the ultimate goal of the program may have been substance abuse treatment for the women in question, the immediate goal of the searches was to generate evidence for law enforcement purposes.

The Court found that the primary purpose of the Charleston program was to use the threat of arrest and prosecution in order to force women into treatment.

Because of police involvement, the strictures of the Fourth Amendment should be strictly adhered. State hospital employees had a duty to inform patients of the potential ramifications of the urinalysis if the specific purpose for the test is to obtain evidence of potential drug abuse.

The maternity patients should have been made aware that their urine drug tests were going to be reported to law enforcement if their urine tested positive for cocaine. The South Carolina case focused on women ingesting drugs or alcohol while pregnant, with the propensity for the women affected to be African American. Gagan (2000) reported that in a rehabilitation program generated for this "criminal" population, "forty-two women arrested under the program between 1989 and 1994 were black [all but one]. The single white woman allegedly had a black boyfriend, a fact which was noted on her chart".

Fried (1990) suggests that gender discrimination plays a role in these cases, in that a woman is being charged for criminal activities against the fetus while men who commit equal or greater degrees of violence are not prosecuted. Fried (1990) illustrates this in an example: While the behavior of pregnant women has, in some cases, led to criminal prosecution, there have been no prosecutorial efforts to arrest men for the damage that secondhand cigarette smoke may cause to a fetus; men have not been required to avoid exposure to drugs or chemicals known to cause damage to the sperm; nor have the male partners of pregnant battered women been targeted by prosecutors for their infliction of injury to the fetus in the course of physically abusing the woman.

Efforts to legally establish fetal rights, and particularly life at conception, also threaten the possibility of scientific gains from embryonic stem cell research. Stevens (2003) emphasizes, "Because the Catholic Church, pro-life activists, and other religious groups believe that life starts at conception, they oppose embryonic stem cell research. These groups argue that benefiting from the destruction of a human embryo is 'no less a crime than abortion'".

Questions raised about the ethics of acquiring the embryonic stem cells must be matched with questions of the ethics of withholding possible medical treatments. Regardless of what stance is taken in this debate, medical advances that save lives are valuable.

LEGAL CASES OF ABORTION

The Supreme Court has been the arena for promoting and challenging abortion in the United States. While *Roe* v. *Wade* (1973) established a woman's legal right to obtain an abortion, subsequent cases have addressed efforts to define and restrict that right.

Roe v. *Wade:* A Fundamental Privacy Right

In *Roev. Wade* (1973), the U.S. Supreme Court described a woman's right to have an abortion as part of a fundamental right of privacy, similar to that in

Griswold, and government interference with that right would be subject to strict judicial scrutiny.

Justice William Brennan, writing for the majority, noted that bans on abortion were relatively recent:

It perhaps is not generally appreciated that the restrictive criminal abortion laws in effect in a majority of States today are of relatively recent vintage. Those laws, generally proscribing abortion or its attempt at any time during pregnancy except when necessary to preserve the pregnant woman's life, are not of ancient or even common-law origin. Instead, they derive from statutory changes effected, for the most part, in the latter half of the 19th century....

It is thus apparent that at common law, at the time of the adoption of our Constitution, and throughout the major portion of the 19th century, abortion was viewed with less disfavor than under most American statutes currently in effect. Phrasing it another way, a woman enjoyed a substantially broader right to terminate a pregnancy than she does today. He went on to describe the "person" for whom the Constitution was intended and then introduced the issue of "viability," or the point at which the state has a "compelling interest" in the unborn child:

The Constitution does not define "person" in so many words.... But in nearly all these instances, the use of the word is such that it has application only postnatally None indicates, with any assurance, that it has any possible prenatal application.... In short, the unborn have never been recognized in the law as persons in the whole sense.

... We repeat, however, that the State does have an important and legitimate interest in preserving and protecting the health of the pregnant woman, whether she be a resident of the State or a non-resident who seeks medical consultation and treatment there, and that it has still another important and legitimate interest in protecting the potentiality of human life. *These interests are separate and distinct* [italics added]. Each grows in substantiality as the woman approaches term and, at a point during pregnancy, each becomes "compelling."

... The end of the first trimester mortality in abortion may be less than mortality in normal childbirth. It follows that, from and after this point, a State may regulate the abortion procedure to the extent that the regulation reasonably related to the preservation and protection of maternal health.

With respect to the state's important and legitimate interest in potential life, the "compelling" point is viability.

Doe v. *Bolton:* Health of the Mother

In *Doev. Bolton* (1973), the companion case to *Roev. Wade,* the Supreme Court held that the decision of whether a woman requires an abortion for the health of the mother is a medical judgment to "be exercised in the light of all factors—physical, emotional, psychological, familial, and the woman's age—relevant to the well-being of the patient".

Hyde Amendment and *Maher v. Roe:* Medicaid Funding

Since *Roe* v. *Wade,* the Supreme Court has used abortion cases to refine its position and define the limits to a woman's access to abortion. As states have enacted increasingly restrictive abortion laws, the Supreme Court has had to determine the boundary between a state's legitimate interest and an unreasonable interference in access to abortion.

Federal regulations have also implemented limitations on access and funding of abortions. The Hyde Amendment, passed by Congress in 1976, excludes abortion from the health care coverage provided to low-income women through Medicaid, except when a woman's life is at risk. Congress later amended the Hyde Amendment to allow coverage for abortions in cases of rape or incest.

States enacted legislation with similar restrictions. In *Maher'* v. *Roe* (1977), the Court was presented with the question of whether the right of access to abortion described in *Roe* v. *Wade* included an entitlement to Medicaid payments for abortions that are not medically necessary. At issue in *Maher* was a Connecticut welfare regulation under which Medicaid recipients received payments for medical services incidental to childbirth but not for medical services incidental to non-therapeutic abortions. The Court held that the constitutional freedom recognized in *Wade* and its progeny "protects the woman from unduly burdensome interference with her freedom to decide whether to terminate her pregnancy" such as the severe criminal sanctions at issue in *Roe* v. *Wade,* or the absolute requirement of spousal consent for an abortion challenged in *Planned Parenthood of Central Missouri* v. *Danforth* (1976), but did not prevent Connecticut from being free to make "a value judgment favoring childbirth over abortion, and... implement that judgment by the allocation of public funds" :

Although government may not place obstacles in the path of a woman's exercise of her freedom of choice, it need not remove those not of its own creation. Indigency falls in the latter category. The financial constraints that restrict an indigent woman's ability to enjoy the full range of constitutionally protected freedom of choice are the product not of governmental restrictions on access to abortions, but rather of her indigency.

The Court stated that indigent women do not even have a right to funding for a medically necessary abortion: Although Congress has opted to subsidize medically necessary services generally, but not certain medically necessary abortions, the fact remains that the Hyde Amendment leaves an indigent woman with at least the same range of choice in deciding whether to obtain a medically necessary abortion as she would have had if Congress had chosen to subsidize no health care costs at all. We are thus not persuaded that the Hyde Amendment impinges on the constitutionally protected freedom of choice recognized in Wade.

The Hyde Amendment sets a floor, but permits states to use their own funds to underwrite abortions for low-income women. As of February 2004, only four states (New York, Maryland, Hawaii, and Washington) have done this voluntarily. Thirteen other states have done so under court order. Thirty-two states and the District of Columbia follow the federal standard and provide abortions in cases of life endangerment, rape, or incest. One state, South Dakota, pays for abortions only when necessary to protect the woman's life.

Congress has passed restrictions similar to the Hyde Amendment affecting programs on which an estimated 20 million women rely for their health care or insurance. According to the American Civil Liberties Union (2002), those denied access to federally funded abortion include poor women on Medicaid, Native Americans, federal employees and their dependents, Peace Corps volunteers, low-income residents of Washington, D.C, federal prisoners, and military personnel and their dependents.

New health initiatives are also being burdened by the legacy of the Hyde Amendment. The Children's Health Insurance Program, a program providing expanded health insurance for children aged nineteen or younger, includes a ban on the use of federal funds for abortions unless the pregnancy endangers the teenager's life or results from rape or incest. The Omnibus Appropriations Act for fiscal year 1999 also extended the Hyde Amendment to Medicare for the first time, prohibiting abortion coverage for disabled women, except in cases of rape, incest, or life endangerment (American Civil Liberties Union, 2002).

Planned Parenthood of Central Missouri v. *Danforth:* Spousal Consent

The Court held in this 1976 case that legislative bodies or courts could not properly determine the specific point in the gestational period when viability occurred, holding instead that such a determination varies with each pregnancy and should be left to the individual judgment of the attending physician.

Webster v. *Reproductive Health Services:* Use of Public Facilities and Public Personnel

In *Websterv. Reproductive Health Services* (1989), five state-employed health professionals and two nonprofit corporations brought a class action suit challenging Missouri's 1986 act. The act declared in its preamble that life begins at conception. It prohibited the use of public funds to counsel women to have an abortion unless necessary to save her life, and it prohibited the use of public hospitals or state employees for abortions unless necessary to save the woman's life. It also required physicians to perform viability tests on fetuses after twenty weeks' gestation. The Court articulated the position that a state may make a value judgment, as Missouri did in its preamble, which favored childbirth over abortion. The Supreme Court maintained that this act only restricted "a woman's ability to obtain an abortion to the extent she chooses a public facility" and did not examine the cost differences between a public and private facility, or the actual effect on access to abortion for poor women.

Planned Parenthood of Southeastern Pennsylvania v. *Casey:* Restrictive State Abortion Laws

In *Planned Parenthood of Southeastern Pennsylvania v. Casey* (1992), the Supreme Court reaffirmed the right to an abortion as part of a constitutionally protected right to privacy but simultaneously upheld a state's ability to pass restrictive abortion laws. It also lowered the standard of review for abortion legislation from "strict scrutiny" to "unduly burdensome," making it easier for such restrictions on abortion to be found constitutional.

Under a "strict scrutiny" analysis, legislation infringing on the right to privacy was treated with the most rigorous level of review, reserved for certain fundamental constitutional rights such as free speech, religious freedom, or freedom from racial discrimination. It is rare for legislation infringing on these rights to survive strict scrutiny. By lowering the standard of review to the more ambiguous "unduly burdensome," the Court opened the door to a number of restrictions that would make it more difficult for women to obtain abortions but did not go so far as to prohibit them. At issue in this case were the provisions of the Pennsylvania Abortion Control Act of 1982, which

1. Required informed consent before an abortion and specified that certain information must be provided at least twenty-four hours before the abortion
2. Required consent of one of the parents of a minor seeking an abortion with the option of judicial bypass in certain circumstances
3. Required spousal notification by married women seeking abortions
4. Defined a "medical emergency" as a condition that necessitates an abortion to avoid death or serious, irreversible harm to the mother and exempted women in that condition from the above requirements
5. Imposed various reporting requirements for facilities that perform abortions

Justices Sandra Day O'Connor, Anthony Kennedy, and David Souter, writing for the majority, reaffirmed the essential holding of *Roe* v. *Wade*—a woman's right to an abortion before fetal viability— but rejected its trimester framework. The medical emergency definition and exemption, informed-consent requirement, parental consent requirement (with judicial bypass), and record-keeping provisions were upheld using an "undue burden" standard. The spousal notification requirement was held unconstitutional, because it imposed an undue burden on women who fear abuse from their husbands, as were the reporting requirements pertaining to it.

Public Policy Consequences of Restrictive Abortion Laws

Beginning with *Roe* v. *Wade,* the legal discussion of abortion has been one of physiology. A pregnant woman and her fetus are presented as two beings that happen to be temporarily interconnected. Becker, Bowman, and Torrey (1994) note "that the woman and her life are almost absent from the discussion of abortion in Roe v. Wade, which becomes instead the story of the fetus and the doctor... resulting from the fact that the Court typically reasons about reproductive regulation in physiological paradigms, seeing regulation as state action that concerns women's bodies rather than women's roles, despite the fact that the social role of women was clearly the central concern in the historical debate about abortion".

From the beginning of abortion case law, the Court introduced the idea that the interests of a pregnant woman and those of the "potentiality of human life" are "separate and distinct". This arguably artificial distinction between a pregnant woman and the child she carries encouraged a line of reasoning that would not be acceptable in other areas of the law. While discrimination based on pregnancy has been prohibited by legislation and case law, including discrimination in health insurance, the Court allowed exactly this discrimination in the Hyde Amendment by excluding insurance coverage when the pregnant woman needs an abortion, even when her life or health are at risk, which is surely the definition of "medically necessary."

Current legislation continues to set mother and unborn child against one another, and the value of the mother's life is explicitly disregarded. Before the movement to regulate abortion, when "quickening" was the criterion for a fetus's viability, it was the pregnant mother who determined whether she experienced evidence of life in the unborn child. Since *Roe* v. *Wade,* legislators have increasingly sought to regulate women as if they were simply vessels that happened to be physiologically connected to the unborn child.

Lichtman (2003) argues that states' restrictive abortion laws reduce access to abortions for low-income women and result in increases in unwanted births to low-income women and increases in the number of children needing and receiving public assistance. Underserved women are the first to lose their right to choose, because limitations on funding and access make abortion effectively unavailable to them. Lichtman compared three states: South Dakota, which has the most restrictive abortion laws and only one abortion provider in the entire state, and Vermont and Connecticut, which protect a woman's right to reproductive choice in their state constitutions. She found that by looking at indicators such as abortion rates, birthrates, child poverty levels, and public assistance caseloads, one can identify a link between abortion access and the number of unwanted births to underserved women. In contrast to Vermont and Connecticut, South Dakota has not been able to reduce its high number of children living in poverty. Lichtman states, "While motivations are both political as well as ethical, anti-abortion legislators and judges are imposing their own ethical beliefs on whomever they can control. In most instances, low-income women and minors are those with the least bargaining power and are thus easiest to control. If these anti-abortion legislators impose their moral beliefs about abortion on low-income women, by removing their access to abortion, these women's reproductive right to privacy is terminated".

CURRENT LEGISLATION OF ABORTION

A series of legislative acts have emerged that illustrate the ongoing challenge to *Roe v. Wade* and abortion rights. Rather than trying to overrule the decision in *Roe,* opponents of abortion have used the strategy of incremental legislation, restricting abortion further and further until access is effectively unavailable.

The Partial-Birth Abortion Ban Act of 2003

The Partial-Birth Abortion Ban Act of 2003 represents the most recent challenge to *Roe v. Wade* and is a response to the 2000 Supreme Court decision *Stenberg* v. *Carhart,* in which the Court struck down a similar state law in Nebraska.

In *Planned Parenthood v. Casey* (1992), the Court rejected the *Roe* trimester framework and held that the point of viability is the dividing line for determining when the state's interest in potential life outweighs a woman's interest in choosing whether to have an abortion. The *Casey* Court determined that the state's interest in potential life exists throughout pregnancy and thus a regulation on abortion is constitutional at any point during pregnancy so long as it does not place an "undue burden" on a woman's right to choose.

In *Stenberg,* the Court applied the *Casey* test to a Nebraska statute banning partial birth abortion. The statute in question banned partial birth abortion except when "necessary to save the life of the mother". Though ostensibly aimed at prohibiting the abortion procedure known as "dilation and extraction" (D&X), the Nebraska law did not refer specifically to this procedure, and instead defined partial birth abortion as "an abortion procedure in which the person performing the abortion partially delivers vaginally a living unborn child before killing the unborn child and completing the delivery". The statute specifically prohibited the deliberate and intentional delivery "into the vagina a living unborn child, or a substantial portion thereof, for the purpose of performing a procedure that the person performing such procedure knows will kill the unborn child and does kill the unborn child".

The Court examined the Nebraska statute as it applied to pre-and postviability abortions and found that the statute's vague language rendered it unconstitutional with regard to previability abortions. In examining the definition of partial birth abortion, the Court found that the language applied to both D&X and to a different procedure "dilation and evacuation" (D&E).

D&E is the most common procedure used for previability second-trimester abortions. Because the statute had the effect of banning the previability use of D&E, it constituted an undue burden on a woman's right to choose. In her concurrence in *Stenberg,* Justice O'Connor noted that if the Nebraska statute were limited to D&X and included a health exception, "the question presented would be quite different from the one we face today".

The language of the Partial-Birth Abortion Ban Act of 2003 is substantially the same as that of the Nebraska statute. The bill's drafters claim to have remedied one of the constitutional problems that plagued the Nebraska statute by defining partial birth abortion more precisely so as to exclude D&C procedures from the scope of the bill's prohibition.

Holsinger argues that the bill easily could have been drafted to exclude D&E by specifically limiting the prohibition to either D&X or postviability procedures. Instead, like earlier versions, the bill employs nonmedical terminology to define the procedures prohibited under the bill. This intentional ambiguity is arguably intended to allow the broadest possible interpretation of the prohibition and thus to restrict abortion procedure by procedure.

Carhartv. Ashcwft

The Center for Reproductive Rights legally challenged the federal abortion ban. This case, known as *Carhartv. Ashcwft,* went to trial in 2004 in a Nebraska federal court.

Representing doctors from Nebraska, New York, Virginia, and Iowa, the center argued that the ban on safe abortion procedures violates the U.S. Constitution and puts women's health and lives in serious jeopardy. To stop the federal ban from taking effect, a lawsuit was filed on October 31,2003, on behalf of Dr. LeRoy Carhart, the lead plaintiff in the earlier Supreme Court case. When President Bush signed the new federal law, U.S. District Court Judge Richard G. Kopf, for the District of Nebraska, issued a temporary restraining order blocking enforcement of the abortion ban, allowing Dr. Carhart and the other physicians challenging the law to continue to perform abortions without fear of prosecution.

Pending further legal decisions, the law was blocked by federal courts in Nebraska, New York, and California (Center for Reproductive Rights, 2004). In September 2004, Judge Kopf handed down a decision finding the Partial-Birth Abortion Ban Act of 2003 unconstitutional:

After giving Congress the respectful consideration it is always due, I find and conclude that the ban is unreasonable and not supported by substantial evidence. In truth, "partial-birth abortions," which are medically known as "intact D&E" or "D&X" procedures, are sometimes necessary to preserve the health of a woman seeking an abortion. While the procedure is infrequently used as a relative matter, when it is needed, the health of women frequently hangs in the balance.

Therefore, I declare the "Partial-Birth Abortion Ban Act of 2003" unconstitutional because it does not allow, and instead prohibits, the use of the procedure when necessary to preserve the health of a woman.

In addition, I decide that the ban fails as a result of other constitutional imperfections. As a result, I will also permanently enjoin enforcement of the ban. Importantly, however, because the evidence was sparse regarding postviability, I do not decide whether the law is unconstitutional when the fetus is indisputably viable.

FACE: Freedom of Access to Clinic Entrances Act

Increased family planning and abortion clinic violence compelled Congress to pass the Freedom of Access to Clinic Entrances Act (FACE) in 1994, which prohibits the use of force, threats of force, and physical obstruction of clinic entrances.

FACE appeared to be effective in decreasing the violent attacks on clinics. Although bomb threats, arson, death threats, and stalking still persist at 20 percent of clinics, the figure is down from 52 percent of clinics in 1994.

While there have been challenges to FACE based on the First Amendment freedoms of speech and assembly, the U.S. Supreme Court has refused to hear these challenges. Lower courts have determined that the legislation is content-neutral and is thus is not biased against the expression of a particular viewpoint or political position. Courts have also determined that the First Amendment does not protect the types of activities that FACE seeks to prohibit. In May 2002, an en banc panel of the Ninth Circuit ruled that "wanted-style" posters and an Internet "hit list" identifying abortion providers are also threats under FACE. The court upheld the injunctive relief in the case, but remanded the case for further review regarding the size of the punitive damage award.

RU486

The violence that FACE tried to address also frightened away potential manufacturers of RU486, thereby denying American women a safe and more easily obtained early abortion procedure. According to Eric Schaff, M.D. (1999), the threat of physical violence is a major reason that potential manufacturers of RU486 are reluctant to step forward.

Schaff notes that the escalating violence targeted at abortion providers and abortion facilities has decreased the number of physicians who are willing to risk their lives and careers to provide these services. Eighty-four percent of counties in the United States have no abortion provider. As a result, fewer services make it more difficult for women to access abortion, thus undermining their ability to control their fertility and health.

RU486, also known as mifepristone, represents a new class of medications that block the action of progesterone, a naturally occurring hormone produced by the ovaries. This causes a nonsurgical abortion in over 95 percent of early pregnancies. RU486 has also been shown to have many significant nonabortifacient-related benefits such as emergency contraception, once-a-month contraception, labour induction, and cervical dilation. It has also been used in the treatment of endometriosis, fibroids, meningioma, Cushing's syndrome, and progesterone-sensitive tumors such as some breast cancer, endometrial cancer, and prostate cancer.

In November of 2003, the RU-486 Suspension and Review Act of 2003 was introduced by Sen. Sam Brownback. This legislation was intended to prevent the use of mifepristone and called for a review of the process by which FDA approved the drug. It was not passed.

This legislation was viewed by many as blatantly antichoice politics, rather than reflecting a concern for women's health. The RU-486 Suspension and Review Act challenged the integrity of the FDA to determine the medical and scientific safety of the drugs it approves. In fact, the FDA has approved 557 new drugs since 1995, yet Congress has never attempted to impose such onerous and burdensome distribution requirements on any other drug. Legislating the approval or disapproval of any drug sets a dangerous precedent. The effort to restrict FDA approval of mifepristone on the basis of an antichoice viewpoint undermines the integrity of the drug approval process and prevents FDA's reliance on science as the sole determining factor in judging the safety of drugs. As is the case with all FDA-approved drugs, mifepristone was put through rigorous scientific research to determine its safety and efficacy (American Association of University Women, 2004).

Ideologically driven legislation such as this disregards other possible benefits of nascent medications and limits access both to safer means of abortion and to potentially effective treatments for other disorders, further undermining a woman's right to choose.

7

Prostitution and Trafficking

Feminsts' views on prostitution vary, but many of these perspectives can be loosely arranged into an overarching standpoint that is generally either critical or supportive of prostitution and sex work. Anti-prostitution feminists are strongly opposed to prostitution, as they see the practice as a form of violence against and exploitation of women, and a sign of male dominance over women. Feminists who hold such views on prostitution include Kathleen Barry, Melissa Farley, Julie Bindel, Sheila Jeffreys, Catharine MacKinnon and Laura Lederer; the European Women's Lobby has also condemned prostitution as "an intolerable form of male violence".

Other feminists hold that prostitution and other forms of sex work can be valid choices for women and men who choose to engage in it. In this view, prostitution must be differentiated from forced prostitution, and feminists should support sex worker activism against abuses by both the sex industry and the legal system. The disagreement between these two feminist stances has proven particularly contentious, and may be comparable to the feminist sex wars of the late twentieth century.

Relationship to Political Movements

In the U.S., feminism, when politically active, formerly aligned largely with the political right, e.g., through the National Woman's Party, from the 1910s to the 1960s, and presently aligns largely with the left, e.g., through the National Organization for Women, of the 1960s to the present, although in neither case has the alignment been consistent.

Socialism

Since the early twentieth century some feminists have allied with socialism. In 1907 there was an International Conference of Socialist Women in Stuttgart where suffrage was described as a tool of class struggle. Clara Zetkin of the Social Democratic Party of Germany called for women's suffrage to build a *"socialist order, the only one that allows for a radical solution to the women's question"*. In Britain, the women's movement was allied with the Labour party. In the U.S., Betty Friedan emerged from a radical background to take leadership. Radical Women is the oldest socialist feminist organization in the U.S. and is still active. During the Spanish Civil War, Dolores Ibárruri led the Communist Party of Spain. Although she supported equal rights for women, she opposed women fighting on the front and clashed with the anarcha-feminist Mujeres Libres.

In Latin America, revolutions brought changes in women's status in countries such as Nicaragua, where feminist ideology during the Sandinista Revolution aided women's quality of life but fell short of achieving a social and ideological change.

Science

Some feminists, such as Evelyn Fox Keller, criticize traditional scientific discourse as historically biased towards a masculine perspective, including the idea of scientific objectivity. Primatologist Sarah Blaffer Hrdy notes the prevalence of masculinely coined stereotypes and theories, such as of the non-sexual female, despite "the accumulation of abundant openly available evidence contradicting it".

Many feminist scholars rely on qualitative scientific research methods that emphasize women's subjective and individual experiences, including treating research participants as authorities equal to the researcher. Objectivity is eschewed in favour of open self-reflexivity and the agenda of helping women. Also, part of the feminist research agenda is the uncovering of ways in which power inequities are created and/or reinforced in society and in scientific and academic institutions. A feminist approach to research often involves nontraditional forms of presentation.

Fascism

Scholars have argued that Nazi Germany and the other fascist states of the 1930s and 1940s illustrates the disastrous consequences for society of a state ideology that, in glorifying women, becomes anti-feminist. In Germany after the rise of Nazism in 1933, there was a rapid dissolution of the political rights and economic opportunities that feminists had fought for during the prewar period and to some extent during the 1920s. In Franco's Spain, the right wing Catholic conservatives undid the work of feminists during the Republic. Fascist society was hierarchical with an emphasis and idealization of virility, with women maintaining a largely subordinate position to men.

Biology of Gender

Modern feminist science challenges the biological essentialist view of gender. However, it is increasingly interested in the study of biological sex differences and their effect on human behaviour. For example, Anne Fausto-Sterling's book, *Myths of Gender*, explores the assumptions embodied in scientific research that purports to support a biologically essentialist view of gender. Her second book, *Sexing the Body*, discussed the alleged possibility of more than two *true* biological sexes.

This possibility only exists in yet-unknown extraterrestrial biospheres, as no ratios of true gametes to polar cells other than 4:0 and 1:3 (male and female, respectively) are produced on Earth. However, in *The Female Brain*, Louann Brizendine argues that brain differences between the sexes are a biological reality with significant implications for sex-specific functional differences.

Steven Rhoads illustrated sex-dependent differences across a wide scope. Carol Tavris, in *The Mismeasure of Woman*, uses psychology and sociology to critique theories that use essentialism and biological reductionism to explain differences between men and women.

She argues that "women are not the better sex, the inferior sex or the opposite sex", rather she contends that there are ever-changing hypotheses that justify inequality and perpetuate stereotypes.

Cordelia Fine, in *Delusions of Gender*, argues that there is currently no scientific evidence for innate biological differences between men and women's minds, and that cultural and societal beliefs contribute to commonly perceived sex differences.

Evolutionary Biology

Sarah Kember—drawing from numerous areas such as evolutionary biology, sociobiology, artificial intelligence, and cybernetics in development with a new evolutionism—discusses the biologization of technology. She notes how feminists and sociologists have become suspicious of evolutionary psychology, particularly in as much as sociobiology is subjected to complexity in order to strengthen sexual difference as immutable through pre-existing cultural value judgments about human nature and natural selection.

Where feminist theory is criticized for its "false beliefs about human nature", Kember then argues in conclusion that "feminism is in the interesting position of needing to do more biology and evolutionary theory in order not to simply oppose their renewed hegemony, but in order to understand the conditions that make this possible, and to have a say in the construction of new ideas and artefacts."

Health

Feminism has led to increased participation by women in the health care they receive (e.g., the book *Our Bodies, Ourselves*), deliver (e.g., as doctors and midwives), and seek.

Reactions

Different groups of people have responded to feminism, and both men and women have been among its supporters and critics. Among American university students, for both men and women, support for feminist ideas is more common than self-identification as a feminist. The US media tends to portray feminism negatively and feminists "are less often associated with day-to-day work/leisure activities of regular women."

Criticisms by some Women

During much of its history, feminist movements and theoretical developments were led predominantly by middle-class white women from Western Europe and North America. However, at least since Sojourner Truth's 1851 speech to American feminists, women of other races have proposed alternative feminisms.

This trend accelerated in the 1960s with the civil rights movement in the United States and the collapse of European colonialism in Africa, the Caribbean, parts of Latin America, and Southeast Asia. Since that time, women in developing nations and former colonies and who are of colour or various ethnicities or living in poverty have proposed additional feminisms.

Pro-Feminism

Pro-feminism is the support of feminism without implying that the supporter is a member of the feminist movement. The term is most often used in reference to men who are actively supportive of feminism. The activities of pro-feminist men's groups include anti-violence work with boys and young men in schools, offering sexual harassment workshops in workplaces, running community education campaigns, and counseling male perpetrators of violence. Pro-feminist men also are involved in men's health, activism against pornography including anti-pornography legislation, men's studies, and the development of gender equity curricula in schools.

This work is sometimes in collaboration with feminists and women's services, such as domestic violence and rape crisis centers. Some activists of both genders will not refer to men as "feminists" at all and will refer to all pro-feminist men as "pro-feminists".

Anti-Feminism

Anti-feminism is opposition to feminism in some or all of its forms. In the nineteenth century, anti-feminism was mainly focused on opposition to women's suffrage. Later, opponents of women's entry into institutions of higher learning argued that education was too great a physical burden on women. Other anti-feminists opposed women's entry into the labor force, or their right to join unions, to sit on juries, or to obtain birth control and control of their sexuality. Some people have opposed feminism on the grounds that they believe it is contrary to traditional values or religious beliefs. These anti-feminists argue, for example, that social acceptance of divorce and non-married women is wrong and harmful, and that men and women are fundamentally different and thus their different traditional roles in society should be maintained. Other anti-feminists oppose women's entry into the workforce, political office, and the voting process, as well as the lessening of male authority in families. Writers such as Camille Paglia, Christina Hoff Sommers, Jean Bethke Elshtain, Elizabeth Fox-Genovese and Daphne Patai oppose some forms of feminism, though they identify as feminists. They argue, for example, that feminism often promotes misandry and the elevation of women's interests above men's, and criticize radical feminist positions as harmful to both men and women. Daphne Patai and Noretta Koertge argue that the term "anti-feminist" is used to silence academic debate about feminism.

MIGRATION CONNECTED WITH TRAFFICKING IN WOMEN AND PROSTITUTION

Migration linked to trafficking in women and prostitution is one of the most dark features of the lack of equality between women and men. This form of migration has developed into a gigantic, highly organised criminal trade linked to the exploitation of women. The main reasons for female emigration are poverty, discrimination against women, unemployment, under-education, lack of resources and political and economic instability. Some women are also motivated to leave their country in order to have the opportunity to work abroad and see something of the world. Another reason is that the situation of prostitutes in other countries is sometimes even worse in the countries of origin than in the receiving countries due to their illegal status.

Criminal organisations are often involved in migration linked to the trafficking in women and prostitution. They exploit the fact that while there is high demand for immigrant labour, there are now fewer opportunities for legal migration in Europe. In fact, there is a high demand for workers who don't put their standards too high. Various migration flows linked to trafficking in women and prostitution can be seen in present-day Europe, originating in the Balkans, Central Europe and Eastern Europe. There is also trafficking in women within these countries.

It is essential that European countries react firmly and in a coordinated manner to the problems posed by migration connected with trafficking in women and prostitution.

I. Draft Resolution

1. Migration linked to trafficking in women and prostitution is one of the most dark features of the lack of equality between women and men. The Assembly is alarmed by the development of this form of migration into a gigantic, highly organised international criminal trade linked to the exploitation of women.
2. The Parliamentary Assembly recalls and reaffirms Recommendation 1325 (1997) on traffic in women and forced prostitution in Council of Europe member states and Recommendation 1545 (2002) on a campaign against trafficking in human beings. These Recommendations define trafficking in human beings as a human rights issue, which entails the violation of women's dignity and integrity, their freedom of movement and, in some cases, their right to life.
3. Trafficking in human beings and migration connected to it is blossoming because of the gap between poor and rich countries, the lack of opportunities for young people to build up an existence, and the deprived position of women in many countries, which make them especially vulnerable to exploitation in the sex industry. The poor economic situation in the countries of origin is exploited by organised crime in both the countries of origin and of destination.
4. The Assembly notes that the deficit in labour supply in some countries of destination creates a demand for immigrants. When legal migration does not cover this deficit, the incentive and room for illegal migration and trafficking increases. Repressive migration policies and the resulting illegal status of women in the destination countries made migrant women more dependent on and more vulnerable to various forms of exploitation and abuse.
5. The Assembly recalls its Recommendation 1489 (2001) on transit migration in central and eastern Europe and reiterates the importance of the elaboration of a European strategy in the field of migration policy aimed at developing legitimate migration opportunities. This should allow some women to avoid being trafficked by mitigating any need to engage with traffickers to effect their migration.

6. It is also a matter of urgency to elaborate an effective European common strategy facilitating economic recovery policies, which will increase socio-economic and political stability in countries of origin and will decrease poverty migration and reduce supply factors of trafficking and demand factors of prostitution. The root causes of economic perspectives in the countries of origin should be tackled through economic cooperation, trade expansion, development assistance and conflict prevention.
7. The Assembly is very concerned by the involvement of international organised crime in migration connected with trafficking in women and prostitution. It urges European states to develop legislation for specific trafficking crimes and related offences, which should include harsh penalties for perpetrators of such crimes.
8. The Assembly considers that the main attention in the fight against trafficking in women should be given to the status and rights of victims (e.g. regarding residence and in criminal proceedings), including their physical protection as well as assistance and support. It is important to ensure that victims of trafficking are protected from further victimisation, whether or not they testify against the traffickers.
9. The Assembly accordingly calls on Council of Europe member states to:

A. *General measures:*

i. nominate a national Rapporteur on Trafficking in Human Beings in each member country;

ii. adopt effective measures to improve the economic situation in countries of origin, including the improvement of social protection and the creation of employment opportunities;

iii. better identify imbalances in labour markets in destination countries, and to promote selective immigration and effective integration policies;

iv. take measures to reduce the demand for the activities of persons trafficked for the purposes of sexual exploitation, forced labour or slavery;

B. *Migration policies improvement measures:*

i. take effective decisions in the field of migration policy aimed at developing legitimate migration opportunities ;

ii. encourage the signing of bilateral agreements between the countries of origin and destination countries on short-term labour migration contracts;

iii. adopt migration policies to assist victims of trafficking and migrant prostitution in their rehabilitation and reintegration in society;

iv. regulate and monitor agencies, such as bridal, employment, tourist, au pair and adoption bodies in order to penalise those which cooperate with criminal groups of traffickers;

v. provide the victims of trafficking with residence permits on humanitarian grounds;

C. *Preventive measures:*

i. set up data banks and promote the exchange of information on the various aspects of migration connected to trafficking in human beings;

ii. promote awareness-raising campaigns and understanding of how the traffic operates, and introduce measures to prevent illegal migration;

iii. cooperate with non-governmental organisations which provide expertise in women's human rights, labour rights and anti-trafficking activities;

iv. develop international cooperation between special police units dealing with trafficking in human beings;

v. organise special anti-trafficking sensibilisation programmes for judicial, law enforcement, medical and social workers and consular and immigration services;

vi. develop interpretative commentaries for judges and other officials as well as comprehensive procedural guidelines for police and immigration officers on the prevention and prosecution of trafficking offences;

D. *Legal measures:*

i. at the international level

a. strongly support the idea of the Council of Europe Convention on trafficking in human beings, which will bring an added value to other international instruments with its clear human rights and victim protection focus and the inclusion of a gender perspective;

b. sign and ratify the United Nations Convention Against Transnational Organised Crime and its additional Protocol to Prevent, Suppress and Punish Trafficking in Persons, especially Women and Children (Palermo protocol) if they have not yet done so;

ii. at the national level

a. appoint prosecution officers specially trained to deal with trafficking in human beings in all regional and national prosecutor's offices;

b. introduce harsh penalties for this type of trafficking and forced prostitution;

c. encourage victims of trafficking and witnesses to testify against the traffickers in courts, and provide those willing to testify with security protection during the investigation and trial and any subsequent period when their safety is under threat;

E. *Victim protection measures:*

i. enable female immigrant victims of trafficking and forced prostitution to return home in dignity and security, if they so desire;

ii. elaborate guidelines enabling the rapid identification of victims of trafficking and providing assistance to them;

iii. ensure that victims of trafficking are not held in immigration detention or other forms of custody;

iv. provide all victims of trafficking with the necessary rehabilitation assistance, including accommodation, health care and counselling;

v. provide financial assistance to non-governmental organisations that implement protection programmes and initiatives for victims of trafficking.

II. Draft Recommendation

1. The Parliamentary Assembly refers to its Resolution ... (2003) on migration connected with trafficking in women and prostitution.
2. The Assembly considers that this type of migration, which has developed into a gigantic, highly organised international criminal trade linked to the exploitation of women, cannot be combated effectively by member states acting on their own.
3. Therefore, the Assembly recommends to the Committee of Ministers to:

i. take as soon as possible the decision to begin the drafting of the Council of Europe Convention on trafficking in human beings, which will bring an added value to other international instruments with its clear human rights and victim protection focus and the inclusion of a gender perspective;

ii. closely involve the Parliamentary Assembly in the drafting of the Convention and provide the necessary financial resources to bring this work to a rapid conclusion ;

iii. ask the European Committee for the Prevention of Torture (CPT) to investigate the conditions of detention and deportation of the victims of trafficking in detention centres, prisons and deportation centres of Council of Europe member states;

iv. instruct the relevant intergovernmental committees:
   a. to draft programmes aimed at assisting member states with legal reform initiatives, including drafting comprehensive anti-trafficking laws and amending penal codes and immigration laws in conformity with international law on trafficking in human beings;
   b. to organise a round table on the different views on prostitution in Council of Europe member states.

III. Explanatory memorandum by Ms Zwerver

1. Migration from East to West Europe linked to traffic in women and migrant prostitution has grown since the collapse of the Berlin Wall, as a result of two factors: the opening up of borders in eastern Europe and the poverty of the former communist countries, factors which have directly affected women in those countries. Before the collapse of the Berlin Wall most trafficked women came from South East Asia and Latin America.
2. Another feature of post-1989 Eastern Europe is the increase in organised crime. Taking advantage of western countries' "drawing power", many criminal organisations have set up in the business of "exporting" women to put them to work in sectors where access to information and social assistance is very limited. The European Commission estimates that 120 000 women and children are trafficked into Western Europe each year.
3. Young women are enticed by offers of employment abroad as dancers, bar hostesses or au pairs and end up, sold and in debt, on the pavements of some unknown country. Even those who know that they are heading into prostitution have no idea of the violence in store for them and they are misled about the conditions they have to work in.
4. The phenomenon has taken on such dramatic proportions in Europe and the rest of the world that many European organisations are now considering how to counter a trade which comes third in the league table of profitable crime, behind only drugs and arms smuggling.
5. The Committee on Equal Opportunities for Women and Men organized a colloquy on the migration connected with trafficking in women and prostitution, which was held in The Hague on 14-15 November 2002. The participants of the colloquy held an exchange of views on the situation in different regions of Europe connected to various migration flows linked with women trafficking and prostitution. The representatives of the International Organization on Migration shared their experience in working out world strategies regarding migration

connected to trafficking in human beings and the practical implementation of those strategies in their field offices. The participants of the hearing had a unique possibility to study in details the Dutch example of the legalisations of prostitution and its impact on the situation of legal and illegal prostitutes and the victims of trafficking. They had discussions with the members of the Foundation "de Rode Draad", the foundation of sex workers the main aim of which is to help sex workers in difficult situations, linked with their job and to provide them with legal assistance, shelters and necessary information on working conditions. The Committee also visited the Prostitution Information Centre in Amsterdam. This Centre provides information to all visitors regarding the development of the prostitution business in Amsterdam. It also distributes information on the main rights, working conditions and security of girls working in this business. As a result of this hearing a list of recommendations was drawn up and added to this report.

6. The report seeks to draw further attention to the gravity of the problem of migration linked to traffic in women and prostitution. Even though there are no reliable statistics on the subject it is possible to identify a migration pattern. Countries divide into countries of origin, transit countries and destination countries. (Some countries, like Poland, are countries of origin, transit and destination at the same time.) Council of Europe member states include all three types. Specific measures are needed in relation to each of these groups of countries.

I. Definitions and Council of Europe work in this area

7. Several organisations have produced definitions of trafficking in women – they include the International Organisation for Migration (IOM), Europol and the European Commission. Following on from these organisations' work on the question, the Council of Europe in turn has defined the term.
8. In Recommendation 1325 (1997) the Council of Europe Parliamentary Assembly defined traffic in women and forced prostitution as any legal or illegal transporting of women and/or trade in them, with or without their initial consent, for economic gain, with the purpose of subsequent forced prostitution, forced marriage or other forms of forced sexual exploitation. The use of force may be physical, sexual and/or psychological, and includes intimidation, rape and abuse of authority or of a position of vulnerability.
9. Committee of Ministers Recommendation Rec (2000) 11 of 19 May 2000 defines trafficking in human beings for the purpose of sexual

exploitation as "the procurement by one or more natural or legal persons and/or the organisation of the exploitation and/or transport or migration – legal or illegal – of persons, even with their consent, for the purpose of their sexual exploitation, inter alia by means of coercion, in particular violence or threats, deceit or abuse of authority or of a position of vulnerability".

10. An international definition of trafficking is given in Article 3 of the Protocol to Prevent, Suppress and Punish Trafficking in Persons, especially Women and Children, supplementing the UN Convention against Trans-national Organized Crime (Palermo, 2000). It says that ""trafficking in persons" shall mean the recruitment, transportation, transfer, harbouring or receipt of persons, by means of the threat or use of force or other forms of coercion, of abduction, of fraud, of deception, of the abuse of power or of a position of vulnerability or of the giving or receiving of payments or benefits to achieve the consent of a person having control over another person, for the purpose of exploitation. Exploitation shall include, at a minimum, the exploitation of the prostitution of others or other forms of sexual exploitation, forced labour or services, slavery or practices similar to slavery, servitude or the removal of organs."
11. Speaking about the definition of trafficking in human beings it is important to make a distinction between "illicit labour" and "forced prostitution". Only when a situation is comparable to slavery, exploitation can be regarded as trafficking in human beings.
12. A distinction should also be made between smuggling and human trafficking. Migrant smuggling is assisting people for money or other gain to enter or stay in a country illegally; in this case the territorial integrity of a state is at stake. Sometimes, the conditions under which people are smuggled may be so bad or degrading that the smuggled persons themselves can in fact, in a practical sense also be called victims. Trafficking in human beings is by definition a serious violation of human rights and personal integrity.
13. Migration linked to traffic in women and prostitution has two distinctive aspects: its illegality and the criminal organisation behind it.
14. Most of this migration is controlled by powerful international criminal networks: this is an extremely lucrative market and creates ideal conditions for corruption, even in western European countries.
15. Specifically migratory aspects aside, trafficking in people is primarily a human-rights issue. In recent years, numbers falling victim to the traffic have risen steeply.

16. Overall, obviously, no one country has the resources to solve the problem on its own. The Council of Europe, which has the main countries of origin, transit and destination among its members, seems ideally placed to coordinate such action.
17. The Council of Europe Parliamentary Assembly has raised the issue several times, in particular in the recommendation mentioned above.
18. A good example of the value of international dialogue in migration management was the European Conference against Trafficking in Human Beings, organized in September 2002 by the International organization on Migration and the European Commission. Its "Brussels Declaration" can be considered as a compendium of good practices and lessons learned. After some years of development of a comprehensive policy, the Conference provided yet another important milestone in the fight against human trafficking which invited actors to take the next crucial steps towards reinforcing efforts to implement best practices identified in a comprehensive and coordinated European approach.
19. This Declaration calls upon the coalition of committed governments, international bodies and NGOs to take concrete measures and to intensify cooperation in the fields of prevention, victim protection and assistance, and police and judicial cooperation, in particular with a view to achieving a swift and sustainable reduction of trafficking in human beings.

II. The Present Forms and the Causes of Migration Linked to Trafficking in Women and Prostitution

20. There seems to be a worldwide agreement on the fact that trafficking in human beings and migration connected to it is blossoming because of the gap between poor and rich countries, the lack of opportunities for young people to build up an existence, and the deprived position of women in many countries, which make them especially vulnerable for exploitation in the sex industry. Therefore, the root causes of this problem should be addressed in order to reduce the economic and social inequality and disadvantages, which provoke illegal migration.
21. Working in the sex industry is no mere sum total of personally preferred or privately chosen behaviour patterns but undoubtedly an organised system – which has now been globalised and industrialised – with links to the criminal world. Migrant prostitution and procuring have become more and more inseparable. Procuring is an organised activity of small, medium-sized or large networks, which interlink with criminal organisations. The traffic routes are fully-fledged businesses in which maximum profit is the key objective. Even though many migrant women

working as prostitutes say they are independent, they face various pressures and few do not end up under procurer control of one kind or another. In addition the procurers cover their tracks by using more and more complex transit routes to move from country to country and by constantly increasing the distance – and the number of middlemen – between themselves and the prostitutes they are exploiting.

22. Research in the Netherlands shows that drugs and trafficking in women rarely go together. There is a high risk involved in drug trafficking and much cash is needed. Trafficking in women asks for other investments, especially time. Drugs are very lucrative and very risky; trafficking in women is very labour intensive and only lucrative in high quantities.
23. Migration connected with trafficking in women and prostitution can be explained by lack of prospects in the country of origin, including women's experience of poverty and social exclusion. Unemployment and lack of education, which, in practice, affect women more than men, are further contributory factors. Women in central and eastern European countries have been particularly affected by the rise in unemployment that has followed those countries' painful transition to the market economy. The desire to migrate can seldom be met through legal channels since western countries have clamped down on immigration. The restrictions encourage the setting up of networks that exploit the desire to migrate. In addition, the economic situation means that, without realising the full implications, many women deliberately resort to prostitution as a means of earning a living.
24. Immigrant women tend to be forced to work in sectors where access to information and welfare networks is limited, which makes them even more vulnerable to exploitation and violence. Some women are forced to labour in underground workshops. They have no residence or work permits and are thus totally dependent on their employers administratively and financially. Another form of exploitation is domestic slavery. The inhuman conditions in which the female domestic slave is forced to live are maintained by nothing less than a reign of terror (Parliamentary Assembly Recommendation 1523 (2001)).
25. Procurers' victims are kept under close watch; sometimes the threat to inform the family is enough. Lodged in hotels, prostitutes are frequently guarded by a woman. The people really in charge may be living in a neighbouring country or may remain in their country of origin.
26. Threats of reprisals against the family are a formidable weapon for maintaining a climate of fear. The procurers use it to keep victims under even tighter control and to deter them from talking to the police.

27. Many trafficked women also suffer beatings, rape, psychological coercion, and serious health problems from sexually transmitted diseases. Refusal to obey traffickers and employers can lead to fines, physical violence, and even death.
28. On top of the violence, surveillance and threats, there is the fear, which victims have of being discovered by the police without proper papers.
29. Despite the efforts of the Council of Europe and other international organisations to combat migration linked to traffic in women and prostitution, the migration continues to flourish in Council of Europe member countries.
30. Countries can be divided into countries of origin, transit countries and destination countries. A full assessment of the situation is difficult as a country may be simultaneously a country of origin, a transit country and a destination country. In addition, relevant statistics are incomplete because the migration is illegal and underground, legislation to combat it is lacking, and the victims are unwilling to speak up.
31. In 2000 a new legislative Act came into force in the Netherlands, lifting the ban on brothels. At the same time, the legislation on the unacceptable forms of prostitution has become more severe. Trafficking in people with the aim of forced prostitution and forced prostitution of minors are considered as serious offences. By legalising the employment of prostitutes the government is thought to have more control over the sex industry and more possibilities to counter abuses.
32. The prohibited forms of prostitution tend to take place in the unregulated sector of prostitution (such as streetwalking or mobile forms of prostitution). Forced prostitution and the prostitution of minors are especially at risk in the unregulated sector.
33. One of the first outcomes of an evaluation of the new Act in the Netherlands shows that there is no confirmation for an often assumed large-scale escape of prostitutes into the unregulated sector.

III. Migration Connected with Traffic in Women and Prostitution

1. The former Soviet Union – Russia and the Baltic states

34. According to the IOM, in the past two years Russian border guards have intercepted five thousand Russian women trying to leave the country with non-valid papers. The majority were going to Turkey, Italy, Germany, Bulgaria or Finland. While the interceptions do not necessarily imply involvement of traffickers, Russian women are the third largest group of victims of trafficking into Germany, after Lithuanian and Ukrainian women. IOM statistics on repatriated persons likewise suggest considerable trafficking out of Lithuania.

2. The Balkans

35. The Balkans are a special case when it comes to migration related to traffic in women and prostitution: the main countries of origin are there, while some Balkan countries are also transit and destination countries. The Balkans have what can only be described as women markets. Bosnia's notorious "Arizona Market" is one example – it sells every possible commodity, including women.
36. Traffic in women for sexual exploitation has become a serious problem in Bosnia and Herzegovina. The country is primarily a destination one. According to the International Police Task Force a third of the foreign prostitutes in Bosnia and Herzegovina say they arrived there as a result of trafficking. Most of the trafficking victims are from Moldova, Romania and Ukraine. The age range is sixteen to thirtythree, with an average age of twenty-three. Five per cent are under age. Unable to subsist in their own countries, many of these women succumb to newspaper advertisements promising well-paid employment abroad. Many are sold, purchased in Belgrade and then moved to Bosnia and Herzegovina. The traffickers cow them into submission by isolating them and not allowing them to leave their lodgings without permission or unescorted. Their papers are usually confiscated as soon as they enter the country.
37. In Bosnia and Herzegovina prostitution and the "white slave trade" are a flourishing economic sector because of the presence of the "international community", as the hotchpotch of organisations composed of the United Nations, SFOR (the multinational peacekeeping force) and the OSCE is termed locally. The presence of tens of thousands of foreign military and civilian male personnel in possession of foreign currency guarantees steady demand in the brothels in which an increasing number of women are coerced into selling their bodies.
38. The problem has spread to Kosovo, which has recently become a "prostitution oasis". The market there, a highly complex one, is growing in response to demand, and trafficking has boomed since the end of the conflict. Since June 1999 restaurants and bars have mushroomed in Pristina, with the local clientele as big as the foreign one. According to the IOM almost half of the women brought into Kosovo illegally are from Moldova, and the others from Ukraine, Bulgaria and Romania. Some are taken from Kosovo to Albania, and then sold to organised criminal networks operating in Western Europe. The women's passports are confiscated, and their resistance is broken by rape and ill treatment. Most receive no wages and are kept in servitude on the pretext of supposed debts, which they must repay in full before they can be

released. Such women have few options. If they manage to escape, they find themselves in hostile, unknown territory.

3. *Central Europe*

39. Since the democratic transformation of central Europe in the early 1990s, the region's migration patterns have changed greatly. The recent liberalisation of their migration policies (making it easier to cross borders), their geographical location, improved economic prospects, the resultant opportunities, and their inexperience in combating unlawful immigration all mean that the central European countries now face huge migration connected to traffic in women and prostitution. The problem is exacerbated by those countries' not having visa requirements for entry. Generally speaking, there are two categories of migration here: with the first, the intention is to remain in the central European country for some time; with the second, the aim is to continue to a western destination and the central European states are only transit countries, being adjacent to the main destination countries. They are also countries of origin for trafficking and consequently they fall into all the categories of country connected with traffic in women and migrant prostitution.

40. In 2001 and 2002 there was a tendency for the region to become more attractive as a destination country. For example, the Polish authorities recorded a 202% increase in the number of Afghan nationals detained in that country in 2002. A large percentage of third country nationals entered the region with the assistance of traffickers. In 2001, the number of people claiming asylum in Hungary, Lithuania, Romania and Slovakia rose significantly.

4. *Western Europe*

41. Western European countries are the main destination for migration connected with traffic in women and prostitution. Interpol estimates that there are some 300,000 women from eastern European countries engaged in prostitution in Western Europe.

42. The lack of any specialist monitoring body to prevent and combat the migration facilitates this state of affairs. Migrant prostitution is everywhere on the increase and countries' treatment of it varies. The individual who engages in migrant prostitution is not in fact regarded as committing a crime. In all countries except Spain and the Netherlands, procuring in any form is an offence. Sweden is the only country where the purchase of sexual services is completely outlawed.

43. The lack of reliable data on migration connected with traffic in women and prostitution in various parts of the world, including western Europe,

is another problem but information does exist and, however incomplete, indicates the scale of the phenomenon and the recent developments.

44. According to IOM data 10% to 20% (2,000 to 6,000) of the 20,000 to 30,000 illegal female migrants who enter the sex industry in Italy each year are trafficked. In Greece, research has shown that just over half of trafficked women are from Russia or Ukraine, while a third are from the Balkans and a small percentage from Asia and Africa. Trafficking to Belgium tends to be from Nigeria, China, Albania, Romania, Russia and Bulgaria. The majority of females trafficked to the Netherlands would appear to be from central and eastern Europe. Most victims in Germany were from the former Soviet Union and elsewhere in Eastern Europe. In France, according to the central anti-human-trafficking office, 12,000 to 15,000 people were engaged in prostitution in 2000. All the eastern European nationalities were involved. The Romanian, Hungarian, Bulgarian, Czech, Croatian and Serb women working as prostitutes in the early 1990s had been joined by young Russians, Ukrainians, Slovaks, Moldavians, Slovenes and Latvians. Albanian women from Kosovo, Macedonia and Albania began appearing in 1997.
45. Switzerland is a special case, not being a member of the European Union or the Schengen area. It is a destination country. The countries of origin for migration into Switzerland are Poland, Russia, the Czech Republic, Latvia and Albania. The recent increase in the numbers of sex workers in some parts of the country, especially the cantons of Ticino, Aargau and Solothurn, is worrying on account of deregulation and the increase in uncontrolled prostitution, which is less professional and often concentrated in clubs or discos in outlying parts of cities, along major roads. Competition in this market is fierce and prices have fallen, making prostitutes' working conditions increasingly difficult. Under greater pressure, they are inclined to take more risks and sometimes to offer or agree to unprotected intercourse. The women involved, the vast majority of who are immigrants, are often in Switzerland illegally or on a dancer's permit.
46. In many Western European countries the interests of victims of trafficking still seem to be made completely subordinate to the interests of the prosecution of traffickers. In practice, it means that the victims of trafficking are first exploited by the traffickers and consequently, as "disposable" witnesses by the criminal justice system.
47. Trafficking in women is also identified in Western Europe with illegal migration, shifting the focus from combating violence and abuse to combating illegal entry and residence. Under the denomination of fight against trafficking repressive immigration measures, such as tightening

visa policies, stricter boarder control, closer supervision of mixed marriages, the criminalization of third parties who facilitated illegal entry or stay are taken. These measures are aimed more at protecting the state against illegal migration rather than at protecting women against violence and abuse. Moreover, repressive migration policies and the resulting illegal status of women in the destination country made migrant women more dependent on and more vulnerable to various forms of exploitation and abuse.

IV. Combating the Varieties of Modern Slavery

48. The resources available to the authorities for combating these various types of slavery are grossly inadequate, given the seriousness of the situation. Introducing the collective measures that are needed if international criminal networks are to be countered more effectively has long been hampered by countries' legitimate attachment to their national legal systems.
49. Countries need to be cooperating at pan-European level in the management of migratory flows, and the Council of Europe is best placed to coordinate the efforts. International cooperation should be developed between special police units dealing with trafficking in human beings.
50. The first thing that needs working on is information. We need to set up a data bank and exchange information on the various aspects of this type of migration. Countries' experience needs pooling so that the various methods used to combat this migration can be analysed.
51. No less essential are collective steps to locate and close down the routes by which women are "exported".
52. As will be evident from this report, it is relatively clear which are the countries of origin, the transit countries and the destination countries in migration linked to traffic in women and prostitution. Council of Europe member countries must accordingly step up bilateral and multilateral preventive cooperation. Prevention can be reinforced by developing routine police cooperation on this matter at European level.
53. National migration policy needs harmonising within the Council of Europe area; regard being had to the particular features of the different groups of countries (countries of origin, transit countries and destination countries).
54. In the countries of origin the emphasis must be on prevention. Avoiding young women being lured abroad with false promises is undoubtedly the most effective way of combating trafficking. Good information is needed about working conditions, rights and duties of migrants.

55. Steps also need taking to improve women's lot in the countries of origin.
56. It is equally important to educate the people dealing with this type of migration in the countries of origin, enable them to exchange information and provide them with special training. Sometimes border officials are incapable of detecting trafficking, far less stopping it, for sheer lack of training.
57. Another problem in some countries of origin is shortage of staff. In Moldova, for example, the police unit responsible for combating human trafficking has only nine staff and is thus incapable of taking effective counter-action. This type of country needs more help in staffing the units set up to combat migration of this kind.
58. The transit countries are strategically important in that they have a possible role to play in stopping this type of migration. Here, too, efforts must focus on special training for staff and on transit countries' exchanging information with countries of origin and destination countries.
59. Measures should be adopted to afford victims of trafficking the opportunity to cooperate effectively and safely with law enforcement officials. They should include stays of deportation; exempting trafficked persons from detention and prosecution for offences directly relating to their trafficking; giving them the opportunity to seek justice and compensation for abuses they have suffered; guaranteeing their personal safety and the safety of their family members; facilitating their safe and humane repatriation; and offering alternatives if such repatriation is not possible, including third country resettlement.
60. Aid to victims is one of the areas in which destination countries' law has serious shortcomings. A migration policy towards victims would be a valuable weapon in combating the traffic. If destination countries were to start issuing them with residence permits on humanitarian grounds it might encourage victims to give evidence and help dismantle the migration routes.
61. The problem of deportation of the victims of trafficking from the destination countries should urgently be solved. Some countries ensured an adequate return of victims informing the relevant authorities of the countries of origin, but a lot of countries use a humiliating practice of deportation. The victims of trafficking need special assistance upon their return home.
62. Traffickers and smugglers are in fact exploiting a growing demand in destination countries. Law enforcement efforts should be supported and should address the root causes of migration. Replacing irregular with regular migration is the best way to undercut the appeal of the

traffickers and smugglers. Bilateral agreements could be signed between relevant European countries on short-term labour migration contracts.

63. The relevant governmental authorities of destination countries (Ministry of Interior, Ministry of Foreign Affairs, etc.) should consult with consular authorities of countries from which trafficked women originate in order to inform them on the situation and to coordinate safe, voluntary repatriation of victims of trafficking and assistance to trafficked women.
64. Also important is training for immigration officials, particularly at consulates, which issue visas. Staff needs thorough training in the problem and up-to-date information on the methods, dynamics and trends as regards migration linked to women trafficking and prostitution. Rules likewise need introducing to allow immigration officials to perform mid-visit checks even where visitors to a destination country have the required papers.
65. At pan-European level very careful consideration should be given to harmonising national law, having regard both to human rights and the requirements of combating the traffic. The Assembly accordingly stresses once again the importance of drafting a convention on traffic in women, with the emphasis on protecting the victims.

PROSTITUTION AGAINST WOMEN

The philosophy that prostitution is a human right has been advanced, in international forums such as Beijing, by drawing distinctions between forced and free, adult and child, third world and first world prostitution, and between prostitution and trafficking. These distinctions are then used to make some forms of prostitution acceptable and legitimate, revising the harm that is done to women in prostitution into a consenting act and excluding prostitution from the category of violence against women. The sex industry thrives on this language and these distinctions.

When distinctions are made between forced and free prostitution, for example, it becomes almost insurmountable for many, if not most, women in prostitution to prove that they have been forced. When distinctions are made between child and adult prostitution, the age of consent in some countries is simply reduced. In practice, the age of children in prostitution is becoming lower and lower; Human Rights /Asia, in their report on the trafficking of Nepali girls and women into India (1995, p. 15), states that the average age of the thousands of Nepali girls recruited every year for prostitution in Indian brothels, has dropped from 14-16 years of age during the 1980s, to 10-14 years of age during the 1990s.

NGOs that work to abolish institutionalized trafficking and prostitution per se receive funding only if they adhere to these distinctions; only if they call prostitutes commercial sex workers; only if they refer to prostitution as "forced prostitution;" only if they separate trafficking from prostitution and focus on closed brothels where women are kept in obvious indentured conditions; and only if they work with other groups who accept these conditions and distinctions.

Some governments who have vocally opposed making prostitution a violation of human rights are also funding NGOs, such as the Dutch Foundation Against Trafficking in Women (STV) and its international offshoot, the Global Alliance Against Traffic in Women (GAATW), which take similar positions. Thus governments and funding agencies are able to exert enormous influence over the agenda of what gets counted as violence against women. Increasingly, prostitution per se is declared a violence-free zone.

A lot of NGOs have the right words to say against violence against women. For example, the recent report of Human Rights Watch/Asia, referred to previously and which is entitled Rape for Profit, is a carefully researched and sensitively written report on the trafficking of Nepali Girls and Women into India's Brothels. Yet after documenting the extreme youth, the poverty, the horrendous abuse, the coercion, and outright abduction of young 10-14 year old girls into prostitution in India, the Report goes on to refer to them as "sex workers" (Human Rights Watch/Asia, 1995, e.g., pp. 13, 49, 65). In a footnote designed to show that the researchers are familiar with the controversy over this term, the report says: "...many activists in India who work with trafficking victims object to its use (i.e., the term sex worker or commercial sex worker)..." (Human Rights Watch/Asia, 1995, note 15 at p. 13). However, the Human Rights Watch reporters have obviously sided with those who favor the term sex worker, and that is the term that is used throughout the Report.

What are we to make of this? If reality hangs on the thin thread of language, this debate is no mere semantic quarrel. Many claim they use the term, sex work, to dignify and professionalize the women in prostitution. "The more 'professional' the sex worker, the more care she takes of herself. The more 'legal' or 'legitimate' she feels,... the more she will... be able to develop a degree of professionalism in her work. Is this not an argument in favour of recognition of prostitution as a form of legitimate work?" (Foundation Against Trafficking in Women, 1995, p. 3).

But the term, "sex work," doesn't dignify the worker; all it dignifies is the sex industry--the pimps, procurers and traffickers. And coming from human rights activists and feminists, it gives the sex industry more dignity than it has ever had, or could get anyplace else. The term "sex work" doesn't convey the exploitation of trafficking and prostitution. It ratifies prostitution as simply another form of work, something that has become a way of making a living. But for most of the women and children in prostitution, it's not living; it's barely surviving.

WHISPER, a Minneapolis-based organization of women who have both survived and who are coming out of prostitution, and who are committed to ending prostitution as a form of violence against women, found it difficult to identify job skills gained in prostitution which would advance anyone's career (Gamache, 1991, p.4). They found that the "skills" of prostitution are: performing sex acts, feigning sexual enjoyment, enduring all kinds of bodily violation, and allowing your body to be used in any imaginable way by another person (Giobbe, 1990, p.4). What young girl would we encourage to develop these "skills?" Yet there are now "courses" to teach would-be "sex workers," as they are called, the sexual techniques of prostitution and everything they need to know to become "skilled" in the trade.

What prostituted women must endure in their "employment" is, what in other contexts, would be the accepted definition of sexual harassment and sexual abuse in the workplace--"employer" behaviour that is unwanted and insulting, and unwelcome sexual attention, violence, and conduct that is offensive and threatening. What then happens to women in prostitution whose very "job"--if we term it "commercial sex work"--constitutes, what in any other "workplace," would be defined as sexual harassment and abuse? It is the exchange of money in prostitution that serves to transform what is actually sexual harassment, sexual abuse, and sexual violence into a "job" known as "commercial sex work," a "job" performed primarily by racially and economically disadvantaged women in the so-called first and third worlds, and by overwhelming numbers of women and children who have been the victims of childhood sexual abuse.

Another term that misrepresents the exploitation of prostitution, and the harm that it does to women, is the term "forced prostitution." What does this term mean? It means we are encouraged to distinguish forced prostitution from free prostitution? The Human Rights Watch Report not only consistently uses "forced prostitution" throughout, but also the term "forced trafficking". Are we to assume, then, that there is "free trafficking?" Building on the shaky foundation of consensual prostitution, do we now have "consensual trafficking" where some women and children freely choose to be trafficked from one place to another? Few human rights activists and people of conscience would use the term "forced slavery" or "forced apartheid" but so glibly slip into the language of forced prostitution and, now, forced trafficking.

The sex industry makes no distinctions between forced and free prostitution while encouraging others to do so. The industry is linked financially and politically with groups like COYOTE in the United States to promote prostitution as a woman's personal choice, proclaiming that the worst thing about prostitution is that the women are stigmatized. But the worst thing about prostitution is its violation of and violence against women and children. Although claiming to be a prostitutes rights organization, COYOTE works more for the rights of the customers and the industry, rather than for the rights of women to leave prostitution. The former director of COYOTE, Margo St. James, served as a witness for the defence at the pimping trial of well-known U.S. pornographers, and works to abolish U.S. laws against pimping and soliciting women for the purpose of prostitution.

It is doubtful that COYOTE's membership even includes many women in prostitution. For example, Priscilla Alexander, one of COYOTE's founders, equates prostitution with her own promiscuous dating experiences at Bennington College in Vermont. Referring to this time, Alexander writes: "I never have literally worked as a prostitute...although I was stigmatized as a whore at one time". Yet Alexander worked in the leadership of COYOTE for years building a career for herself as a prostitutes rights spokeswoman, even to the extent of being employed by the WHO (World Health Organization) as a consultant on AIDS/HIV) and prostitution. To all appearances, she has been accepted as speaking on behalf of women in prostitution because she has been there--but she was never in prostitution. The same is true for Margo St. James, another founder of COYOTE who recently ran for an elected seat on the San Francisco City Council.

Furthermore, COYOTE does not reveal its membership or the percentage of its members who are prostitutes, thus making it seem as if COYOTE is an organization of women in prostitution. Even researchers who write in praise of COYOTE and agree with its positions have alluded to the "institutionalizing [of] an organizational myth" upon which COYOTE is built. For example, author Valerie Jenness states that "Contrary to COYOTE's public image, only a small percentage of its members have worked as prostitutes, and an even smaller percentage are active prostitutes who are also active in the organization. On occasion, St. James has admitted that COYOTE is not an organization of and for prostitutes". COYOTE capitalizes on this lie with its spokeswomen promoting the image of COYOTE as an organization by and for prostitutes.

Meanwhile, groups who truly represent prostituted women--groups such as WHISPER and the Council for Prostitution Alternatives in the United States--are composed of many women who are survivors of prostitution, or women currently in prostitution trying to leave. Whenever I speak in the United States on the topic of prostitution, the question inevitably arises who represents the concerns of women in prostitution. Most of the audience has heard of COYOTE and immediately assumes that COYOTE speaks for all women in prostitution. Very few know about the work of WHISPER in Minneapolis; the Council for Prostitution Alternatives in Portland; PROMISE is San Francisco; Genesis House in Chicago; RESPECT in Madison; and SAGE in San Francisco. These are several of the groups advocating for women in prostitution--who are composed of many survivors of prostitution, who oppose prostitution per se as a human rights violation, who are not linked with the sex industry, and who work primarily to help women out of prostitution and create sustainable alternatives to prostitution in women's lives. Because such groups are not supported financially and politically by the sex industry, and thus do not have the resources to publicize their policies and positions, they do not receive the same public attention and prominence as the pro-prostitution industry groups.

A lot of NGOs are now working for women's rights to better their conditions in prostitution instead of helping them out of prostitution. Annabel Fan, a US lawyer, spoke of her impressions after completing a research trip to Thailand. "A lot of the NGOs whom I met with talked about ending the exploitation of women. Nowhere did I get the impression that prostitution itself is being targeted, to stop the practice. Definitely, what NGOs are concerned about is women's rights to determine how they work as prostitutes...Also, my sense is that there is not a lot of alternatives being offered by NGOs, but rather that the work done tends to maintain the system. The empowerment of women seems to be in the context of prostitution...It is empowerment in prostitution and not separate from prostitution...a lot of organizations I talked to do not want the criminalization of anybody, not clients, not pimps, no one, because they say, if you penalize the clients and pimps, then you disadvantage the women in the way they operate...Brothels are everywhere in Thailand...There are more brothels than schools" (Fan, 1995, p.3). Such NGO groups talk about women's empowerment in prostitution and primarily teach women how to perform better as prostitutes, how to negotiate with customers, and how to get men to use condoms and make it part of the sex, but they don't offer women a way out. Why? Because it's easier to believe that prostitution is a choice for these women. And talking about women's empowerment in prostitution means you don't have to confront the controversial issue of the customer.

In fact, the silent participant who is actually a silent perpetrator of prostitution, is the customer. He is often depicted, like the woman in prostitution, as a victim too, but this sentimentalizes his reality as opposed to hers. Surely, the question is not why do women choose to enter prostitution, but why do so many men choose to buy women and children in prostitution?

If the issue of choice must be raised, let it be raised in the context of the men who buy the sex of prostitution. Why do men choose to buy the bodies of millions of women and children, call it sex, and seemingly get tremendous pleasure literally over their bought bodies?

Opponents of making prostitution a human rights violation argue that past attempts to abolish prostitution have been repressive and worked against women. This is true, but only because such legislation has punished the women in prostitution and not the pimps, procurers and customers.

To argue that prostitution and trafficking are violations of a person's human rights means that we cannot regulate prostitution into categories of good and bad prostitution. We cannot create a zone of brothels or "eros centres," the usual approach to regulating prostitution, within which anything goes. Germany, for example, restricts prostitution activity to specific "eros centres," or large prostitution buildings--a type of barracks mentality--which are the designated sex zones in cities with populations over 20,000, the cities in Germany where prostitution is legal. "Red-light" districts, or zoned areas in which brothels, as well as other forms of sex "entertainment," may function are found in many countries as diverse as Turkey, Tunisia, Holland, Belgium, and South Korea. The U.S. version of zoned prostitution is Nevada where regulated prostitution functions throughout the state except in Reno and Las Vegas. Brothels, such as the infamous Mustang Ranch on the outskirts of Reno, were located outside the city limits, so as not to violate the law.

The regulationist system has been a failure because:

1. It doesn't work. Most women do not want to be registered officially as "sex workers," thus creating a permanent record of their prostitution.
2. It increases the extent of illegal prostitution. Particularly, it promotes the illegal trafficking of women into regulationist countries from poorer countries in the third world for the purpose of cheaper sex.

"The normalization of prostitution in European regulationist countries has actually promoted trafficking in women to the Netherlands. Neo-regulation relaxes the policing of prostitution, making it easier for traffickers to move in and out of the country. Trafficking from the Philippines, Latin America, and Eastern Europe has expanded in the Netherlands as it did a few decades earlier when Germany legalized prostitution". In fact, the case can be made that when a country regulates prostitution, the number of unregistered and unregulated women in prostitution increases simply because women are pressured into identifying as prostitutes, paying taxes on paltry earnings, and undergoing non-elective and often demeaning health screening and testing. "The regulations governing prostitution (medical, check-ups, card and brothels) were historically one of the main causes of the prostitution of women, and still are, because they do not allow them to abandon this activity and return to their social group. Because of the regulations, they come to form a separate category of women living on the fringes of society, who are vulnerable and 'marked for life' ".

The reality is that during the 1980s as the sex industry in several European countries underwent notable development, commercialization, and legitimation through regulationist legislation, it also became an international business. "In certain parts of the world...prostitution is...a 'planned' and 'institutionalized' part of it [the national income]...in South-East Asia and Europe, the existence of mass prostitution and the structure of the market, which makes use of the media, airlines, hotel chains, international communication and the banks, mean that it could neither exist nor develop without the tacit or implicit agreement of the institutions". This kind of trafficking in women for prostitution is linked with economic development policies of so-called "promotional states" which directly or indirectly foster sex tourism for the remission of foreign currency.

Additionally, Asian women bear the brunt of migration policies which channel them into gendered jobs, such as domestic labour and "entertainment" that often become sexually exploitative. The internationalization of the labour markets, and free trade, has also meant the internationalization of women's bodies for sex (de Dios, 1993, pp.3-11). Migration, turned into migrant trafficking, has also become a bonanza for organized crime. Large numbers of women from developing countries and, with the end of the cold war, from Russia and eastern Europe are illegally brought into western European countries for sex. Major John Alleart of the Belgian national police states that these international crime syndicates are "...very sophisticated, far-flung networks with acccess to high-tech communications equipment and the best legal advice money can buy".

Women became goods and services in an industry without national borders. The sex industry treats women as moveable property, passing them from one club to another, from one district to another, and from one country to another.

The presence of legalized or regulated brothels, eros zones, sex clubs, and recruitment agencies made all this possible--ready made and legitimate locations for the flesh handlers and trade. It was regulation that, in large part, made possible increased trafficking in women from developing countries into Europe. Sex businesses had to cut costs to compete in the sexual marketplace for cheaper and more exotic male tastes and demands so they imported women from developing countries to meet the demand (De Stoop, 1992). It has been estimated that there are between 200,000 and 400,000 prostitutes in Germany,

60 per cent of whom are foreigners, and most who work illegally within the regulated eros zones (De Stoop, 1992, p. 119). The Netherlands, which has a specific policy against trafficking in women but at the same time regulates prostitution, has an active and thriving sex industry that promotes demand for cheaper and more exotic women from developing countries.

"The Netherlands differentiated between Dutch women...and Third World women...Making the distinction between 'free' and 'forced' prostitution, their economic interests are apparent. Third World and Eastern European immigrant women in the Netherlands, Germany, and other regulationist countries lower the prostitution market value of local Dutch and German women. The price of immigrant prostitution is so low that local women's prices go down, reducing the pimps' and brothels' cuts. The result: a movement against 'trafficking in women' that promotes local prostitution on the basis of an erroneous distinction between 'free' and 'forced' prostitution to protect market prices". A large number of Dutch towns and villages have their sex clubs or their sex farms offering women deemed to be "exotic" and mostly from developing countries. Rife with contradictions, the anti-trafficking policy of the Netherlands makes it easier for traffickers to move in and out of the country because of the ready-made set up for prostitution and the relaxing of policing.

What kind of public policy and legislation do we need? For one thing, we need to encourage more countries to ratify the 1949 Convention for the Suppression of the Traffic in Persons and of the Exploitation of the Prostitution of Others, and to add a new protocol to the Convention whereby countries that have ratified it are made accountable for enforcing its provisions.

Most importantly, we need to reinforce and expand the 1949 Convention with a new Convention Against All Forms of Sexual Exploitation that, among other things, makes all prostitution and trafficking violations of a person's human rights; that de-criminalizes the women in prostitution; and that punishes pimps, procurers and customers. This new Convention also addresses the social services, educational opportunities and economic alternatives necessary for survivors of sexual exploitation.

Any feminist or human rights activist knows that legislation alone is not the answer. But legislation that punishes the perpetrators and not the victims of the crime of prostitution is necessary; together with political activism, education, economic alternatives and social services aimed at helping women in prostitution. A new Convention Against All Forms of Sexual Exploitation speaks to the seriousness of the violation of merchandising women and children sexually. It proclaims that the international community will not tolerate this abuse, regardless of the victim's age, consent, race or geography. It declares for the first time that all sexual exploitation is a violation of a person's human rights. It promotes social and economic remedies for women in prostitution, without minimizing the enforcement measures that are necessary to thwart and punish the perpetrators and customers. And it provides mechanisms for international supervision.

This new Convention Against All Forms of Sexual Exploitation recognizes that there can be no supply of women and children without the male demand for the sex of prostitution; without the sex industry's commodification of women and children; without the direct and/or tacit approval of governments in fostering sex tourism, for example, or zoned areas of prostitution; and without the exporting of a western sexual liberalism that depicts prostitution as sexual pleasure and liberation, calls it work, and tells us that prostitution is about a woman's right to control her own body!

The new Convention Against All Forms of Sexual Exploitation recognizes that women's human rights are seriously threatened by the massive and growing sexual exploitation of women, and that international policy and legislation must be made more effective in the struggle against sexual exploitation. Finally, it affirms that all women have the right to sexual autonomy and integrity.

THE VARIOUS TYPES OF VIOLATIONS

The number of deaths related to combat and the collateral damage caused by warfare are only a small part of the tremendous amount of suffering and devastation caused by conflicts. Over the course of protracted conflict, assaults on political rights and the fundamental right to life are typically widespread. Some of the gravest violations of the right to life are massacres, the starvation of entire populations, and genocide. Genocide is commonly understood as the intentional extermination of a single ethnic, racial, or religious group. Killing group members, causing them serious bodily or mental harm, imposing measures to prevent birth, or forcibly transferring children are all ways to bring about the destruction of a group. Genocide is often regarded as the most offensive crime against humanity.

The term "war crime" refers to a violation of the rules of jus in bello (justice in war) by any individual, whether military or civilian. The laws of armed conflict prohibit attacks on civilians and the use of weapons that cause unnecessary suffering or long-term environmental damage. Other war crimes include taking hostages, firing on localities that are undefended and without military significance, such as hospitals or schools, inhuman treatment of prisoners, including biological experiments, and the pillage or purposeless destruction of property. Although clearly outlawed by international law, such war crimes are common. According to Kofi Annan, Secretary-General of the United Nations, it is increasingly true that "the main aim...[of conflicts]... is the destruction not of armies but of civilians and entire ethnic groups."

Women and girls are often raped by soldiers or forced into prostitution. For a long time, the international community has failed to address the problem of sexual violence during armed conflict. However, sexual assaults, which often involve sexual mutilation, sexual humiliation, and forced pregnancy, are quite common. Such crimes are motivated in part by the long-held view that women are the "spoils" of war to which soldiers are entitled. Trafficking in women is a form of sexual slavery in which women are transported across national borders and marketed for prostitution. These so-called "comfort women" are another example of institutionalized sexual violence against women during wartime. Sexual violence is sometimes viewed as a way to destroy male and community pride or humiliate men who cannot "protect" their women. It is also used to silence women who are politically active, or simply inflict terror upon the population at large. Mass rapes may also form part of a genocidal strategy, designed to impose conditions that lead to the destruction of an entire group of people. For example, during the 1990s, the media reported that "rape and other sexual atrocities were a deliberate and systematic part of the Bosnian Serb campaign for victory in the war" in the former Yugoslavia.

Rather than simply killing off whole populations, government forces may carry out programs of torture. Torture can be either physical or psychological, and aims at the "humiliation or annihilation of the dignity of the person." Physical torture might include mutilation, beatings, and electric shocks to lips, gums, and genitals. In psychological torture, detainees are sometimes deprived of food and water for long periods, kept standing upright for hours, deprived of sleep, or tormented by high-level noise.

Torture is used in some cases as a way to carry out interrogations and extract confessions or information. Today, it is increasingly used as a means of suppressing political and ideological dissent, or for punishing political opponents who do not share the ideology of the ruling group.

In addition to torture, tens of thousands of people detained in connection with conflicts "disappear" each year, and are usually killed and buried in secret. Government forces "take people into custody, hold them in secret, and then refuse to acknowledge responsibility for their whereabouts or fate." This abduction of persons is typically intended to secure information and spread terror. In most cases, interrogations involve threats and torture, and those who are arrested are subsequently killed. Corpses are buried in unmarked graves or left at dumpsites in an attempt to conceal acts of torture and summary execution of those in custody. Because people disappear without any trace, families do not know whether their loved ones are alive or dead.

Various lesser forms of political oppression are often enacted as well. Individuals who pose a threat to those in power or do not share their political views may be arbitrarily imprisoned, and either never brought to trial or subject to grossly unfair trial procedures. Mass groups of people may be denied the right to vote or excluded from all forms of political participation. Or, measures restricting people's freedom of movement may be enforced. These include forcible relocations, mass expulsions, and denials of the right to seek asylum or return to one's home.

Political oppression may also take the form of discrimination. When this occurs, basic rights may be denied on the basis of religion, ethnicity, race, or gender. Apartheid, which denies political rights on the basis of race, is perhaps one of the most severe forms of discrimination. The system of apartheid in South Africa institutionalized extreme racial segregation that involved laws against interracial marriage or sexual relations and requirements for the races to live in different territorial areas. Certain individuals were held to be inferior by definition, and not regarded as full human beings under the law. The laws established under this system aimed at social control, and brought about a society divided along racial lines and characterized by a systematic disregard for human rights.

In addition, women are uniquely vulnerable to certain types of human rights abuses — in addition to the sexual abuse mentioned above, entrenched discrimination against women is prevalent in many parts of the world and leads to various forms of political and social oppression. This includes strict dress codes and harsh punishments for sexual "transgressions," which impose severe limitations on women's basic liberties. In addition, women in some regions (Africa, for example) suffer greater poverty than men and are denied political influence, education, and job training.

Human Rights Violations and Intractable Conflict

Many have noted the strong interdependence between human rights violations and intractable conflict. Abuse of human rights often leads to conflict, and conflict typically results in human rights violations. It is not surprising, then, that human rights abuses are often at the center of wars and that protection of human rights is central to conflict resolution.

Violations of political and economic rights are the root causes of many crises. When rights to adequate food, housing, employment, and cultural life are denied, and large groups of people are excluded from the society's decision-making processes, there is likely to be great social unrest. Such conditions often give rise to justice conflicts, in which parties demand that their basic needs be met. Indeed, many conflicts are sparked or spread by violations of human rights. For example, massacres or torture may inflame hatred and strengthen an adversary's determination to continue fighting. Violations may also lead to further violence from the other side and can contribute to a conflict's spiraling out of control.

On the flip side, armed conflict often leads to the breakdown of infrastructure and civic institutions, which in turn undermines a broad range of rights. When hospitals and schools are closed, rights to adequate health and education are threatened. The collapse of economic infrastructure often results in pollution, food shortages, and overall poverty. These various forms of economic breakdown and oppression violate rights to self-determination and often contribute to further human tragedy in the form of sickness, starvation, and lack of basic shelter. The breakdown of government institutions results in denials of civil rights, including the rights to privacy, fair trial, and freedom of movement. In many cases, the government is increasingly militarized, and police and judicial systems are corrupted. Abductions, arbitrary arrests, detentions without trial, political executions, assassinations, and torture often follow.

In cases where extreme violations of human rights have occurred, reconciliation and peacebuilding become much more difficult. Unresolved human rights issues can serve as obstacles to peace negotiations. This is because it is difficult for parties to move toward conflict transformation and forgiveness when memories of severe violence and atrocity are still primary in their minds.

What Can Be Done?

International humanitarian law has been enacted to preserve humanity in all circumstances, even during conflicts. Such law "creates areas of peace in the midst of conflict, imposes the principle of a common humanity, and calls for dialogue." It rules out unlimited force or total war and seeks to limit the use of violence in the hopes of maintaining the necessary conditions for a return to peace. Various international committees are in place to monitor compliance with human rights standards and report any violations. When breaches do occur, they are brought to the attention of international tribunals or tried in an international court or war crimes tribunal.

But conflicts sometimes progress beyond the state at which international law can help. As the number of victims grows and more individuals are taken prisoner, tortured, or executed, it becomes more difficult to resort to the legal path. In addition, it is often difficult to "reconcile the safeguarding of human rights with conflict resolution."

Many peacekeeping and conflict-prevention initiatives have failed both to protect human rights and help the parties towards conflict resolution. In part this is due to the fact that while wars between states have diminished, wars within states have escalated. Many internal conflicts involve a surge in organized violence. Genocide, crimes against humanity, and aggression against civilians have become a central part of warfare in these "internal" conflicts. Such violence often arises out of identity issues — in-group/out-group dynamics — and attempts of one ethnic or religious group to gain and maintain political control and to exclude other groups. Such conflicts are often not fought over principles or ideas, but rather focus on differences. The "outsiders" are dehumanized, making human rights violations such as severe discrimination or ethnic cleansing all the more psychologically feasible. Thus, attacks on human rights are often at the very heart of these internal conflicts.

In response, public authorities must regain control of organized violence. This means a re-establishment of the rule of law and a rebuilding of trust in public authorities. In addition, more inclusive, democratic values are needed to defuse exclusivist ideals. In the face of such violations, leaders must champion international legal norms and human rights. These human rights norms are central to the maintenance of civil society, and necessary for grounding attitudes of tolerance and mutual respect within communities. Serious difficulties arise, however, when those in power are responsible for human rights violations. In this case, outside intervention is necessary to stop the abuse.

DEFINING 'TRAFFICKING'

The definition of trafficking can be found in the various sections of ITPA. Section 5 speaks about procuring, taking and even inducing a person for the sake of prostitution. Even attempt to procure and attempt to take or cause a person to carry on prostitution amounts to trafficking. Therefore 'trafficking' has been given a broad scope.

Though it is focused on child trafficking, the definition is comprehensive. Under section 2, "child trafficking" means "the procurement, recruitment, transportation, transfer, harbouring or receipt of persons, legally or illegally, within or across borders, by means of threat or use of force or other forms of coercion, of abduction, of fraud, of deception, of the abuse of power or of a position of vulnerability or of giving or receiving payments or benefits to achieve the consent of a person having control over another person, for monetary gain or otherwise".

The Offence of Trafficking, Essentially, has the Following Ingredients

The displacement could be from one house to another, one village to another, one district to another, one state to another or from one country to another. Displacement is also possible within the same building. An example will clarify the point. Presume that the brothel keeper controls several young women who are inmates and that one of the women has a teenage daughter staying with her. If the brothel keeper, by duress or bribe, manages to get the mother to agree to allow the teenager to be used for CSE, the teenager has been moved out of the 'mother's community' and into the 'brothel community'. This displacement is adequate to constitute trafficking.

Exploitation of the Trafficked Person

The ITPA and related laws envisage sexual exploitation of the trafficked person. The process of exploitation may be manifest, as in a brothel, or latent, as in certain massage parlours, dance bars, etc, where it takes place under the facade of a legitimate commercial activity.

Commercialization of Exploitation and Commodification of the Victim

The trafficked victim is exploited as if she is a commodity. The exploiters generate revenue out of the exploitation. They may share a part of the revenue with the victim too. The victim who is getting a share of the money generated is often 'branded' as an accomplice and arrested/charge-sheeted and even convicted.

The trafficked victim, whose freedom even to think, let alone move out, is dictated by the exploiters, should never be treated as an accomplice. Even if she gets a share of the 'earnings', the fact that she has been trafficked to CSE does not alter her status as a victim.

The organized crime of trafficking

Human trafficking is a crime of crimes. It is a basket of crimes. In this basket one can dig out the elements of abduction, kidnapping, illegal detainment, illegal confinement, criminal intimidation, hurt, grievous hurt, sexual assault, outraging modesty, rape, unnatural offences, selling and buying of human beings, servitude, criminal conspiracy, abetment etc. Therefore, multiple abuse and abusers located at different points of time and place together constitute the organized crime of trafficking. A host of human rights violations like denial of privacy, denial of justice, denial of access to justice, deprivation of basis rights and dignity etc constitute other part of the exploitation. Therefore, there is no doubt that trafficking is an organized crime.

The trafficked person

In the context of ITPA and related laws, a trafficked person could be a male or a female of any age who has been trafficked for CSE in a brothel or any place where CSE takes place. ITPA provides punishment even for attempt to traffic a person. Therefore, even before the person is physically trafficked, the law comes into operation.

Child

Child is a person who has not attained the age of 18 years. Any child who is vulnerable to trafficking is considered a "person in need of care and protection" under the Juvenile Justice Act, 2000.

Law enforcement agencies are duty bound to rescue such children, produce them before the Child Welfare Committee and extend all care and attention.

Trafficked adult

Regarding adults, the mere consent of the person does not exclude the possibility of trafficking. If the consent was obtained under duress, coercion, fear or any pressure, then the consent has no meaning and, therefore, all such instances amount to trafficking. Thus, even when an adult woman is 'picked up' from a brothel on the charge of 'soliciting', it cannot be presumed that she is guilty of soliciting unless and until the 'mens rea' is investigated. A woman trafficked for CSE is a victim of CSE and not an accused.

Traffickers and other exploiters

Trafficking is an organized crime. There are several persons involved at several places, starting with place of recruitment, places of transit and places of exploitation.

Therefore, the list of exploiters includes the following:

- The brothel in charge and other exploiters in the brothel, or the final place of exploitation, which would also include:
  - The brothel "madam" or the person in charge of the 'dance bar' or 'massage parlour' or such other place where exploitation takes place.
  - The 'managers' and all other dramatis personae in such places.
  - The hoteliers or persons in charge of hotels, etc where exploitation takes place. This includes keepers of places/vehicles used as a brothel, persons who allow premises to be used as a brothel, persons who detain victims in brothels and other places of exploitation, and those who allow public places to be used for prostitution.
- The "customer" or "clientele", who is the abuser of the trafficked

woman, is undoubtedly, an exploiter. He is the one who perpetuates 'demand' and CSE and is, therefore liable under ITPA and other laws..

- *The financiers*: All those who finance the various processes involved in trafficking are part of the nexus. This may include those who finance recruitment, transportation, stay, accommodation, and even those who indulge in money lending and borrowing at the brothels.
- *The abettors*: All those who abet or support the exploitation or any process involved in trafficking are triable under ITPA.
- *Those who are living on the earnings of CSE*: Any person who knowingly lives, wholly or partly, on the earnings of prostitution is liable. This includes all those who have a share in the illegal benefits derived from the exploitation. The financiers who lend or collect money from the brothels and do business out of such transaction are also liable under this part. The hotelier who profits from the exploitation of girls is undoubtedly an accused u/s 4 ITPA.
  - The spotter, the recruiter, the seller, the purchaser, the contractor, the agent or anybody acting on their behalf.
  - The transporters, the harbourers and those who provide shelter are also part of the racket.
- *All conspirators*: In nearly all trafficking situations, several persons conspire at the various stages involved in the process of exploitation, thereby constituting a case of conspiracy. If there is a meeting of minds, followed by an overt act in pursuance thereof, the law of conspiracy is attracted. The ITPA, those who conspire to allow any premises to be used as a brothel or those who live on the earnings of exploitation, even partly, or those who procure or induce or take the person for prostitution are all considered conspirators.

Therefore, the list of exploiters and abusers is inevitably long, undulated and not always apparent at first glance. Only professional investigation can expose the linkages involved and bring all such persons to book.

Registering the Crime (FIR) at the Police Station (PS)

- There should not be any delay in registering FIR.
- The FIR has to be on the statement of the complainant. The statement cannot be altered or amended by the police. If the complainant is the victim herself, she may be traumatized and, therefore, may not be able to recall the events which constitute specific offences. The police officer can help her to recall such events. Even otherwise, the statement of the victim u/s 161 or 164 CrPC, recorded in due course, should bring in all details, including those which have been missed out in the FIR.

- Anybody can be the complainant. If nobody comes forth, the police official should be the complainant.
- Jurisdiction of the PS need not be disputed. As trafficking is a continuing offence, the FIR can be lodged at the source or destination. Both courts have jurisdiction. This has been specifically provided u/s 5(3) ITPA. However if two or more FIRs are lodged at different PS on the same issue, the police officials can consult each other and transfer the evidence and case documents to one of the PS, who can follow it up thereafter.
- The copy of the FIR has to be given free of cost to the complainant.
- Female witnesses/victims are to be interviewed at the place of their choice. Police should go to them for the interview, and not vice versa.
- No female witness should be summoned to the police station after sunset.
- Do not deny the right of the victim/complainant to know the progress of information.
- Do maintain proper and regular contact with the victim and her well wishers, including the NGO who is attending to her.
- FIR is the first document in the process of justice delivery. The steps that follow are mostly dependent on the FIR. Distorted FIR where the victim has been shown as accused entails further violations and harm to the victim. Therefore, victim must be projected as victim and this be done loud and clear from the FIR onwards.
- Do register cases under the relevant provisions of ITPA and other laws which are applicable, IPC, special legislations like Bonded Labour System Act,1976, Child Labour Act 1986, Children Act 1933, Maharashtra Control of Organised Crime Act 1999 etc.
- All cases of trafficking be treated as 'Grave Crimes' or 'Special Report' Crimes and be investigated and supervised by senior police officials, specially those who are sensitized and trained for the same. The SP/DCP can take initiative in this.
- Do understand the abuser-abused dynamics involved. All steps should be oriented accordingly.

Prosecutor Role in Prevention of Trafficking

The prosecutor has a large role to play in preventing trafficking.

- If the trafficker is convicted and kept behind bars, as a corollary, the trafficker is being deprived from indulging in trafficking. Therefore, by aggressive law enforcement, prosecutors can ensure prevention of trafficking.
- If the post conviction measures are taken properly against the trafficker

and other exploiters, it will make a tremendous impact in preventing trafficking.

- Eviction of brothels and such other places of commercial sexual exploitation carried out effectively, is another method of preventing trafficking. Prosecutor should take initiative u/s 18 ITPA.
- Post rescue care and attention of victims and survivors, if carried out properly, in such a way that they are rehabilitated just as to their best interest, would mean prevention of re-trafficking. Prosecutors can play a role in such post rescue activities by involving the government department or the civil society either directly or by taking up with the concerned Magistrate depending on the issues concerned and getting an appropriate direction issued by the Magistrate to the concerned government agency/NGO.

CRIMINAL ACTS AND RIGHTS VIOLATIONS ON THE TRAFFICKED PERSONS

In the existing scenario, trafficking is usually confused with prostitution and therefore, there is no proper understanding of the seriousness of trafficking. It would be appropriate here to list out the wrongs, violations, harms and crimes that are committed by various persons on a trafficked victim.

These violations can be realised only during a careful interview of a trafficked person. Once the victim is allowed, facilitated and promoted to speak, the unheard story will reveal a long list of violating acts perpetrated on her. As a typical example, under the Indian Penal Code, a trafficked girl child has been subjected to a multitude of violations. She has been:

- Displaced from her community, which tantamounts to kidnapping/ abduction
- Procured illegally.
- Sold by somebody
- Bought by somebody
- Imported from a foreign country
- Wrongfully restrained
- Wrongfully confined
- Physically tortured/injured
- Subjected to criminal force
- Mentally tortured/harassed/assaulted
- Criminally intimidated
- Outraged of her modesty
- Raped/gang raped/repeatedly raped

- Subjected to perverse sexual exploitation
- Defamed
- Subjected to unlawful compulsory labour
- Victim of criminal conspiracy

This list is only illustrative and not exhaustive. Undoubtedly, in every case, the trafficked person is a victim of at least one or more of the violations. Oftentimes victims become pregnant as they are subjected to non-protective sex. If the victim has been subjected to miscarriage then the liability of the offender falls under the Sections 312 to 318 IPC.

In some cases, the process of exploitation has proven fatal wherein the victim succumbs to the direct effects of the harm or to the consequential problems arising thereof. This means that the offence of homicide/murder is also attracted. The offences envisaged under the ITPA are specific to the context of CSE. They are briefly listed out below:

- Keeping or managing a brothel or allowing premises to be used as a brothel
- Living on earnings of prostitution.
- Procuring, inducing, trafficking or taking persons for the sake of prostitution. Even attempt to procure or take would constitute the offence.
- Detaining a person in any premises where prostitution is carried out
- Anybody who carries on prostitution, or anybody with whom such prostitution is carried on, in the vicinity of public places
- Seducing or soliciting for the purpose of prostitution in any public place or within sight of a public place
- Seduction of a person in custody.

The Juvenile Justice Act, 2000 also has penal provisions. Anybody in control of a child who assaults, abandons, exposes or willfully neglects the child or procures him to be assaulted, abandoned or exposed causing the child unnecessary mental or physical suffering, is liable under S. 23 JJ Act There are so many Human Rights violations that take place on trafficked person. The list includes the following:

- Deprivation of the right to life.
- Deprivation of the right to security.
- Deprivation of dignity.
- Deprivation of the right to access to justice and redressal of grievances.
- Denial of access to health services.
- Denial of right to self determination.
- Denial of right to return to own community.

- Double jeopardy.
- Denial of right to representation.
- Denial of right to be heard before decision making.

The list of rights violations is long and several such violations can be listed out depending on the provisions of the Constitution/Protocols/Conventions etc.

Which law to use and when

ITPA, being a special legislation, has comprehensive, stringent and effective provisions to address the issues in trafficking and consequent exploitation. However, there is no bar in utilizing the provisions of ITPA along with IPC etc.

In any given context, the investigating police officer should file charge-sheet against the accused under the graver parts of all laws which are applicable. Do not hesitate to involve the provisions of ITPA along with IPC, JJ Act, and other legislations which would apply to the facts and circumstances of the case under investigation. One has to be careful in applying proper sections of law. Never victimize a trafficked woman u/s 8 ITPA or any other section of any law. When investigation brings home the point that she has been sexually exploited against her informed consent, charge sheet be filed against all her exploiters not only under ITPA, but also under the relevant sections of IPC, dealing with sexual assault.

Consent obtained under lure, deceit, duress, coercion, compulsion, force etc. is not 'consent' in the legal sense. Furthermore, if the victim is a girl child, the offence is complete even if there was consent.

THE STRENGTHS OF ITPA AND HOW BEST TO USE THEM

ITPA is a comprehensive legislation which gives power and strength to the law enforcement/justice delivery agencies to combat and prevent trafficking.

Since its enactment in 1956, the legislation was amended by the Indian Parliament twice, in 1978 and 1986. The latter amendment focused on prevention, a provision which is not so common in the legal regime across the world. However, for various reasons, the different provisions of this special law are not being used and, furthermore are often misused and abused. One of the main reasons, as research has shown, is ignorance and lack of understanding of these provisions.

Therefore this checklist is a reference guide to the law enforcement agencies and other stake-holders, providing answers to several frequently asked questions and frequently overlooked aspects. *The legal regime relevant in the context of trafficking*

- Immoral Traffic Act, 1956.
- The Juvenile Justice Act, 2000.
- The Goa Children's Act, 2003.
- The Indian Penal Code, 1860.
- Procedural laws.
- Preventive Sections of CrPC.
- Other special laws relevant to the context.

The inherent strengths of ITPA

General Provisions

- The law applies to trafficking of males and females.
- Commercial sexual exploitation of anybody is an offence.
- The law gives specific attention to women's rights and child rights.
- The law provides a specific mandate for NGO's and civil society in addressing trafficking. Perhaps there is no parallel where NGOs have been given powers in law enforcement on anti human trafficking.
- The thrust of the law is addressing trafficking and not prostitution, as is often misunderstood.
- This legislation gives specific powers to judicial magistrates and also to executive magistrates.
- This legislation gives special protection to the police officers and NGOs taking part in search, rescue etc. from any criminal or civil proceedings against them.

The Offences Under ITPA

- *S.3 ITPA*: Keeping or managing a brothel or allowing premises including vehicles to be used as a brothel.
- *S.4 ITPA*: Living on the earnings of prostitution.
- *S. 5 ITPA*: Procuring, inducing, trafficking or taking persons for the sake of prostitution. Even attempt to procure or take would constitute this offence.
- *S.6 ITPA*: Detaining a person in any premises where prostitution is carried out.
- *S.7 ITPA*: Any body who carries on prostitution, or any body with whom such prostitution is carried on, in the vicinity of public places.
- *S.8 ITPA*: Seducing or soliciting for the purpose of prostitution in any public place or within sight of a public place.
- *S.9 ITPA*: Seduction of a person in custody.

Whether "Clientele" is Liable

The answer is yes. Firstly, he should be booked u/s 5(1) (d) and u/s 7(1) ITPA. He is a person who 'causes' or 'induces' another person to carry on prostitution and is, therefore, liable u/s 5(1)(d).

Moreover he is a person "with whom prostitution is carried on" and is therefore liable u/s 7(1). Further subsection IA of section 7 ITPA makes it clear that if the offence of 'prostitution' is committed in respect to a child or minor then the person committing the offence is liable for a graver punishment and fine with a mandatory minimum imprisonment of 7 years.

Besides these provisions of ITPA, he is an abettor to all violations on the victim, which attracts S.114 IPC. If the victim is a child, S.376 IPC should be added to the charges against the "customer". If the victim is an adult, S.376 IPC will come into operation if it can be established that she had not given informed or willing consent. Moreover perverse sexual acts on the victim invite liability under S.377 IPC.

Liability of Traffickers

U/S 5 ITPA, trafficking committed, contemplated or even attempted is punishable, regardless of consent of the trafficked person. The modus operandi could include procuring, attempting to procure, inducing, taking, attempting to take, causing a person to be taken, causing or inducing a person to prostitute etc.

If the offence of trafficking is committed against the will of the person, then the offender is liable for graver punishment. If the trafficked victim is a child, the minimum punishment is 7 years of rigorous imprisonment. Depending on the facts and circumstances of the case, the traffickers are also liable u/s 4, 6, 9 ITPA. Moreover as abettors and/or conspirators they are also liable under IPC.

Jurisdiction of Police and Courts

In which police station can a trafficking offence be registered? Which Court has jurisdiction? Trafficking is a 'continuing offence' and therefore may be tried in either of the following places:

- The place from where the person has been procured, induced to go, taken or caused to be taken or from where an attempt to procure or take the person is made. This means the place where trafficking took place *i.e,* the source point.
- At the place to which the person may have gone as a result of the inducement or to which he is taken or caused to be taken or an attempt

to take him is made. This means the destination point or the point of exploitation and the transit points where the exploitation continues.

Since the court of law has jurisdiction in the source, transit and the destination points, the police stations in all these points also have jurisdiction. In this context, the following are the do's and dont's.

- In a case of trafficking, police agencies at the source point, the transit point and at the destination point have a duty and responsibility to register FIR in their police station.
- There is no legal bar in having FIRs registered both at the source point and destination point if the former is only on charge of trafficking and the latter is only on the charge of sexual exploitation. However, the best situation would be to have the FIR at one of the two places and, thereafter, the investigation should cover the entire spectrum of the offences from its origin to the last part.
- In the event of registration of two FIRs at both the source and destination points, the investigation can be clubbed together, as and when the linkage is established in evidence. Thereafter, police is free to file a charge report before the court of law at either place and simultaneously close the investigation in the other place, so as to avoid double jeopardy.
- Since attempt to trafficking is also a specific offence under this section, it gives very strong weapon to the law enforcement agencies to bring to book the traffickers as well as abettors and conspirators in trafficking.

Law of double jeopardy will not be attracted if the offences alleged are independently acted upon. For *e.g.*, there is no legal wrong if the FIR in one place is u/s 5 ITPA for trafficking and the FIR in another place is for exploitation u/s 7 ITPA, 376 IPC etc., both with respect to the same victim.

The Doctrine of Presumption As a Good Weapon for Preventing and Combating Trafficking

ITPA gives so much strength to the law enforcement agencies by virtue of the fact that the specific provisions of presumption casts onus of proof on the accused.

The following are the provisions.

- Section 3 provides punishment for keeping a brothel or allowing premises to be used as a brothel. It shall be presumed, u/s 3 (2A), that the concerned person has knowledge of the same if:
  - A report is published in a newspaper with local circulation that the premises concerned are being used for prostitution, as revealed during a search.
  - A copy of the search list is made available to the person concerned.

- If any person A, over 18 years of age, is proved to have exercised control, direction or influence over the movements of another person B, in such a manner as to show that A is aiding, abetting or compelling B to prostitute, it shall be presumed that A is knowingly living on the earnings of prostitution of another person and is liable u/s 4 ITPA.
- If a person is found with a child in a brothel, it will be presumed that the person has detained the child for CSE and is, therefore, liable for the same u/s 6(2) ITPA.
- If the medical examination shows that the child, who has been detained in a brothel, was sexually assaulted, it will be presumed u/s 6 (2A) ITPA that the child was detained for CSE and was sexually exploited. This legal presumption is a good tool to establish liability of the person.
- S.6 (3) ITPA, a person shall be presumed to have detained a woman or girl (of any age) in a brothel or upon any premises for CSE, if the person withholds from her any of her property with intent to compel/induce her to remain there. He is also liable if he threatens her with action if she takes away any such property lent/supplied to her by, or on the direction of, such a person.

CSE of Child/Minor

Law views CSE of children/minors as a grave offence and therefore, has the following special provisions u/s 7 ITPA:

- Consent is immaterial.
- Enhanced punishment for prostituting a child/minor.
- Minimum punishment is rigorous imprisonment for 7 years.
- Mandatory fine along with jail.
- If sexual exploitation of a child takes place in a Hotel, the hotel license can be cancelled..

Who can Order Rescue of a Trafficked Person

S.16 ITPA authorizes rescue of any person who is made to carry on prostitution in a brothel. The powers are given to both Judicial Magistrates and Executive Magistrates. Therefore, any of these officials may be moved for an order for the rescue of any such person. The Magistrate can order rescue of any person if he has reason to believe that any person is carrying on or is being made to carry on prostitution in a brothel. S.15 ITPA gives powers to Special Police Officers to search without warrant and carry out rescue u/s 15(4). This gives enormous powers to SPO.

Can Any Civilian Move the Magistrate and Seek Orders for Rescue of Any Person

The answer is yes. u/s 16, the Magistrate has powers to direct any police officer to rescue any person if the Magistrate has reason to believe that the rescue is required.

The source of information for the Magistrate could be government agencies or otherwise and, therefore, it includes any of the following:

- Police
- Any person authorized by the State Government
- Any NGO
- Any other source

If a Notified Police Officer is Not Available, is Rescue Possible

Yes u/s 16 ITPA, the Magistrate can authorize any police officer provided the police officer is of the rank of SI of police.

How to Prevent/Combat Misuse of Public Places

The legal provisions u/s 7 ITPA envisage a very important role of law enforcement agencies in not only taking action against the offenders who misuse public places, but also in preventing such misuse. In this context, the following aspects be taken note of.

What is a Public Place

Public place, u/s 7 ITPA, includes the following:

- Any premises within an area notified by the Government.
- Any premises within a distance of 200 metres of any place of public worship, educational institution, hotel, hospital, nursing home or other official/public domain.
- Any hotel.
- Any transport or vehicle to which public has access.
- "Any place intended for use by, or accessible to the public" is a public place. "It is not necessary that it must be public property", "Even if it is a private property, it is sufficient that the place is accessible to public". Gaurav Jain vs UOI, AIR 1997 SC 3021.

Can a Hotel Licence Be Suspended if Prostitution is Carried on in the Hotel

Yes, u/s 7(2) (c) ITPA, if the public place which is misused happens to be a hotel, the hotel licence may be suspended for a period not less than 3 months and may be extended to one year. Therefore in such circumstances, the police officer should move the concerned court for the suspension of the hotel licence.

Can the Hotel Licence be Cancelled

Yes, u/s 7(2) (c)ITPA, if it can be proved that the victim of prostitution or CSE in the hotel happens to be a child or minor, then the hotel licence is liable to be cancelled. The police officer has to move the court of the District Magistrate for the same.

Who are All Liable for Misuse of Public Places

U/s 7 ITPA, the persons liable are:

- Any person who carries on prostitution.
- Any person with whom such prostitution is carried on.
- Any keeper of a public place who permits such misuse.
- Any tenant, lessee, occupier or person in charge of any premises who permits the place or part thereof for misuse.
- Any owner, lesser, landlord of any such place, or their agents, who lets the place or part thereof for misuse or is willfully a party to the same.

Closure and Eviction of Brothels After Notice

- The District Magistrate u/s 18(1) ITPA, can act on information from police or NGO or anybody else. The Commissioner of Police or any other official who has been vested with the powers of DM is also empowered to take action under this section of law.
- The information should be that any house, room, place or portion thereof, located within a distance of 200 metres of any public place is being used as a brothel by any person, or is being used for commercial sexual exploitation of anybody.
- DM can issue notice to the owner, lesser, landlord or their agent, as well as the tenant, lessee, occupier of, or any other person in charge of such house, room, place or portion thereof.
- The notice sent to them by the DM directs that show cause be filed within 7 days of the receipt of the notice stating why the property should not be attached for misuse.
- The DM should hear the party before taking a decision.
- After hearing, if the DM is satisfied about the misuse, he can direct eviction of the occupier within 7 days of the order and direct that prior approval of the DM be obtained before letting out the place again during the following one year.
- The order of the DM is non appealable nor stayable as per S. 18(3) ITPA.

- Since closure of brothel would entail loss of 'income' for the exploiters, and no relief is available by way of appeal, this is a stringent section of law which the administrators, police, prosecutors and NGO's can effectively utilize to combat and prevent trafficking.
- The Sub Divisional Magistrate (SDM) also can exercise all these powers.

Closure and Eviction of Brothels Without Notice

S.18 (2) ITPA, the court convicting a person of any offence under S.3 ITPA or S.7 ITPA, may pass orders of closure and eviction without any notice to any such person. Therefore in the event of a conviction u/s 3 or 7 ITPA, the police/ prosecutor should immediately move the court for closure/eviction u/s 18 ITPA. However, the eviction order of the judicial magistrate is a sequel to the conviction of the person to be evicted, and cannot preceed conviction

No Appeal Against Order of Closure/Eviction

S. 18 (3) ITPA, orders passed by the DM u/s 18(1)ITPA and orders by the convicting court u/s 18(2)ITPA shall not be subject to appeal and shall not be stayed or set aside by any court, civil or criminal.

Therefore, the finality of order by a competent court is a very powerful tool to combat CSE.

Special Provisions Against CSE of Child (Under 16) and Minor (Under 18)

Anybody involved in CSE of a child/minor is liable for conviction for a minimum term of 7 years imprisonment which may go upto life imprisonment, u/s 7(1A).

- In such convictions, along with imprisonment, fine is also mandatory.
- If the abuse takes place in a hotel, and the victim is a child or minor, the hotel license shall be liable to be cancelled u/s 7(2) (c) ITPA.

Surveillance of Convicted Persons

ITPA, any person, who has earlier been convicted under ITPA or relevant sections of IPC is again convicted under ITPA, for a period of 2 years or more, may be subjected by the court to notify, just as to the rules made by the State Government in this regard, of any change of his residence or any absence from such residence after release, for a period upto 5 years. If the State rules exist, this is a potent weapon for the law enforcing agencies to keep surveillance on the movement and activity of the convicted person so as to prevent any such crime in future. If there are no rules, the state government be moved for bringing out comprehensive Rules under ITPA.

Externment of Convicted Persons

ITPA, the District Magistrate, Sub-Divisional Magistrate, or an Executive Magistrate authorized by the State Govt, has power to extern a convicted person to another place within or outside the limits of his jurisdiction. This is a powerful weapon against convicted exploiters so that they are prevented from carrying on further exploitation. The police has to move the concerned Magistrate immediately after conviction so that the Magistrate can start the externment proceedings.

Finality of Proceedings and Fast-Track Mechanisms

ITPA is a special legislation which has certain inherent provisions to ensure that the legal proceedings are not long drawn.

These provisions and restrictions are meant to be invoked by the agencies concerned so that the trial is expedited and justice is delivered without delay. The following are the provisions:

- U/s 18 ITPA, there is neither appeal nor stay against the order of eviction by a Magistrate or Court.
- Any appeal against the order for protective custody u/s 17 (4) ITPA, issued by the Magistrate shall go to the Court of Sessions, whose decision shall be final. Therefore, there is no appeal beyond the Sessions Court.
- Special Courts for the trial of offences under ITPA can be constituted not only by State Government but also by the Central Government.
- *Summary Trial*: Whenever necessary, the State Government may authorize the Court to try cases summarily. However, the maximum punishment in Summary Trial is up to 1 year. If the Court thinks that enhanced punishment is called for, then the case can be reverted to regular trial.

Special Police Officer of the State Government

U/s 13 (1) ITPA the State Government can notify one or more police officers, not below the rank of Inspector of Police, as SPO having powers over a specific jurisdiction, which may include the entire state.

Since many trafficking cases have inter-district and even inter-state ramifications, it is better to issue such notifications, without jurisdictional restrictions.

The jurisdiction of the SPO is to be at least co-terminus with "that of the offender" so that the SPO can carry out unrestricted investigation.

Shortage of Police Officers

Yes, S.13 (2A) ITPA authorizes the District Magistrate to notify any retired police officer or any retired military officer as SPO.It is advisable that the Superintendent of Police identifies appropriate retired officials and moves the DM for notification.

Police Officer Essential

U/s 13(3) (a) ITPA, the SPO notified by the State government shall be assisted by an adequate number of Subordinate Police Officers including women police officers, wherever practicable. The best situation would be to notify a combination of male and female police officers for each unit. Wherever women police officers of the rank of Inspector or above are available, they should be notified as SPO.If woman police official is not available, the SPO should take assistance of woman NGO/social worker.

India Notify Special Police Officers Under ITPA

U/s 13(3) (4) ITPA, Govt. of India can notify Anti-trafficking police officers with powers throughout India. Such ATPO can be appointed for investigating offences:

- Under ITPA
- Under any law dealing with sexual exploitation of persons committed in more than one State. Therefore, a notified ATPO will have powers to investigate, crimes relating to not only trafficking but also other such crimes, relating to pornographic rackets, 'sale' and 'purchase' of women etc., which have inter-state and international ramifications.

The Government of India has appointed officers of and above the rank of Inspector of Police in CBI as Trafficking Police Officers having jurisdiction throughout India to investigate any offence under ITPA or any other law dealing with sexual exploitation of persons committed in more than one State.

How to Invoke CBI Investigation

Since CBI derives its strength under the DSPE Act, and since law and order is a 'State subject' under the Constitution of India, the State Govt has to issue notification u/s 6 DSPE Act authorizing CBI to take over such crimes. This is to be followed by a notification of Govt. of India u/s 5 DSPE Act, extending the powers of CBI to carry out the task.

Therefore, despite the notification dated 28 August 2001 by the Govt. of India, CBI takes over investigation of a crime of trafficking when the State Police, having original jurisdiction over the case, hands over the case file to

CBI. However, if there is an order by the Supreme Court or any High Court, directing CBI to take over such a case, CBI cannot and will not wait for the notifications by the Govt. Often such directions of the High Court or the Apex Court arise out of Public Interest Litigation.

Law Enforcement and Justice Delivery Under ITPA

ITPA is a social legislation which envisages a large role for NGOs/CBOs and social workers. The following are noteworthy:

- *Advisory Body*: The State Govt. may notify, u/s 13(3) (b) ITPA, a nonofficial advisory body of leading social workers including women social workers. This body has powers to advise the SPO on questions of general importance, regarding the working of ITPA. Therefore, this body can advise and facilitate the police to carry out rescue, ensure that the rights of rescued persons are protected initiate steps for victims' best care and attention, keeping in view victims' best interests, take steps for empowerment and rehabilitation of victims take steps for stringent action against traffickers and other exploiters and initiate and implement steps for prevention of trafficking and network with all concerned government and non government agencies.
- *Accompanying Police during search*: The SPO while carrying out search for victims or even accused persons should arrange two or more respectable persons of the locality (one of whom should be a woman, as provided u/s 15(2) ITPA to attend and witness the searches. NGOs are the appropriate agencies to be contacted by police in such situations. The male witness should be from the locality, whereas the female witness could be from any where, vide proviso to S.15 (2) ITPA. It would be better to take a lady social activist along. Police officials should maintain a list (ready reckoner) of women activists and NGO's, whose services can be called upon in such situations. This section gives a legal right to NGOs to be part of the rescue process.
- *Interviewing rescued/removed persons*: U/s 15(6A) ITPA, any female person rescued or removed during a search can be interviewed by the police officer only in the presence of a female police officer or a female member of NGO.This gives a legal right to NGOs to be part of the investigation process.
- *Home verification of rescued persons*: A mandatory duty is cast upon the Magistrate u/s 17(2) ITPA to cause home verification of the rescued person before taking a final decision regarding her rehabilitation. Direction is to be given to the Probation Officer. The Magistrate can call upon NGOs to carry out the task. Even the Probation Officer who has been tasked for the same can, in turn, entrust the job to NGOs. This

gives a legal right to NGOs to be part of the rehabilitation process.

- *NGOs to advise Magistrate on rehabilitation*: The Magistrate may, as provided u/s 17(5) ITPA. Summon a panel of five respectable persons, three of whom shall be women, to assist him in taking decision in home verification and rehabilitation of the rescued person. It would be better that the Magistrate is provided with a list of NGOs who are working in the field so that their services can be utilized at the appropriate time. This section also gives a legal right to NGOs to be part of the justice delivery process and an opportunity to ensure that the processes confirm to the principles of human rights and the decisions are in the best interest of the rescued person.

Refuse to Cooperate with Police in Search and Rescue

As per S.15 (3) ITPA, any person who, without reasonable cause, refuses or neglects, to attend and witness a search when called upon to do so by an order in writing, delivered or tendered to him, shall be deemed to have committed an offence u/s 187 IPC. Though, it is a non-cognizable and bailable offence, it entails punishment upto 6 months imprisonment and fine.

Verification of the Rescued Persons

As per the mandatory requirements u/s 17(2) ITPA, Home verification of the rescued person needs to be carried out. The points of verification include the correctness of age, character and antecedents, the suitability of the parents/ guardian/husband for taking charge of the person, the nature of the influence which the condition in the home is likely to have on the person if she is sent home, the personality of the person and the prospects of rehabilitation u/s 17(5) ITPA. Since the task of verification can be entrusted to NGO's, the law enforcement officials need to network with appropriate NGO's and bring to the notice of the Magistrate the name, address and other details of the NGO's. Once the task is assigned to the NGO's, it needs to be facilitated and followed up so that the verification is expedited. Objectivity is called for in the process of verification.

The verifying authority should consult the victim, her well-wishers, friends, parents, guardians, neighbours and all persons who can share information. There are instances where the guardians themselves have indulged in trafficking. Therefore extreme care is called for in arriving at conclusions.

Police Officers and NGO's against Litigation

S. 15(6) ITPA provides a safety clause for bonafide work. The authorized police officer, the witnesses, and the NGOs who take part, attend, or witness a search shall not be liable to any litigation, civil or criminal proceedings, against them for any bonafide work in connection with or for purposes of the search being carried out u/s 15 ITPA.

PREVENTION OF TRAFFICKING: DO'S AND DON'TS

Prention is the sumum bonum of all activities that one can do to address trafficking. It includes prevention of re-trafficking too.

- Law enforcement processes should be integrated and comprehensive. There should be a combination of steps for Prosecution, alongwith Protection and Prevention. An integrated P-P-P model is essential. Adequate attention should be paid to all the three legs and the efforts should be dove-tailed.
- Prevention of trafficking requires attention at all the scenes of crime. Accordingly they can be classified into three:
    - Prevention at the demand point: This requires proper investigation, prosecution, conviction, addressing the demand effectively and all post conviction measures. This also involves proper care and protection of victims to ensure prevention of re-trafficking.
    - Prevention at the transit area: Trafficking when carried out from one place to another involves transit places. The major hub of such transit are railway junctions, bus stops, ports, border entry posts etc. 'Rights intervention centre' started by the NGO 'SEWA' of Gorakhpur at Sanauli, with the partnership of local police, is a classic example of prevention of trafficking. In a span of nine months, 65 girls could be prevented from exploitation, by interception at the transits place. Effective surveillance and watch on suspects at the transit places by deputing spotters in association with NGOs can be a good method. The details of transit routes, mode of transport and the names of persons involved could be gathered on careful interviewing of victims and interrogation of suspects.
    - Prevention at the source point requires several steps, like addressing vulnerabilities, attending to missing persons, networking with the civil society and Panchayati Raj institutions, empowering the vulnerable sections along with other police strategies on prevention. The details of these strategies are discussed below:

(a) Do ensure conviction, punishment and stringent action against traffickers and all exploiters.

(b) Do ensure post conviction steps. This includes closure and eviction of brothels and other places of exploitation, externment of the convicted persons, surveillance and dossiers on convicted and suspected persons, confiscation of illegal assets etc.

that in one year more than 30,000 children are reported missing and one-third of them remain untraced. This study has established with examples that many of these 'missing children are, in fact, trafficked. Hence prevention of trafficking requires the following:

- Do realise the linkage between 'missing' persons and 'trafficked' persons, because many who are 'reported missing' have been, in fact, trafficked.
- Do cross-check the list of persons rescued from brothels and other places of exploitation with the list of persons reported missing from anywhere in India.
- The linkage will also help to expose the traffickers, trafficking routes and trafficking processes.
- Do follow up missing women and children till a logical conclusion is arrived at. Constitute special teams to go into the root of the issue and ensure rescue/return/recovery of the missing person. Follow-up all the leads in this process to ensure that those responsible for making the person missing are brought to book. Any slight suspicion should immediately be taken cognizance of a proper FIR registered, followed by sustained investigation.
- It is often seen that the trafficked person is blamed 'as if he/she is responsible for being 'missing'. One should realise that more often children who were missing are from the vulnerable sections of the society and are essentially 'children in need of care and protection'.
- Provide the details of missing children to the police agencies and NGOs who are working in the rescue of trafficked persons so that they could also follow up.
- Network with NGOs/Helpline/Child line, etc. to identify the linkage. Expand the database of missing persons to link it up with trafficked and rescued persons.
- Do a mapping of missing persons for a specific time in a particular place and undertake special operations to locate them. One linkage to a brothel elsewhere in the country could be a clue for locating many who are still missing.

- *Utilizing preventive sections of CrPC*: Section 110 CrPC provides enough scope for preventing offences. Executives Magistrates are vested with the powers. The Magistrate can bind down the persons for ensuring good behaviour. Steps u/s 111, 116, 121, 122 CrPC will further affirm the preventive actions against likely offenders.
- *Helplines*: The Police Managers should establish proper and functional networks with the existing help-lines like child-line, Women's helpline

etc. Such help-lines should be linked up to the police control rooms and police stations for prompt response.

- *Strengthening Police Stations*: Institutionalization of the response systems requires that the police stations, being the fundamental unit of police administration and public service, be strengthened. Besides empowering the police stations with the required human and material resources, their capabilities need to be enriched by regular training and discussions. The methodology prescribed for the functioning and training of STF are applicable here too.
- *Involving local self government agencies*: The Panchayat Raj Institutions have lot of sway over the local public. Therefore their services can be effectively channelised towards the prevention strategies. Tamil Nadu has started this process through a Government order issued in 2002 followed by training/orientation programmes for PRI members on preventing trafficking. This model could be adopted by others too. Police officers should network with the PRI's, orient them, sensitize them and involve them in the anti trafficking processes. District level and village level Monitoring Committees could be set up by the DM/SP, involving all stake holders and PRI's.
- *Data-base*: One of the essential ingredients of crime management is to develop a proper data base. It is utmost essential for not only combating trafficking but also prevention of trafficking. As of today lack of database is one of the major impediments in law enforcement. Since theInvestigating officials are more or less confined to their limited jurisdictions, the police managers like SP/DCP and other higher formations should take initiative in developing the data base, not only on traffickers and exploiters, but also on victims and survivors. The data should include the profile of the offenders, the area of operations of the traffickers, their networks, the details of source, transit, destination etc. This should be regularly updated. The second aspect of data base is data analysis. This would facilitate in developing criminal intelligence. The third aspect of data base is sharing of criminal intelligence with all concerned and initiating appropriate action for combating and preventing trafficking. Collation, analysis and dissemination of data and intelligence are professional aspects of policing and therefore the responsibility for the same is with the police managers. It is advisable to involve appropriate NGOs working in the field and associate them fully in all activities.
- *Anti Human Trafficking Unit*: An in-depth understanding of the dimension of trafficking will clearly bring to focus the essentiality of multi stake holder partnership in preventing and combating trafficking.

The law enforcement agencies need to have close association with other departments like health, social welfare, labour, department of women and child, department of correctional administration, development department, panchayati raj institutions etc. These government agencies need to have symbiotic partnership with the NGOs working in this field. The police managers especially the SP/DCP should take initiative in setting up an AHTU by developing close partnership of the police with all these responders. Such an AHTU will be the best mechanism in the given situation to prevent and combat trafficking. The officials and NGOs who are put in the AHTU should be specially trained and oriented. Protocols should be drawn up to demarcate the role of each stake holder. The scope of AHTU can be widened to include Corporates so that they could lend the services of their corporate social responsibility for not only funding the programmes but also giving appropriate back up support in empowering the survivors, utilizing the services for productive activities, marketing their produces etc.

Sexual Exploitation

Forced Prostitution: Prostitution is the most documented and visible form of trafficking. In the case of children, it is always forced prostitution and therefore must not be used interchangeably with 'sex-work', which may be undertaken voluntarily also.

Their playground is the brothel, they are the playthings and toys of lust. India reportedly has the world's largest concentration of child prostitutes, accounting for one in every four of the global number. India's children are no strangers to exploitation, but none of it is as brutuish as the terror to which these particularly unfortunate kids have been subjected. Raped at 10, tortured and starved to submission at 11, an abortion at 12 —and sexually violated 15 times a day till age and AIDS throws them on to the streets.

A large number of child prostitutes in India are girls from Nepal and Bangladesh. Almost 15 per cent of the prostitutes enter the profession before the age of 15, and 25 per cent enter between 15 and 18 years.

Around 60 per cent of the prostitutes belong to the scheduled castes, tribes and backward classes Amongst those trafficked into India from Nepal for prostitution, it is said, "most females are girls under 16. Many are also between 12 and 15 years, some as young as 8. Young girls are lucrative sale. Majority of the Indian girls into prostitution belong to the Scheduled Caste and Scheduled Tribe communities. A significant number of children in prostitution are children of prostitutes.

Religious Prostitution

Religious prostitution is practised in various parts of India and Nepal. Devadasi cults are found in Southern India and there are reports of temple prostitution being also practised in other parts of the country such as Uttar Pradesh and Orissa. Pre-pubertal girls, aged between five and nine years, from poor, low caste homes go through an initiation rite at the local temple during full moon where they are dedicated to the diety. After a girl is married to the deity by the tali rite, she is branded with a hot iron on both shoulders and her breast.

The temple priest then employs her. Sometimes, even before menarche, she is auctioned for her virginity; the deflowering ceremony known as udilumbuvadu becomes the privilege of the highest bidder. The market value of a girl falls after she attains puberty, when she is said to have no recourse other than prostitution.

Yellama is represented as the principal goddess who is worshipped but, as recent research has shown, the practice of devadasi is prevalent in many other temple towns and other deities such as Meenakshi, Jagannath and Hanuman are also propitiated.

Religious prostitution is known by different names such as Venkatasani, Jogini, Nailis, Muralis and Theradiyan. The victims of religious prostitution, the Jogins and Devadasis join at a very early age. 95 per cent of Harijan familes send about 5-10 thousand girls every year in this practice.

Sex-tourism

Any child without a physical handicap, irrespective of caste or class can be pushed into satisfying the sexual needs of the tourists. Conversations with groups working on sex tourism reveal that the tourists lure children with small toys, trinkets and fancy gifts. Goa, one of the hottest tourist spots in the country is known for child-sex tourism. "Goa is a known destination for sex tourists", says the Special Rapporteur, Ms. Ofelia Calcetas-Santos. There are now reports of tourists moving from Goa to areas of North Karnataka such as Gokarna and Karwar, which are presently being developed for tourism. Foreign tourists have settled permanently in the Om and Kudle beaches, which have become hideout points and these are also areas where the tourists are sexually exploiting children. Another two popular destinations that are emerging for paedophilic activity are Kovalam and Mamallapuram.

Puri in Orissa is also another haven for the commercial sexual abuse of children. Other areas in the North, especially along the highways are also spots where trafficking of children happens.

The golden triangle of tourism on the Agra-Delhi-Jaipur belt has spawned a flourishing trade in child prostitution among Rajasthan's nomadic tribes of entertainers, with middlemen coercing the tribal communities to send girls as young as 10 years to serve in sex shops along the highway. The dalals, with an eye on the booming market among tourists, travelling businessmen and truck drivers who believe that sex with a young child may keep them safe from diseases, are forcing the community to send out their girl children, most of whom are between the age 10-14. "10 year old tribals forced into sex trade in Rajasthan". With the spread of the sex-tourism networks to all the well-known tourist destinations and with the alarming rise in HIV/AIDS in the country, the need to tackle this problem is becoming even more crucial. Recognising that children from Kovalam are being used for sex tourism, activists have found that people from other parts of Kerala are refusing to marry persons from there.

Pornography

Street children or children from poor families and middle class families fall prey to foreigners who attract them through the riches of the world and lure them into such exploitation. In 1991, in Goa, Freddy Albert Peat was booked for using children for pornography and selling young boys to foreign paedophiles. He had managed to stay away from law, from being caught for over 25 years..

In December 2000, Forum Against Child Sexual Exploitation, a Mumbai based NGO, helped the police unearth a child pornography racket being operated by a Swiss Couple from a posh hotel "the Resort' at Marve Road, Madh Island, Mumbai.

Illegal Activities

Begging

The children with a handicap are more vulnerable in a situation where trafficking is for the purpose of begging. Poverty and handicap is the ideal combination for the children to be trafficked in the belief that the handicap will induce sympathy in the giver. That belief puts the child beggar at serious risk of being deliberately maimed in order to increase his or her earning potential. Street children, who are easily available to be picked up, are another vulnerable category.

Organ Trading

Although very little information is available on this aspect of trafficking, newspaper reports and anecdotal reports from persons working on trafficking issues clearly indicate that trafficking of children for organ replacements for persons who can afford to buy them is a "lucrative business" for the traffickers.

Drug Peddling and Smuggling

Use of children for drug peddling is common because it is assumed that they would be suspected the least. Children are initiated into drugs and then used as conduits for peddling. It appears that the major factor pushing girls from Nagaland in the North East towards sex trade is drugs. A study carried out by Butterflies, a Delhi based NGO, reveals that "girl children as young as nine or ten are initiated into drugs and sexually abused. They are also used as couriers, as they are rarely frisked by the cops"

TRAFFICKING FOR AND THROUGH MARRIAGE

Trafficking for marriage is an inter-country and intra-country phenomenon. What makes this form of trafficking very difficult to challenge under law is that there is formalisation of the marriage. Young girls from poor families are taken in marriage to another state or country. Adhikar, a human rights group based in Bhubaneswar, discovered that a number of girls were being taken as brides from the Nayagarh district of Orissa, after paying bride price, and married to young men in Jhansi.

They managed to rescue some of them, but there are still many who are untraced. From Bangladesh, women are trafficked out to India for marriage to Indian men who find it difficult to marry for reasons of dower payment. In Chapainabaganj alone, over 10,000 women have been trafficked to Lucknow, Firozabad, and other places in India for marriage reasons during last 15 years. In this case, women includes young adolescent girls.

"Hundreds of Bengali women and teenage girls are routinely brought into the Kashmir Valley every year to be sold to aspiring grooms, who are often poor, old and physically disabled and thus unable to find a local bride. Some aspirants prefer to marry in such a fashion because they cannot afford the huge expenditure involved in performing local customs. In most Kashmiri villages, a groom has to meet the expenses of marriage and even buy gold ornaments and other expensive gifts for the bride.

Dalals were very active before the onset of militancy and would smuggle women into the Kashmir Valley mainly from West Bengal's Murshidabad district in large numbers. Their activities had seen a shrimp when military had reached its peak. However, with some improvement in the law and order situation, the middlemen have resurfaced. Some women form part of the racket involved in the sex-trade. These women are recruits of dalals who sell and resell them to prospective grooms on commission basis. Each girl or woman, depending on her age and physical features, is bought between Rs, 2,000 and Rs. 15,000, and then sold to a customer for double that amount. The racketeers lure the poor parents of underage girls in West Bengal and Bihar with promises that their daughters will be married off to wealthy people in Kashmir. The parents, stricken by poverty, fall prey to such enticements. In order to avoid penal action under the laws pertaining to trafficking in women, the sale is given a legal colour by solemnizing the 'marriage' through the institution of nikah". Not all trafficking that happens in the name of 'marriage' is for the purpose of marriage.

Marriage may also be a means to get young girls into prostitution or for labour. Clearly, the nature of the problem is wide in spectrum and the cruelty of the situation varies just as to the form and purpose of child trafficking. The report of the South Asian Workshop on Trafficking in Women and Children, Formulating Strategies of Resistance stressed: "It is important to distinguish between different forms of trafficking in terms of the final use of the 'goods', as the traffickers say. This distinction is necessary to understand that it may not be always useful to discuss the internal and trans-boundary migration of people under a single term like "trafficking". It is obvious that the issue such as organ trade requires completely different type of attention than other forms of trafficking. The children and women are ending up being sexual slaves, but there are also cases where they are legally or illegally married to a person".

Bibliography

Aghatise, E.: *Violence Against Women,* Maharashtra: Pune Publication, 2004.

Bertozzi, S.: *Demography and Sex Work Characteristics of Female Sex Workers in India,* Maharashtra: Pune Publication, 2006.

Boud, D., Feletti, G.: *The Challenge of Problem-based Learning*, London, Kogan, 1991.

Bowlby, J.: *A Secure Base: Parent-child Attachment and Healthy Human Development,* New York, Basic Books, 1990.

Chesler, Phyllis: *Women and Madness*. New York: Harvest, 1982.

Cockburn, A.: *Combating Trafficking of Women and Children,* New Delhi: Long Life Publication, 2006.

Cox, Jr., T.: *Cultural Diversity in Organizations: Theory, Research & Practice,* San Francisco, Berrett-Koehler Publishers, 1993.

D'Cunha, J.: *Trafficking in Persons: A Gender and Rights Perspective*, Toronto: Thomson Nelson, 2008.

Damon, William: *Social and Personality Development: Infancy through Adolescence,* New York, Norton, 1983.

Denhardt, R. B.: *Managing Human Behavior in Public & Nonprofit Organizations,* Thousand Oaks, Sage, 2002.

Derrett, J. : *Religion, Law, and the State in India,* London, Faber, 1968.

Fine, M.: *Women with Disabilities: Essays in Psychology, Culture, and Politics,* Philadelphia, Temple University Press, 1988.

Fleenor, Juliann: *The Female Gothic*. London: Eden Press, 1983.

Glover, J.: *The Philosophy and Psychology of Personal Identity*, London, Penguin, 1988.

Graham, G. : *Philosophical Psychopathology,* Cambridge, MIT Press, 1994.

Guillaumin, Colette: *Racism, Sexism, Power and Ideology* Routledge, 1995.

Harvey, C.: *Understanding Diversity: Readings, Cases, and Exercises,* New York, HarperCollins College Publishers, 1995.

Homans, Margaret: *Women Writers and Poetic Identity*. Princeton: Princeton University Press, 1980.

Jana, S.: *A Tale of Two Cities: Shifting the Paradigm of Anti-Trafficking Programmes,* New Delhi: Long Life Publication, 2003.

John, R.: *Subpersonalities: the People inside Us*, London, Routledge, 1990.

Jordan, J. V.: *Women's Growth in Diversity,* New York, Guilford Press, 1997.

Kapur, Rajesh.: *Collateral Damage: Sacrificing Legitimacy in the Search for Justice,* Maharashtra: Pune Publication, 2001.

Kathleen, V.: *Real People : Personal Identity without thought Experiments,* Oxford, Clarendon Press, 1988.

Kelly, G.A.: *Theory of Personality : The Psychology of Personal Constructs,* New York, W.W. Norton, 1955.

Kempadoo, K.: *Global Sex Workers: Rights, Resistance, Redefinition*, Hyderabad: Self Publication, 2000.

King, Margaret L." *Women of the Renaissance*. Chicago: University of Chicago Press, 1991.

Langbauer, Laurie: *Women and Romance: The Consolations of Gender in the English Novel* Ithaca: Cornell, 1990.

Levin, David Michael: *Pathologies of the Modern Self,* New York, NYU Press, 1988.

Madhusudana, B.: *Internal Trafficking of Women into Sex Work in India: Problems in Rehabilitation and Reintegration,* Hyderabad: Economic and Political Weekly Press, 2002.

Matsumodo, D.: *People: Psychology from a Cultural Perspective,* Pacific Grove, Brooks/Cole, 1994.

Mead, G. H.: *Mind, Self, and Society from the Standpoint of a Social Behaviorist,* Chicago, University of Chicago Press, 1967.

Michael, S.: *Attachment in Adults: Clinical and Developmental Perspectives,* New York, Guilford Press, 1994.

Nag, M.: *Sex Workers of India: Diversity in Practice of Prostitution and Ways of Life,* Hyderabad: Economic and Political Weekly Press, 2006.

Nath, P.M.: *Human Trafficking: Dimensions, Challenges and Responses*, Toronto: Thomson Nelson, 2010.

Parker, Michael: *India's other Virus: Human Trafficking and the Spread of HIV,* New Delhi: Long Life Publication, 2003.

Philippy, Patricia: *Women, Death and Literature in Post-Reformation England*. Cambridge, UK: Cambridge UP 2002.

Rubin, Kenneth: *Social, Emotional, and Personality Development,* New York, Wiley, 1998.

Schuster, C.: *The Process of Human Development,* Boston, Little, Brown & Co., 1980.

Stephen, L.: *The Unity of the Self,* Cambridge, MIT Press, 1991.

Vicinus, Martha: *Suffer and be Still: Women in the Victorian Age*. London: Macmillan, 1972.

Weinberg, R. : *Women Anthropologists,* Westport, CT: Greenwood, 1988.

White, Stephen L.: *The Unity of the Self,* Cambridge, MIT Press, 1991.

Wilkes, Kathleen V.: *Real People : Personal Identity without thought Experiments*, Oxford, Clarendon Press, 1988.

Yount, Lisa : *Contemporary Women Scientists*, New York, Facts on File, 1994.

Index

Q

R

S

T

V

W

❑❑❑